# 501
# ESSENTIAL
# BACKGAMMON
# PROBLEMS

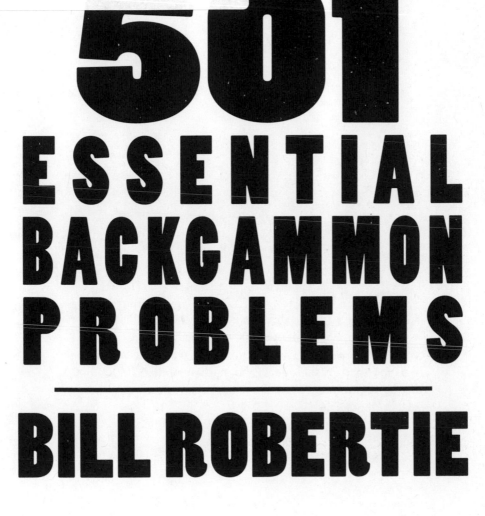

# 501
# ESSENTIAL
# BACKGAMMON
# PROBLEMS

---

## BILL ROBERTIE

# CARDOZA PUBLISHING

Cardoza Publishing is the foremost gaming publisher in the world, with a library of over 200 up-to-date and easy-to-read books and strategies. These authoritative works are written by the top experts in their fields and, with more than 10,000,000 books in print, represent the best-selling and most popular gaming books anywhere.

**NEW 2017 EDITION**
Copyright © 2000, 2017 by Bill Robertie
- All Rights Reserved-

Library of Congress Catalog Card No: 2017940740
ISBN 13: 978-1-58042-349-6

Visit our website or write for a full list of Cardoza Publishing books and advanced strategies.

**CARDOZA PUBLISHING**
P.O. Box 98115, Las Vegas, NV 89193
Toll-Free Phone (800)577-WINS
email: cardozabooks@aol.com
**www.cardozabooks.com**

## ABOUT THE AUTHOR

Bill Robertie is the world's best backgammon player and the only two-time winner of the Monte Carlo World Championships. In addition to this book, Robertie is the author of six other books on winning at backgammon and the co-publisher of *Inside Backgammon*, the world's foremost backgammon magazine. He's also a chess master, winner of the U.S. Speed Chess Championship, and the author of six chess books.

His club and tournament winnings have allowed him to travel the world in style. Robertie currently makes his home in Arlington, Massachusetts.

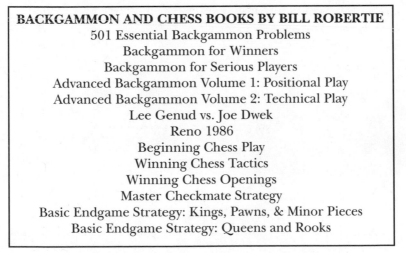

**BACKGAMMON AND CHESS BOOKS BY BILL ROBERTIE**
501 Essential Backgammon Problems
Backgammon for Winners
Backgammon for Serious Players
Advanced Backgammon Volume 1: Positional Play
Advanced Backgammon Volume 2: Technical Play
Lee Genud vs. Joe Dwek
Reno 1986
Beginning Chess Play
Winning Chess Tactics
Winning Chess Openings
Master Checkmate Strategy
Basic Endgame Strategy: Kings, Pawns, & Minor Pieces
Basic Endgame Strategy: Queens and Rooks

# TABLE OF CONTENTS

**1. INTRODUCTION**   **11**

**2. HOW TO USE THIS BOOK**   **12**

**3. BACKGAMMON NOTATION**   **14**

**4. GENERAL PRINCIPLES**   **17**

Counting Dice Combinations   17
Counting Dice Rolls   18
Counting Pips   20
Doubling   22
Taking a Double   23
Offering a Double   24
Too Good to Double   25
Beavers   26

**5. THE OPENING**   **28**

Problems 1-59   29
Solutions   49

**6. FLEXIBILITY**   **65**

Problems 60-84   66
Solutions   75

**7. THE MIDDLE GAME**   **82**

Problems 85-162   84
Solutions   110

**8. THE 5-POINT**   **131**

Problems 163-172   132
Solutions   136

**9. THE BLITZ**   **139**

Problems 173-206   140
Solutions   152

## 10. ONE MAN BACK    161
Problems 207-216    162
Solutions    166

## 11. HOLDING GAMES    169
Problems 217-244    170
Solutions    180

## 12. PRIMING GAMES    188
Problems 245-267    189
Solutions    197

## 13. CONNECTIVITY    204
Problems 268-275    205
Solutions    208

## 14. HIT OR NOT?    211
Problems 276-283    212
Solutions    215

## 15. BREAKING ANCHOR    217
Problems 284-287    218
Solutions    220

## 16. CRUNCH POSITIONS    221
Problems 288-290    222
Solutions    223

## 17. ACTION DOUBLES    224
Problems 291-295    225
Solutions    227

## 18. LATE GAME BLITZ    229
Problems 296-300    230
Solutions    232

## 19. POST-BLITZ TURNAROUND GAMES    234
Problems 301-307    235
Solutions    238

## 20. TOO GOOD TO DOUBLE?    240
Problems 308-312    241
Solutions    243

## 21. ACE-POINT GAMES — 245
Problems 313-335 — 246
Solutions — 254

## 22. BACK GAMES — 260
Problems 336-368 — 262
Solutions — 273

## 23. THE CONTAINMENT GAME — 283
Problems 369-384 — 284
Solutions — 290

## 24. POST-ACE-POINT GAMES — 295
Problems 385-418 — 296
Solutions — 308

## 25. PLAYING FOR A GAMMON — 316
Problems 419-423 — 317
Solutions — 319

## 26. SAVING THE GAMMON — 321
Problems 424-429 — 322
Solutions — 324

## 27. BEARING OFF AGAINST CONTACT — 326
Problems 430-450 — 327
Solutions — 334

## 28. VARIOUS ENDGAMES — 340
Problems 451-459 — 341
Solutions — 344

## 29. THE RACE — 347
Problems 460-469 — 348
Solutions — 352

## 30. THE BEAROFF — 355
Problems 470-501 — 356
Solutions — 367

## 31. NEXT STEPS — 377

# 1

# INTRODUCTION

At first glance, backgammon looks like a simple game. Run your checkers around the board, play safe and don't get hit, and throw high numbers on the dice so you can bear off first. Apparently, nothing to it. Many players play all their lives and never progress beyond this simple-minded approach to the game.

But there's another way to play, one that's a lot more interesting. Instead of always running, you use your dice rolls to make key points. You take shrewd chances to block your opponent. You maneuver to prevent yourself from being blocked. If your opponent leaves you an opening, you swoop in with a deadly blitz attack. And you never forget to double the stakes when the game looks promising for you!

As you might guess, the second way is the winning way. But it's not easy to implement. You'll need to master the strategy and tactics of the game, learning when risks are justified and when they're not. That's what this book is all about. I'll show the key ideas behind today's style of dynamic, aggressive backgammon. You'll learn when to play loose and when to play tight, when to attack and when to hold back, and how to save a bad position with a well-timed back game. You'll also learn the secrets of good doubling and aggressive taking.

Armed with the weapons in this book, your untutored opponents, playing yesterday's style, won't have a chance. But be warned — don't win all their money too quickly, or they just might stop playing with you!

# HOW TO USE THIS BOOK

This is a book of backgammon problems. The problems have been carefully chosen to illustrate key situations and concepts that occur over and over again. Master the problems in this book, and you'll be well on your way to becoming a top-flight player.

My first book, *Backgammon for Winners*, gave you a solid foundation for mastering the basic strategies of the game. My second book, *Backgammon for Serious Players*, analyzed some games of world-class professionals, giving you a feel for what top-flight backgammon looked like.

In this book we're going to show you the real guts of the game. You'll learn the secrets of backgammon strategy and tactics that enable the pros to clobber the casual player. Armed with the weapons in this book, you'll find yourself able to dominate the players you meet in clubs and tournaments.

If this is your first backgammon book, start with Chapter 3, *Backgammon Notation*. It explains how the points are numbered and how moves are described.

Chapter 4, *General Principles*, shows you how to calculate dice combinations, how to use the pip count to count races, and what the doubling cube is all about.

The next 26 chapters explain different phases of the game, starting with *Openings and Flexibility* and finishing with *Races and Bearoffs*. You should treat each chapter like a short quiz. Read the introduction to get a general idea of what's going on, then look at the problems and write down what you would play over the board. When you've gone through all the problems this way, check your answers against the solutions and explanations. I'd recommend writing all your answers on a separate sheet of paper, so that later you can quiz yourself again.

# BACKGAMMON NOTATION

Backgammon games are recorded using a method called **backgammon notation**. It's easy to learn, and it lets us replay a backgammon game whenever we want to. Let's see how it works.

Diagram A shows the starting position of a backgammon game:

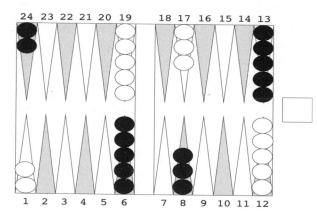

Notice that we've numbered all the points on the board, starting with point number 1 in the lower left and going all the way to point number 24 in the upper left. Using these point numbers, we can describe all the moves of a backgammon game.

In Diagram A, Black is moving **clockwise**. His pieces move from the upper left quadrant, to the right across the top half of the board, then to the left along the lower half, ending up in the quadrant on the lower left. Black's pieces always move from higher numbered points to lower numbered points.

White's pieces move in the opposite direction, **counter-clockwise**. White's pieces end up in the upper left quadrant.

Suppose Black won the opening roll with a 31 (Black rolled a 3 and White rolled a 1, so Black would move first), and wanted to make his 5-point. In backgammon notation, we would write

**1. Black 31: 8/5 6/5** - This says: On the first roll of the game, Black rolled 31, and moved a piece from the 8-point to the 5-point, and another piece from the 6-point to the 5-point. The resulting position would look like this:

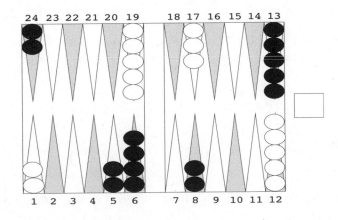

Now suppose that White rolled a 63, and elected to run with one of his two checkers on the 1-point. We'd write

**2. White 63: 1/10** - and the position would now look like this:

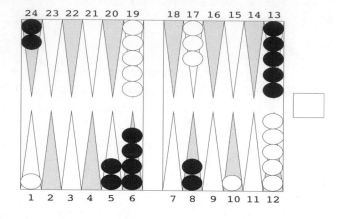

If you've understood this so far, congratulations! You've mastered backgammon notation.

There are a couple of more shorthand notations that you'll see throughout the book. Here they are:

**Rolling doubles**. When a player rolls doubles and moves his checkers in pairs, the move looks like this:

**3. White 11: 19/20(2) 17/18(2)** - This means White moved two checkers from the 19-point to the 20-point, and two more from the 18-point to the 17-point.

**Hitting a blot**. When someone hits a blot, we use the symbol *, like this:

**4. Black 63: 24/15*** - This means Black moved a checker from the 24-point to the 15-point, hitting a blot and sending it to the bar.

**Bearing off**. We indicate that checkers were borne off with the notation /off. For instance:

**24. Black 65: 6/off 5/off** - This means Black rolled a 65 and bore off two checkers.

That's all there is to it! When you play through the games, compare the position on your board at home with the diagrams in the book. WIthin a very short time you'll be reading the notation flawlessly.

# GENERAL PRINCIPLES

The problems in the rest of the book are broken down by category: openings, bearoffs, back games, and so forth. In this chapter, you'll learn some ideas and techniques that are important in all positions, such as how to count pips and what doubling is all about. Don't skip this chapter, even if you're an experienced player. The ideas here will help you make sense of everything that comes afterward.

## Counting Dice Combinations

Whenever you roll two die, there are 36 possible dice combinations that can result. To see this, imagine that the two dice are different colors, with the first die red and the second die blue. The red die can land in any of six different ways. For each way the red die can land, the blue die can also land in six different ways. So the total number of dice combinations is six times six, or 36.

A roll of a double, like double-ones, can occur in only one way. You'll need an ace on the red die and an ace on the blue die. So the probability of a specific double is 1 in 36.

A non-double, like five-four for instance, can actually occur in two different ways: You could get a five on the red die and a four on the blue die, or a five on the blue die and a four on the red die. The probability of throwing a specific non-double is twice as likely as a specific double; 2 in 36.

## Counting Dice Rolls

In many backgammon situations, you'll need to count the number of rolls that accomplish some particular purpose. You might want to count the number of rolls that bear off all your checkers, or count the number of ways that you might be hit, or the number of ways to make a point. Let's look at a couple of examples.

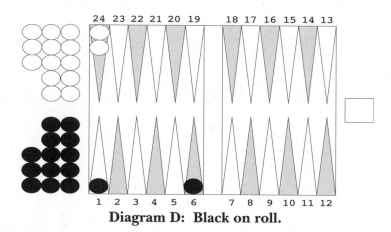

**Diagram D: Black on roll.**

Black has two checkers left and is thinking about doubling. Since it's the last roll of the game, he wants to double if he's the favorite. To figure out if he's the favorite or not, he needs to count the rolls that actually bear off both checkers. Let's see what they are.

We'll look at the non-doubles first. The roll of 65 bears off both men. But as we just saw, 65 is really two rolls: six on the first die and five on the second, or five on the first and six on the second. So 65 counts as two rolls. In the same way, 64, 63, 62, and 61 each count as two rolls. So we now have a total of 10 rolls that win.

Among the doubles, 66, 55, 44, 33, and 22 bear off both checkers. Since there's only one way for a double to happen, each of these five count as one roll. So we have a total of 10 + 5 = 15 rolls that bear off both Black checkers.

Since we know the total number of dice combinations on any throw is 36, we'd need to have 18 combinations working for us to be even money, and 19 or more to be a favorite. With only 15 good rolls, we're actually an underdog in the position. Our percentage winning chances are 15/36 = 41.7%. Not too good. So Black correctly refrains from doubling.

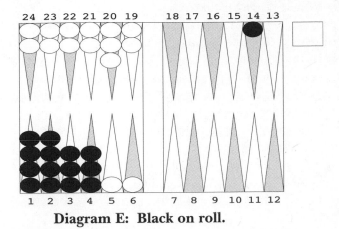

24 23 22 21 20 19    18 17 16 15 14 13

1  2  3  4  5  6    7  8  9  10 11 12

**Diagram E:  Black on roll.**

In Position E, Black has a 61 to play.  He has no choice with the six: he must play 14/8.  With the ace, he has a choice.  He can play 8/7, giving White aces and deuces to hit, or play something like 4/3, giving White twos and threes.  Which is better?

For all intents and purposes, this is the last roll of the game.  If White hits this shot, he will win easily, and if he misses, Black will win a single game but not a gammon.  So Black wants to make sure that White has as few rolls that hit as possible.  To determine this, he counts the hitting rolls after each play.

After 14/8/7, White hits with any roll containing a one or a two. The rolls containing a one are 61, 51, 41, 31, 21, and 11.  The five non-doubles each count as two rolls, making a total of 10, and the single double counts as one roll, making a total of 11 rolls containing an ace.  (That's a good number to commit to memory: there are 11 ways out of 36 to throw any specific number — about 31%.)

Now we'll count the deuces, but we have to remember not to count the roll 21 — we counted that already among the aces.  The rolls containing a deuce but not an ace are 62, 52, 42, 32, and 22, a total of nine additional numbers.  That makes a grand total of 20 hitting numbers containing an ace or a deuce.  (Another very good number to remember.  The number of ways of rolling any two specific numbers is 20 out of 36, or about 55%.)

So if we play 14/8/7, we'll be hit 20 times out of 36.  Suppose instead we play 14/8 4/3.  Is that better or worse?

Now White has twos and threes to hit. Since we now know that there are 20 chances out of 36 to roll either of two specific numbers, we know White has 20 ways to roll a two or a three. But — are there any numbers which hit but don't contain a two or a three?

Yes. White could roll a 11 and also hit. So his total number of hits is 21, which makes this play (14/8 4/3) worse than 14/8/7.

By the way, there's a general principle at work here. To minimize the number of shots, move as close as possible to the checkers that are shooting at you. That reduces the number of combination shots, like 11 in this example.

That's the basic idea of counting shots in backgammon. Most positions don't require it, but when you need to count, it's good to know how.

## Counting Pips

Another key skill in backgammon is the ability to figure out who's ahead in the race, and by how much. To do it, you'll need to know how to execute what's called "the pip count."

The pip count is just a measure of how many pips you have to throw on your dice to bear off all your men, with no wastage. Look back to Diagram D. Black has two checkers left, on his 6-point and 1-point. The minimum number of pips Black needs to throw to bear off both these checkers is seven, so Black's pip count in this position is seven.

What about White's pip count in the same position? White has two checkers that need to travel one pip apiece to bear off, so his pip count is two.

Pip counts get more complicated when the checkers have farther to travel. Let's do a pip count for the starting position:

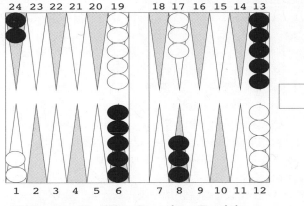

**Diagram F: The Starting Position**

We'll count Black's pips. (Since the positions are symmetrical, we know White's pip count will be the same as Black's.)

Black has two checkers on the 24-point. Each of those will have to travel 24 pips to bear off, so the checkers on that point represent 48 pips. In the same way, the five checkers on the 13-point represent 65 pips, the three checkers on the 8-point are 24 pips, and the five checkers on the 6-point are 30 pips. The total pip count for the Black position is

$$48 + 65 + 24 + 30 = 167$$

And White's pip count is also 167.

Pip counts are important because being ahead in the race is, in the vast majority of positions, a major asset. Having a positional advantage combined with a lead in the pip count is often a doubling combination, whereas a positional advantage all by itself might not be.

Being skilled at counting pips quickly and accurately is a big advantage for a backgammon player. You should try to practice counting pips until you're very good at it. In many positions in this book, I've given the pip count as part of the explanation. Try counting the pips yourself in those positions and see if you can get the right answer.

## Doubling

Backgammon in various forms has been around for about two thousand years. The doubling cube, however, is quite a recent addition to the game. It appeared in 1926 or 1927 in New York, probably in one of the chess and gambling clubs of the Lower East Side. (The most likely candidate location for the cube's invention was the Stuyvesant Chess Club, at the corner of Second Avenue and 14th Street — a smoky den above an old brownstone where wealthy games players from the uptown clubs would mingle and battle with Jewish and Italian immigrants from lower Manhattan over chess, backgammon, and cards.)

The doubling cube revolutionized backgammon by forcing players to quantify their advantage during the game and rewarding the player who could best act on that knowledge. With the doubling cube, backgammon mutated from a moderately interesting game of racing and blocking to a great two-player game of strategy, tactics, and probability.

The doubling cube is slightly larger than a regular die. Its six sides are marked with the powers of two — 2, 4, 8, 16, 32, and 64, and its function is to mark the value of the game.

At the beginning of each game, the cube is placed in the center of the bar with the "64" side face up. This indicates that the value of the game is one unit. At any point in the game, the player *on roll* can, instead of rolling, turn the cube to "2" and say "I double," or words to that effect. This is called "offering a double."

The opponent now has two choices. He can give up the game, lose one point (the old value of the cube), and set up the pieces for the next game. Or he can accept the cube, after which the cube sits on his side at the 2-level and the value of all results of the game are doubled. (A single win is now worth two points, a gammon is worth four points, and a backgammon is worth six points.) Having accepted the cube, only he has the right to redouble to the 4-level at some future point if the game turns around again.

In practice, among experienced players, most games end at the 1, 2, or 4-level. In a session of a few hours, you might see a few 8-cubes. Games reaching the 16-level are quite rare. A session with 16 and 32-cubes floating around indicates a bunch of players who don't know what they are doing.

## Taking a Double

You should be willing to take a double if you have at least a 25% chance of winning the game, as long as you're unlikely to lose a gammon or backgammon. Many players are surprised by the 25% number. "Why should I take a double if I'm an underdog?," you might ask. But that's not the right way to think about the situation.

Take a look at Position G:

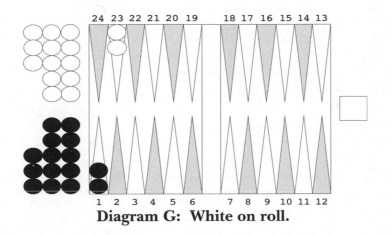

**Diagram G:  White on roll.**

It's White's turn, and instead of rolling, he doubles Black by giving him the cube at 2. Black can give up and lose a point, or take the cube at the 2-level. If he takes, White will roll. White will win most, but not all of the time.

Black's first job is to figure out just what his winning chances actually are. White will win unless he throws a number containing an ace, except for 11, which will also win. White's losers are 61, 51, 41, 31, and 21. That's five non-doubles, or a total of 10 rolls out of 36. White will win the other 26 games out of 36.

So Black's a 26-10 underdog. Not too good. But should he give up or play on? To understand the decision, let's imagine Black reaches this situation in 36 different games.

Suppose Black drops the double in 36 games. Then he loses one point in each game, for a total of 36 points lost.

Now suppose he takes the cube at 2 in all 36 games. On average, he loses 26 of these games, for a loss of 52 points. But he wins 10 games, for a gain of 20 points.

His **net** loss is:
- 52 + 20 = - 32 points

Losing 32 points isn't good, but it's a little better than the 36 points he would have lost by dropping. Taking is correct, not because it makes Black a winner, but because it makes him less of a loser.

When you're doubled, you're offered two choices. Neither of those choices is going to be profitable, but they're the only two choices you have, so you must pick the least bad choice. Evaluating the dropping choice is easy; you know exactly what that choice will cost you. Evaluating the taking choice is more difficult. Study the examples in this book, and you'll start to get a feel for what assets you need to save one game in four.

One last point about taking. If you can be gammoned, you'll need better than one chance in four to take. Exactly how much more depends on how likely you are to lose a gammon. Again, pay careful attention to the problems, and you'll get a feel for correct takes in the face of possible gammons.

## Offering a Double

Offering a double is trickier than accepting a double. You don't want to double too late, because your opponents will give up, and you'll only win one point instead of a possible two or four. But you don't want to double too early either, because your opponents will then have too many chances to turn the game around.

Technically speaking, you'd like to offer an initial double if your winning chances are in the 68% to 69% or better range. You'd like to offer a redouble if your chances are better than about 71% to 72%. (Note that you need to be a slightly bigger favorite to redouble. This is because the cube is a powerful asset when only you have access to it.)

Over the board, there's no way to calculate your percentage chance of winning with such precision. You have to make a reasonable estimate, and the better you get at estimating, the stronger a player you will be.

When thinking about doubling, ask yourself these two questions:

(1) **Do I have a better position?** (Am I ahead in the race? Do I have more blocking points? Are my back checkers more advanced? Is my opponent on the bar?)

(2) **Could the position change decisively in my favor on the next roll?** (Am I threatening to do something crushing?)

If the answer to both questions is "Yes," you probably have a good double or redouble.

## Too Good to Double

Just because you can double with the sure knowledge that your opponent will pass doesn't mean you should double. Take a look at Position H:

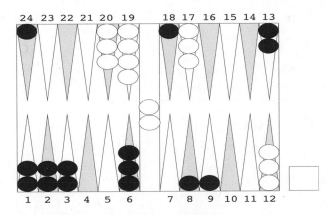

**Diagram H: Black on roll.**

If Black redoubles, White will surely pass. The threat of a gammon is very high, and White's winning chances are slim.

But it would be a mistake for Black to give White the chance to drop! True, Black could cash a sure two points. But his proper play is to keep the cube and play on, hoping to win a gammon and four points. (If he's very lucky, he might win a backgammon and six points.)

Position H is an example of a position that's too good to double. In general, if you think you're more than twice as likely to win a gammon as you are to actually lose the game, it's correct to play on without doubling.

One note:  In most backgammon clubs around the country, chouettes and head-to-head games are played with the Jacoby rule in effect, which states that no gammon can be scored unless a double has been made and accepted.  It's a good rule, which speeds up play and prevents long dull games.  But it also means that you can only play on for a gammon if you already own the cube, not if the cube is still centered.  By the way, the Jacoby rule is not used in tournament play.

## The Beaver

The beaver is an extra twist to the doubling rules, a way of punishing a player who gives a grossly incorrect double.  Take a look at Position I:

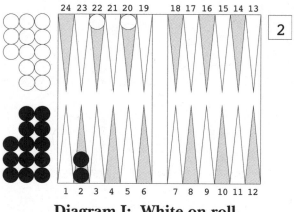

**Diagram I:  White on roll.**

White, owning the cube on 2, decides to double to 4.  It's a bad mistake, and Black knows it.  Instead of just taking the cube on 4, Black takes the cube, turns it one more notch to 8, and keeps it on his side, announcing "I beaver!"  Next turn, he's free to redouble to 16 if he wants.

The beaver rule allows you, when doubled, to turn the cube one extra level and still retain ownership.  You must beaver immediately upon being doubled.  (No, you can't wait a roll or two to see how things turn out!)  After you beaver, the cube is yours and you can subsequently redouble in the normal fashion.

**26**

Note that not all incorrect doubles are beavers. You should only beaver if your opponent's bad double has actually left you the favorite in the game.

The beaver is a great weapon for punishing the foolish doubler. It adds an extra measure of skill to the game, and is allowed in all backgammon clubs in chouettes and heads-up games. If you're playing in a private game, you should ask if beavers are permitted. Beavers are never permitted in tournaments.

# THE OPENING

In the opening, the two players mobilize their armies and prepare for the battles to come. The large stacks of checkers on the 6-point and the midpoint have to be turned into blocking formations. The rear checkers on the 24-point have to be advanced and connected to the rest of the army. All the while, you're looking for some enemy blots to hit.

The opening is the most difficult and important phase of the game, because so many choices are possible. If you play too safely, you'll enter the middle game with few points and fewer prospects. Play too aggressively, and you'll find yourself trailing in too many races. The key to successful opening play is balance. You've got to balance offense and defense, risk and reward, aggression and prudence. In this chapter, we'll show you how. Here are some good general guidelines to get you through the forest of opening plays:

• Don't stack up your checkers just to play safe. You need to be flexible, to enhance your chances of making points.

• If your opponent splits to your 4-point or 5-point, you'll want to attack him there.

• Double-hits are often strong plays.

• Hitting and making points are the two major goals in the opening.

• Hitting is usually slightly more important than making a point.

• If you have a choice of points to make, try to figure out which one is more valuable in the position at hand.

• If you have to leave a blot, slot the most valuable point available.

• When you're under pressure, look for a hit that will take away half your opponent's next roll.

• When your opponent is weak, play strong; when he is strong, regroup.

• Don't strip your midpoint.

• Prime two checkers; attack one checker.

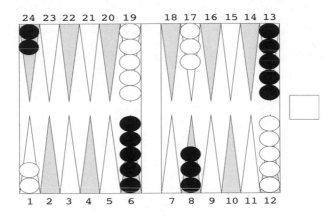

**Problem 1: Black to play 21.**

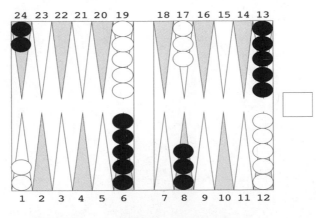

**Problem 2: Black to play 62.**

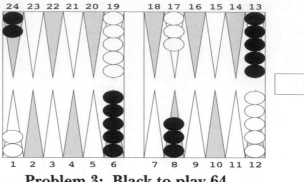

**Problem 3: Black to play 64.**

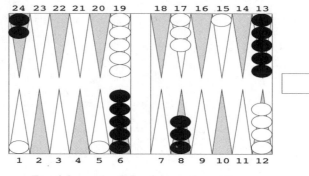

**Problem 4: Black to play 41.**

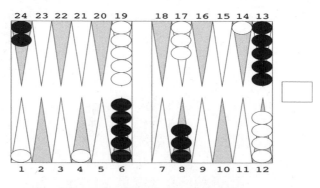

**Problem 5: Black to play 52.**

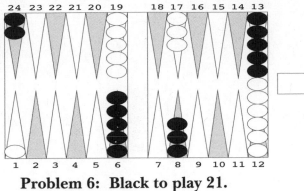

**Problem 6: Black to play 21.**

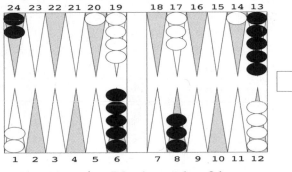

**Problem 7: Black to play 21.**

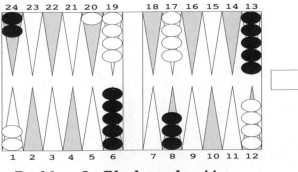

**Problem 8: Black to play 44.**

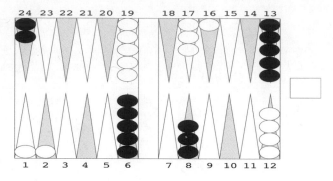

**Problem 9: Black to play 44.**

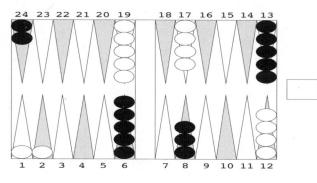

**Problem 10: Black to play 52.**

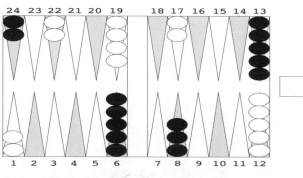

**Problem 11: Black to play 43.**

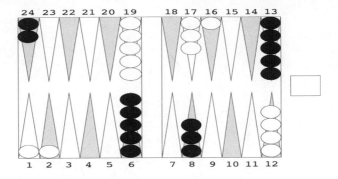

Problem 12: Black to play 41.

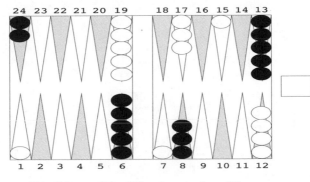

Problem 13: Black to play 65.

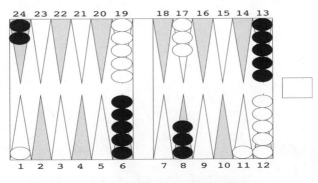

Problem 14: Black to play 55.

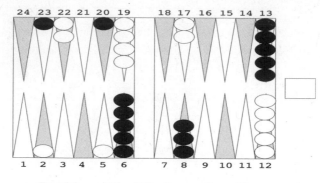

**Problem 15: Black to play 42.**

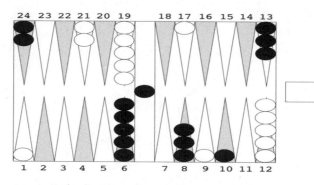

**Problem 16: Black to play 53.**

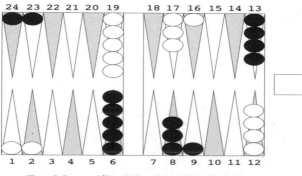

**Problem 17: Black to play 61.**

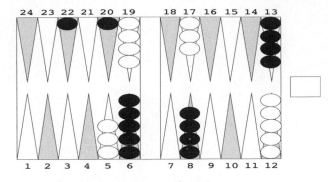

Problem 18: Black to play 21.

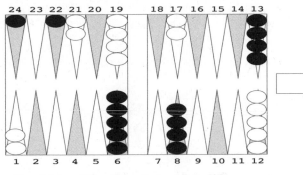

Problem 19: Black to play 52.

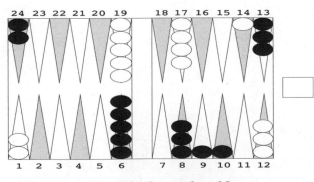

Problem 20: Black to play 62.

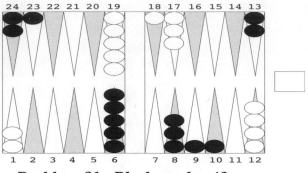

**Problem 21: Black to play 43.**

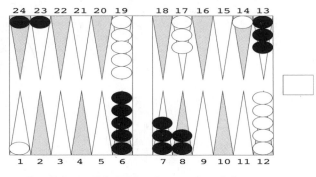

**Problem 22: Black to play 21.**

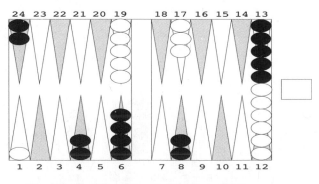

**Problem 23: Black to play 33.**

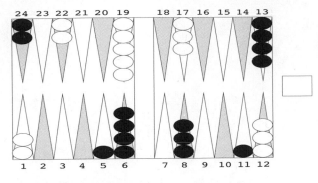

**Problem 24:  Black to play 66.**

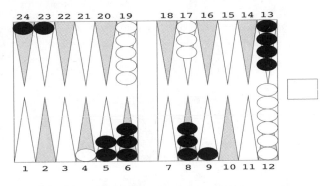

**Problem 25:  Black to play 31.**

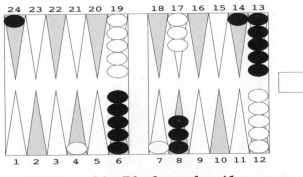

**Problem 26:  Black to play 41.**

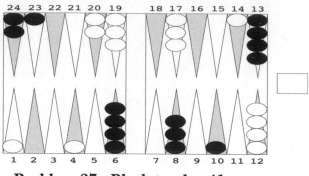

**Problem 27: Black to play 41.**

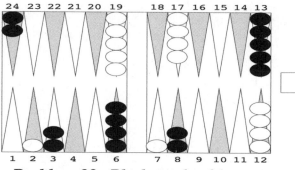

**Problem 28: Black to play 21.**

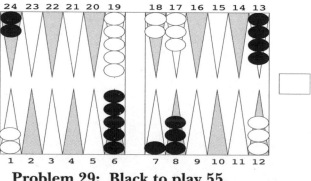

**Problem 29: Black to play 55.**

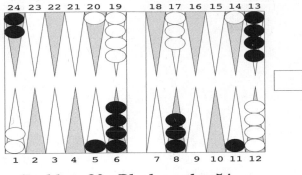

**Problem 30: Black to play 54.**

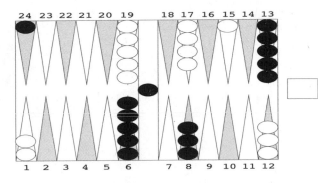

**Problem 31: Black to play 61.**

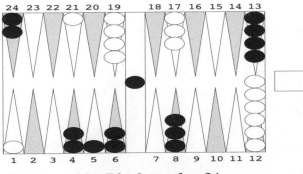

**Problem 32: Black to play 64.**

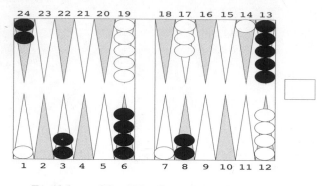

Problem 33:  Black to play 53.

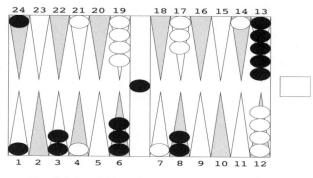

Problem 34:  Black to play 52.

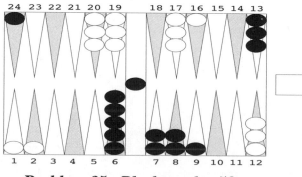

Problem 35:  Black to play 53.

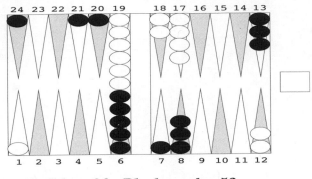

**Problem 36:  Black to play 52.**

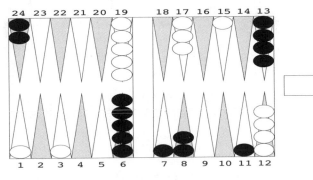

**Problem 37:  Black to play 52.**

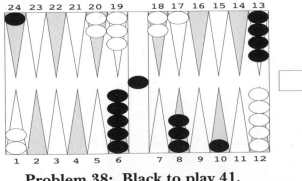

**Problem 38:  Black to play 41.**

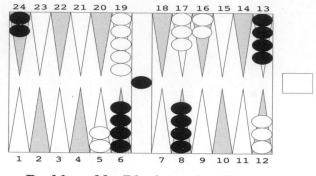

Problem 39: Black to play 51.

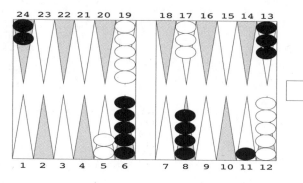

Problem 40: Black to play 61.

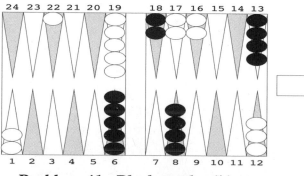

Problem 41: Black to play 54.

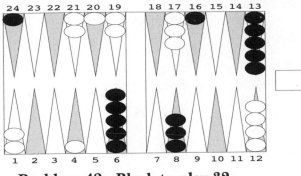

Problem 42: Black to play 32.

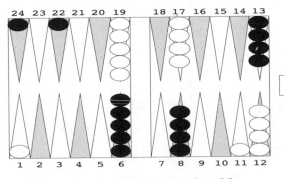

Problem 43: Black to play 32.

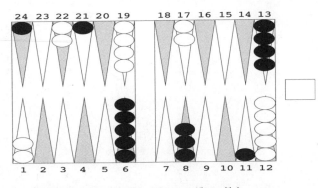

Problem 44: Black to play 54.

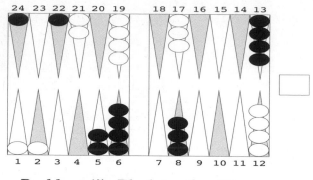

Problem 45: Black to play 32.

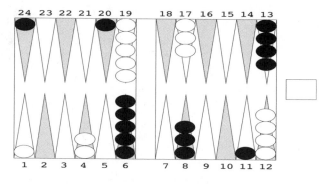

Problem 46: Black to play 52.

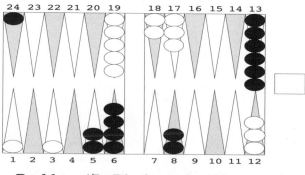

Problem 47: Black to play 66.

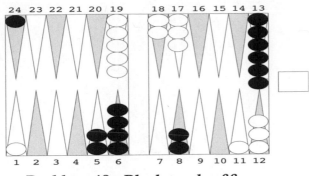

Problem 48: Black to play 66.

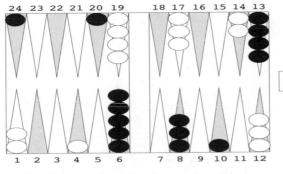

Problem 49: Black to play 41.

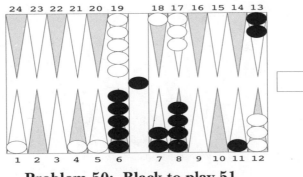

Problem 50: Black to play 51.

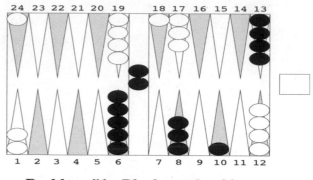

**Problem 51: Black to play 22.**

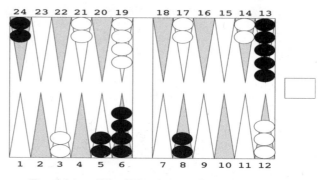

**Problem 52: Black to play 21.**

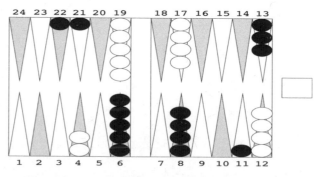

**Problem 53: Black to play 55.**

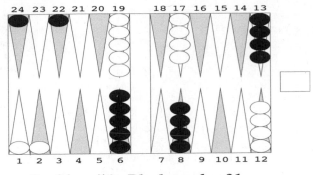

Problem 54: Black to play 31.

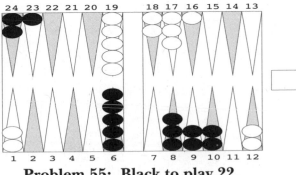

Problem 55: Black to play 22.

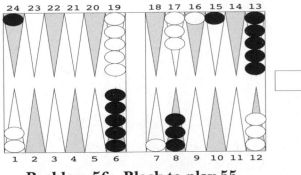

Problem 56: Black to play 55.

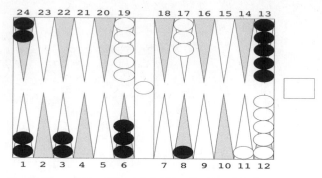

**Problem 57: Should Black double?**
**Should White take if doubled?**

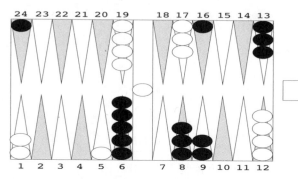

**Problem 58: Should Black double?**
**Should White take if doubled?**

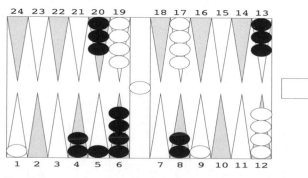

**Problem 59: Should Black double?**
**Should White take if doubled?**

## SOLUTIONS

**Problem 1: Opening roll, Black to play 21.**
Play 13/11 with the 2 and slot the 5-point by playing 6/5 with the ace. The 5-point is the most important point in the early stage, and this play lets you slot it while distributing your checkers off the big stacks. Aggressive and strong.

**Problem 2: Opening roll, Black to play 62.**
The best way to handle an opening 62 is with a combination of splitting and building: 24/18 and 13/11. The split starts to fight for a good anchor on White's bar-point, at a time when White has minimal development. The builder gives Black a bunch of constructive new rolls, like 41 and 63, plus all deuces.

You'll see this roll played a couple of other ways, which are not as good. Some players will run all the way, 24/16. If this checker gets hit, Black will have wasted his opening roll, and he won't have a lot of return shots. If it's missed, Black will try to safety it next turn. That means several rolls will pass without Black's making an inside point, which could hand the initiative over to White.

Some players like the play 13/5, slotting the 5-point. The problem here is not that the 5-point isn't valuable enough to slot (it is), but this play slots it with the wrong checker. Black wants to use the checkers on the 6-point to make the 4 and 5-points, while the checkers on the midpoint should build outer-board points. If Black plays 13/5, then covers next turn with a three, he'll be left with an awkward and undeveloped stack of checkers on the 6-point.

**Problem 3: Opening roll, Black to play 64.**
Black should play 24/18 with the 6, and 13/9 with the 4. Splitting to the 18-point is a powerful maneuver which starts a good anchor while constricting White's choices. 13/9 creates an excellent builder for new inner board points.

**Problem 4: Black to play 41.**
The right play is 6/5* 24/20. Fighting for the 5-point is crucial in the early stages, so Black must hit with the ace rather than give up his 5-point without a fight. By playing 24/20, he leaves himself with a possibility of making **both** 5-points next turn. That's stronger than hitting a second checker with 5/1*.

**Problem 5: Black to play 52.**

Here's a good rule for attacking in your inner board in the early stages of the game: Fight for the 5-point and the 4-point; be reluctant to hit on the 3-point; avoid hitting on the 1-point or 2-point unless absolutely necessary.

Here Black should fight for his 4-point by hitting with 6/4*. He could also hit on the 1-point, but that's not necessary, so he avoids sticking a checker that deep. Instead he balances his distribution with 13/8.

**Problem 6: Black to play 21.**

Many players who slot the 5-point with an opening 21 are reluctant to do so once the opponent has escaped a checker. They usually resort to a splitting play like 13/11 24/23 or 24/21 instead.

But in fact, you should be even more eager to slot in this position than in the opening position! Here's the reason. If you slot in the opening position and get hit, the hit accomplishes two good things: it gains 20 pips in the race, and it starts the 5-point for White, in preparation for making an anchor next turn. Once White has run a checker out, there's no anchor that can be made, so the hit isn't as effective. The right play is still 13/11 and 6/5.

**Problem 7: Black to play 21.**

What do you do when your opponent has slotted a key point and you miss? Counterslot!

Black should play 13/11 6/5!, counterslotting his own 5-point. White has very few rolls that both hit your blot and cover his own. Unless he does both you'll be able to equalize.

**Problem 8: Black to play 44.**

Black has just rolled his best number in Position 8 — 44. But he must be sure to play it correctly.

He can't go wrong by playing 24/20*(2). He hits a blot, gains 20 pips in the race, and secures a key anchor. With the last two fours, he should play 13/9(2), rather than the obvious 8/4(2).

The trouble with making the 4-point is that Black overruns the play a bit. He doesn't actually make an additional point — he had to give up the 8-point to make the 4-point. And he hasn't done anything about the stacks on his 6-point and 13-point, while he's left a blot exposed on the 8-point. After 13/9(2), he's unstacked the midpoint, made a good new point, and provided a nice combination of builders to keep making good points in the future. It's an effective, balanced play.

**Problem 9:  Black to play 44.**

You won't go wrong in the opening if you look for plays that simply must be right, because what they accomplish is both powerful and difficult to do. Black has many possible plays here, and it's impossible to play such a great shot in a way that doesn't markedly improve the position. What's the best way?  Black should move 24/16* (hitting, gaining 16 pips in the race, and escaping a back checker) and 6/2*(2) (hitting and making an inner point). Other plays are good, but no other play accomplishes quite this much.

**Problem 10:  Black to play 52.**

On the opening roll, it's a tossup whether 52 should be played 13/8 13/11 or 13/8 24/22. Once your opponent has split his back men, however, the choice is clear. A blot on the 11-point is now subject to six hits (64, 63, and 54) rather than just two hits (64). That's more risk than necessary, so Black should just play 13/8 24/22.

**Problem 11:  Black to play 43.**

On the opening roll, it's a tossup whether you play 43 by bringing two men down from the midpoint (good for priming) or splitting the back men (good for building an anchor).

Once your opponent has moved, the choice probably isn't a tossup anymore. Look at what your opponent's opening move has done for his position, and decide accordingly.

Here White has made his 3-point with an opening 53. Now what should Black do with his 43? The advantages of pulling two men down (13/9 13/10) haven't changed. But splitting has been seriously affected. White's position, with an extra inner board point, is less effective for building a blocking prime, so one reason for splitting has been weakened. But White's game is now better for attacking any split checkers (stronger inner board), so a new reason has been added against splitting.

Conclusion: don't split, which just allows White to attack more effectively. Just play 13/9 13/10.

**Problem 12:  Black to play 41.**
Black should play 6/2*/1*.  Putting two checkers up in the air is often a strong play in the opening, with the potential of leading to a blitzing game.  It's the best way of handling what has become an awkward roll.

**Problem 13:  Black to play 65.**
Black should grab the initiative by hitting two men:  13/7* and 6/1*.  White will have to lose some time entering his men, and Black might be able to launch a blitz or make his bar point with a good block.  Don't miss chances to knock your opponent off balance in the early stages.

**Problem 14:  Black to play 55.**
Black should make two inner points by playing 8/3(2) 6/1*(2).  This is always a powerful opening play with 55 when your opponent has split his back men.

**Problem 15:  Black to play 42.**
Opening play is governed by two basic rules:  (1) Hit Blots;  (2) Make Points.

If you can do only one of these two things, that will almost always be the right play.  If you can do both, or neither, then you might have a tough decision.

Here Black was scared of being attacked and ran with 20/14.  But there was a point to be made, and that's top priority.  The right move is 8/4 6/4.

**Problem 16:  Black to play 53.**
In the opening, you want to make points when you can, and hit blots when you can.  What happens when you can do both?

Usually, given a choice between making a point and hitting a shot, you want to hit.  Hitting accomplishes two things:  it gains ground in the race and prevents your opponent from using his whole roll to make a point of his own.  You might even get really lucky and have him stay out altogether, losing his whole turn.  Here the right play for Black is Bar/17*, rather than Bar/20 13/10.

**Problem 17: Black to play 61.**

The right idea here is to hit and gain ground in the race by playing 23/16*. Note that Black could also make his bar-point with 13/7 8/7. In the opening, when faced with a choice between hitting on the opponent's side of the board or making a good blocking point, the hit is usually slightly better. It does two good things (gaining in the race and escaping a back checker), while making the block does only one good thing.

**Problem 18: Black to play 21.**

Anchors are powerful, permanent assets. It's worth taking some risks in the race to secure an anchor for the long term.

Here Black can play safely and risk little in the race with either 6/3 or 6/4 22/21. But the right play is 22/20 8/7!, locking down the anchor. Black won't like it if White rolls a deuce next, but he'll be delighted if White doesn't, and he'll be delighted for a long time.

**Problem 19: Black to play 52.**

In the early stages, give more weight to an anchor than running out a back checker. Here 22/15 looks inviting, but a sounder play is 24/22 13/8.

**Problem 20: Black to play 62.**

Inner board points are stronger than outer board points.

Black can make the 7-point (13/7 8/7) or the 4-point (10/4 6/4). The 4-point is more important. As an inner point, it serves to block any checker on the bar from entering the home board. And since the 6-point is awkwardly stacked (five checkers right now), making the 4-point helps to smooth out Black's position.

**Problem 21: Black to play 43.**

When you have a choice of points to make, you'll have to decide which one is more valuable, at that moment.

Here Black has a choice of making either the 20-point or the 5-point. Both are strong points. To decide on the best play, Black will have to look at a few other features of the position:

• Black has three men back to White's two. That calls for a defensive play, hence favors making the 20-point.

• After making the 5-point, the 8-point is left stripped, hence not useful for making future points.

• The checkers on the 6-point want to be used to make the 5-point (and the 4-point). By making the 5-point with checkers on the 8 and 9-points, the checkers on the 6-point become less useful.

The positional considerations all favor playing 24/20 23/20 — the best play by far.

**Problem 22: Black to play 21.**

When you have a choice of building an offensive or defensive point, see which side of the board needs more work.

Black's offense is hampered by the big stack on the 6-point. His defense is working well, with his rear checkers in no danger yet and covering White's side of the board very well. His offense needs the most help, so play 7/5 6/5.

**Problem 23: Black to play 33.**

In the opening, small changes to the position can alter what would otherwise be a standard play. Be alert for these situations.

Here Black has a 33 to play. In most opening situations 33 is played by making the 10-point and the 21-point. But Black has already made his 4-point (with a 42) and White has escaped a checker (with a 65). These developments change Black's priorities.

Now moving to the 10-point is less effective than before. The 10-point doesn't provide as much building power, since the 4-point is already made, and making a new point using the 8-point leaves a blot behind. At the same time the defensive 21-point goes down in value because a new, very strong offensive possibility has arisen.

Instead, Black should now play 8/5(2) 6/3(2)! This was the second-best way to play 33 as a reply to the opening roll, but with the making of the 4-point this play moves to the top of the list. The super-strong inner board that Black creates puts enormous pressure on White to play carefully and safe, because any hit could immediately become a winner for Black.

Watch how each move in the opening alters the balance of the position, and you'll spot these moves more easily.

**Problem 24: Black to play 66.**

Double-sixes is a great shot in position 24, but Black can't do everything he wants. If he had five sixes, he could make his 5-point and both bars. But with only four, he has to leave one key point unmade. Which one?

Since his 5-point is the best point on the board, Black grabs that first with 11/5. The next two are easy: 24/18 and 13/7. Then comes the hard part: his offensive bar-point or the defensive 18-point.

Black has to realize that he's off to a great start in this game, and offense comes first. If he plays 13/7 with his last six, he's guaranteed an excellent position even if he gets hit on the 18-point. But if he plays 24/18 and then gets hit on the 7-point, he has nothing. 13/7 is the way to go.

**Problem 25: Black to play 31.**

Against a single checker — attack, don't block.

Black should play 8/4* rather than the blocking play 13/9. Why? Two reasons — a prime isn't as good against one checker, because a single good roll can escape; and a single checker can't anchor, so the blitz can go on until the checker actually gets away.

**Problem 26: Black to play 41.**

Black started off by running with 64, and White responded with an odd-looking 63, played 24/18 24/21. You'll see these sorts of double-splits with the back men occasionally. In the backgammon world, they're known as "Middle Eastern plays," because they're commonly seen in that part of the world.

It's inherently dangerous to put your checkers on points that your opponent very much wants to make. These plays work well against timid players, not so well against aggressive ones. (Which you should be by now!) The right response is the double-hit: 8/4* 8/7*, which could lead to a quick blitz.

**Problem 27: Black to play 41.**

Here's a case where you don't fight for the 4-point. Two reasons argue against it: White has a stronger board, having already made his 5-point; and there's a strong point to be made for free. Black should grab what's been offered to him and play 13/9 10/9.

**Problem 28: Black to play 21.**

In the opening, breaking key points to hit is mostly a bad idea, but there are exceptions. Black sees he can hit and start an attack with 8/7* 13/11, but he's reluctant because the 8-point is usually a valuable point to hold, and White will have 18 return shots from the bar. But the key is that Black's other plays are very passive (24/21 is the best alternative) and if White fails to hit back Black's game is very strong. Go ahead and hit.

**Problem 29: Black to play 55.**

When you have to leave a blot, leave it on the most valuable point available. That way, if you're not hit, you have a chance to make a great point.

Here Black has a choice between 13/3 8/3 7/2, leaving fewest shots by slotting the 2-point, or 13/3(2), leaving a couple of extra shots but leaving the key 7-point slotted. The right play is to leave the blot where it is, and hope to make the 7-point next turn.

**Problem 30: Black to play 54.**

When you hit your opponent's slot, you generally want to stay on the point and try to make it next turn.

Here 24/20*/15 doesn't do much. Black would love to actually make the 20-point, so the right play is 24/20* 13/8.

**Problem 31: Black to play 61.**

Black will enter with the one (it's forced) and then have a choice of three legal sixes. Dumping a checker in the board with 8/2 can be rejected immediately. Although it's the play that's least likely to be hit, the 2-point is a worthless point at this stage. The real choice is between 13/7 and 24/18.

The right play is 24/18. If Black starts his own 7-point, a hit will cost him 18 pips in the race. If he goes to the 18-point, a hit will cost only 7 pips. In addition, Black may have a lot of profitable return shots at a White blot on the 18-point. When in doubt, start the other guy's bar-point.

**Problem 32: Black to play 64.**

With an awkward six in the opening, move to the other guy's bar.

Here Black should enter with the four, Bar/21*. With the six, his best play is 24/18. Playing to his own bar, 13/7, looks aggressive but rates to lose too much ground in the race. Running out with 21/15 leaves the back checkers disconnected from the rest of the army. Playing 24/18 minimizes risk and maintains connectivity.

**Problem 33: Black to play 53.**
Hitting on the ace-point with a five is sometimes an effective tactic, especially if you have five or more checkers on your 6-point. If you don't have a big stack on your 6-point and your opponent doesn't have many threats, just leave him alone and make a normal developing play. Here the right move is 24/21 13/8, splitting your back men and putting a valuable spare on your 8-point.

**Problem 34: Black to play 52.**
Once you've hit on the ace-point in the early going, you probably can't play a positional priming game. The continued presence of a blot in your inner board will cause you too many awkward problems later on. Instead, the right idea is to cover the blot as soon as possible and play for an attacking game. Here the right move is Bar/23 6/1.

**Problem 35: Black to play 53.**
Black has to enter with the 3, playing Bar/22. His best choice with the 5 is the active play, 6/1*, knocking White off balance by hitting. Any passive play allows White to use his active builders on his 5, 6, 8, and 9-points to attack. By hitting, Black buys time to consolidate.

**Problem 36: Black to play 52.**
Here's a case where hitting on the 1-point makes good sense. Black has a bad position with four blots strung around the board, and he's just thrown a terrible number, which doesn't consolidate anything. He can't afford to let White play his whole number. Instead the right idea is 6/1* 13/11, keeping White partly off balance, and hoping to button up next turn.

### Problem 37: Black to play 52.

If you don't have a board yet, a double-hit play doesn't rate to be very strong. But it's not weak either, and it may be the best available move.

Here Black should play 8/3*/1*. It's not a powerhouse punch, but it might lead to a blitz, and everything else is lousy.

### Problem 38: Black to play 41.

When your opponent gets off to a fast start building his prime, you need to try for an anchor quickly, before his position gets too dangerous.

The right play for Black is the bold Bar/21 24/23, immediately going for the anchor, rather than the safe but passive Bar/24 13/9. By moving to the 21-point now, before White has a lot of builders in play, Black has the best possible chance of making it. Look at it this way: splitting won't get any safer in the future.

Playing 24/23 with the ace is technically accurate. If White makes the 4-point with a roll like 32, for instance, Black will be able to hit back with 5s and 6s. Also, Black may later have to anchor on the 23-point, which gives him a more viable position than an anchor on the 24-point.

### Problem 39: Black to play 51.

Although the game's just a couple of moves old in Position 39, Black's already in big trouble. He has to take drastic steps now to get a playable game, else he could quickly be doubled out. The safe but passive Bar/24 13/8 isn't worth considering. Black should play Bar/20 24/23!, taking a risk now to try to get an anchor. If the play works, Black will be right back in the game.

### Problem 40: Black to play 61.

Don't take a chance without knowing what you're getting for it. Black made what he thought was an aggressive play: he played 13/7 8/7, leaving the blot on the 11-point exposed but making the bar point.

But the right play was just 11/4, leaving no blots. Since White already has an advanced anchor, the 7-point doesn't really block anything. If Black had noticed that, he wouldn't have left a shot for nothing.

**Problem 41: Black to play 54.**

A lot of players get panicky when they holding the 18-point anchor, and look for a chance to run off it as soon as possible. They
remember all the games where they held that anchor too long, and
lost by getting trapped off it at an awkward moment. In position
41, Black fell victim to his fears and played 18/13 18/14.

The trick is to grab the 18-point, then try to build a good home
board. When your board is at maximum strength, then you run
from the 18-point. Here Black should just play 13/8 13/9, and try
to build some points. There will be plenty of time to run later.

**Problem 42: Black to play 32.**

A blot in your opponent's board is a sign you can play more
aggressively. If you get hit, your opponent will probably not cover
his blot at the same time, so you'll have a chance to reenter with
a hit.

Here Black should make a big play, 6/4* 13/10. Hitting fights
for the important 4-point, while 13/10 unstacks and gives Black
some good sixes next turn. White's only good numbers are 4s
and 3s, so other combinations leave him without much to do. Play
strong when the other guy has weaknesses.

**Problem 43: Black to play 32.**

Obviously Black will hit with the deuce; then he needs to consider the best three. The choices are 13/10 and 24/21. (11/8 is
safe but much too passive.)

"Don't strip the midpoint too quickly" is a good rule to follow
in the opening. Keeping a third checker on the midpoint enables
you to hit runners that your opponent may send into your outer
board, without breaking your midpoint in the process. Eventually,
of course, you'll have to play that third checker, but there's no need
to rush. Black should play 24/21 with his three.

**Problem 44: Black to play 54.**

Put your blots in front of stripped points, not in front of big
stacks. White's big stack on his midpoint cries to be developed, so
Black doesn't want to stick checkers in White's outfield if he can
avoid it. White's stripped 8-point is weak, so Black can sit in front
of it with relative impunity. The right play is 13/8 24/20.

**Problem 45: Black to play 32.**

Black's two is very clear: His back men are starting to come under pressure, so he should play 24/22, securing a good anchor. The three is more difficult. His choices are 13/10 or 8/5.

13/10 is a good-looking play which creates many new point-making combinations: 62 and 64 now make the 4-point, while 31 and 63 make the bar-point. In addition, 41 makes the 9-point, while any three would make the 10-point itself, which is potentially part of an outside prime. There's a cost for these building opportunities, however. Black will get hit next turn if White rolls a 62, 53, or 63.

8/5 is completely safe, and seems to create new building opportunities as well. Does that make it the right play?

Not really. The problem with 8/5 is that it doesn't really create a new builder. If Black subsequently makes the 4-point with 41 or 42, he does so at the cost of leaving a vulnerable blot on the 8-point. Making the bar-point with a later 61 now also comes at the cost of leaving the same blot on the 8-point. Moving the checker to the 5-point does create some new attacking numbers on the 1-point and 2-point, but it's premature for Black to be aiming for a blitz attack.

Moral: In the opening you need to take a few chances to build your priming game. Six indirect shots in the outfield is a good tradeoff for creating a powerful new builder.

**Problem 46: Black to play 52.**

A new point is worth a little extra trouble in the opening.

Here Black has a choice between 20/13, safetying the blot, and 20/15 13/11, leaving a shot but building the 11-point. If this were just a choice between a safe play and a risky play, it would be a close call. But in fact, neither play is "safe." After 20/15 13/11, White has all 3s plus 21 (13 shots) to hit on the 15-point. But after 20/13, White has all 7s plus 64 (8 shots) to hit on the 11-point. Seen this way, 20/13 is only slightly safer. But it's worth a few extra shots to nail down a point, even an outside point. The right play is 20/15 13/11.

**Problem 47: Black to play 66.**

An early 66 in the opening often gives the choice between a priming play and an attacking play. The correct choice usually depends on the number of men your opponent has in your home board.

If he has two or more men back, a prime causes him real problems. Here Black should play 13/7(4).

**Problem 48: Black to play 66.**

If the defender has only one man back, an attack is more powerful since even when the defender enters from the bar, he can't create an anchor and so is still vulnerable to attack next turn. Here Black should play 13/1*(2).

**Problem 49: Black to play 41.**

When you've got a solid lead in the race, make some effort to hold onto it, unless the only safe plays leave you very awkward.

In problem 49, Black is off to a nice start and leads by 18 pips before the roll. He'd like to hold onto that lead if he can. Black might normally consider attacking the blot on the 4-point with a play like 8/4* 10/9, but here that play mostly causes Black to lose his racing lead.

Another possibility is the solid 24/20 10/9, which avoids disasters. But that gives White plenty of numbers to hit on the 9-point, taking a lead in the race.

The right play is 13/9 10/9!, which consolidates the race by making a good blocking point. Black will be unhappy if White can make the 20-point on his head, but White's only about 25% to do so. Otherwise, Black's doing very well.

**Problem 50: Black to play 51.**

Don't bother fighting for the 5-point if the play is very unlikely to work. Here Black can play Bar/20 6/5*, fighting for the 5-point. But that just rates to give away his racing lead, since White can hit him back with 25 out of 36 numbers. (The only misses are 16, 26, 36, 46, 33, and 66.) He should just try to consolidate his big lead with Bar/24 11/6.

**Problem 51: Black to play 22.**

In the opening your primary task is *balance* — make the play that results in the best overall improvement in your game. Don't blind yourself to possibilities by focusing on just one objective.

In a New York chouette, Black (the team captain) quickly played Bar/23(2)/21(2). He explained to his teammates that whatever happened, he was going to get a good anchor.

His play was easy to understand. A second before, he was sitting with two checkers on the bar, wondering if he was about to be blitzed. His orientation was defensive — he just wanted to survive. So when he rolled a great shot from the bar, he used it to make an impregnable defensive position.

But it wasn't the best play. Once he played Bar/23(2), his defense was already secure. If he had looked at the position with a fresh eye, he might have seen that leaving those checkers alone and playing 6/4(2) gave him the biggest overall improvement in his game. He'd then have the security of an anchor (albeit a modest one), combined with a better home board and an unstacked, flexible front game. *Balance* is the key to strong opening play.

**Problem 52: Black to play 21.**

One goal in the early game is to improve those parts of your game that are weakest. Black has two weaknesses in Position 52: his big stack of checkers on the midpoint, and his two back checkers, which haven't started to move and which are in some danger of being blocked. Black can work on both problems by playing 13/11 24/23! His back checkers start to move, while the builder on the 11-point creates new blocking combinations for the 7-point and 9-point.

**Problem 53: Black to play 55.**

55 is a great roll in Problem 53, but Black must play it accurately. Two of the 5s are clear: Black should move 21/11, making the useful 11-point while escaping a checker. With the last two, he has a choice between 6/1(2) and 8/3(2). Although making the ace-point leaves a better distribution of spares than making the 3-point, Black should play 8/3(2). The 3-point is a much better point than the ace-point, and right now this game could go in many different directions. In most of those games, Black will have a stronger position if he makes the better point now.

**Problem 54: Black to play 31.**

Many times in the opening of a game we're asked to make a choice between offense and defense. Here Black can build his front game with 8/5 6/5 (offense), or secure an anchor against an eventual attack (defense). Which should he play?

To decide, consider which side of the board requires the most improvement. Does Black need to make a defensive play? Not really, since White hasn't achieved a threatening position yet. On the other hand, Black has no development at all on the offensive side of the board, so it's time to make an improvement in that area. Black should play 8/5 6/5.

**Problem 55: Black to play 22.**

Double-deuces is a great shot for Black in problem 55. He has several ways to play it, all which give him a strong position.

- All-out offense with 6/4(2) 9/7(2), giving him a strong blocking position.
- Solid defense with 24/20(2), securing the best anchor.
- A little of both, with 6/4(2) 24/22(2).

While both the offensive and defensive plays look good, the right idea is to play a little of both by making the 22-point and the 4-point. Look at it this way: if you start off playing 24/22(2), which pairs of twos improve your game more — continuing on to the 20-point, or unstacking while making the 4-point? Clearing unstacking is the right idea.

Coming up to the 22-point is especially good since, by attacking the blot on the 16-point, it greatly hampers White's ability to make threats next turn. If he rolls a 31 or 42 and makes an inner point, Black will still have a chance to roll a six and hit the blot.

**Problem 56: Black to play 55.**

Three of Black's fives are pretty clear: he plays 13/8 and 8/3(2), making an inner point. With the last five he has a choice between 15/10 and 13/8. Some players would start calculating how likely they are to get hit after each play, how likely they are to make a point next turn, and so forth. The trick is to see that this is really a simple problem. Black has to leave a blot exposed either way. But playing 15/10 leaves him with two spares on the midpoint and no spares on the 8-point, while 13/8 leaves a spare on both points.

That's the right play.  Remember — balance your position.

### Problem 57:  Should Black double?
### Should White take if doubled?

White started the game by running with a 64.  Black then threw 55, making two inside points, and White danced.  Black should double and White should take.  Black has real chances to win a gammon, especially if he can roll a 2 and hit White's other blot.  White has just enough chances to enter and anchor to venture a take.

### Problem 58:  Should Black double?
### Should White take if doubled?

Under just the right circumstances, you can offer an opening double with no new points in your home board.  Here's a good example.  Black has a big lead in the race (42 pips), one White checker is still on the bar, and Black has 10 combinations that make the 5-point next turn, while almost every roll hits loose there.  Black has a solid chance of pinning White in an ace-point game or some sort of back game, so he has a good double now.  White has a take, of course, since Black hasn't actually done any of those things yet.

### Problem 59:  Should Black double?
### Should White take if doubled?

This is a problem which could fool most players.  It might look like Black is offering an early double, but before you take, look more closely.  Black is ahead in every phase of the game.  He's up 21 pips in the race, White is on the bar, Black has 1s, 3s, and 8s to cover his 5-point, 4s and 11s hit, 55 makes the 5-point, and 66 makes the 1-point.  Black also has a strong anchor, while White hasn't made a point yet.  Double and clear pass.

# FLEXIBILITY

With only 15 checkers at your disposal, you need to make sure that every checker is working to its maximum to create new points and block your opponent. That means you can't just run your checkers to safety and hope to automatically throw good numbers. You have to place your checkers so that more of your future numbers will be useful. Playing this way creates a mobile, flexible position.

In this chapter we'll look at some ways to create good positions, including

• **Diversifying**: If there's a key point to be made, make sure you create as many builders as possible bearing on that point. Often there's no cost involved in creating an extra builder, just ingenuity.

• **Unstacking**: Huge stacks cut future flexibility. Look to move off stacks.

• **Duplication**: Give your opponent the same good number in different parts of the board, rather than different good numbers.

• **Slotting**: Put a checker on a point you need to make, with the idea of covering it next turn.

**PROBLEMS**

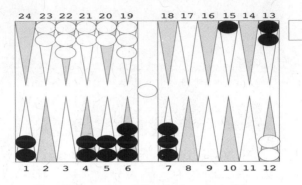

Problem 60: Black to play 11.

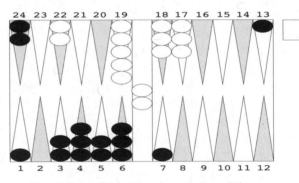

Problem 61: Black to play 65.

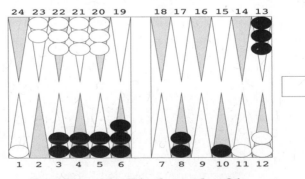

Problem 62: Black to play 21.

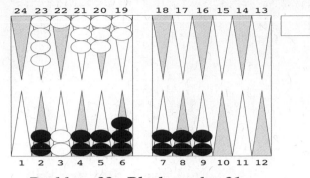

Problem 63: Black to play 31.

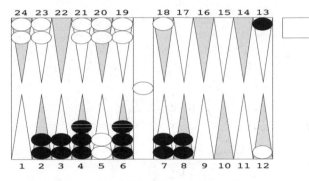

Problem 64: Black to play 41.

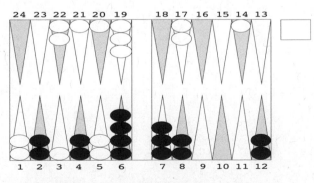

Problem 65: Black to play 22.

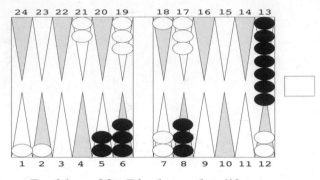

**Problem 66: Black to play 53.**

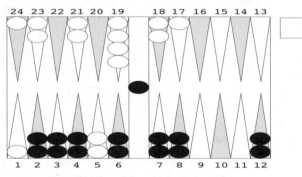

**Problem 67: Black to play 11.**

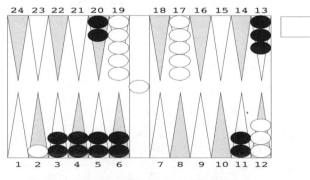

**Problem 68: Black to play 32.**

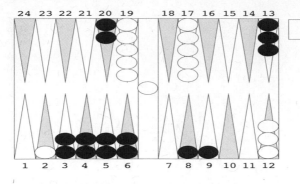

Problem 69:  Black to play 65.

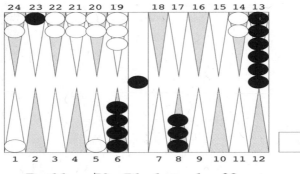

Problem 70:  Black to play 32.

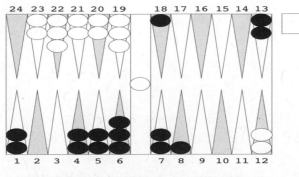

Problem 71:  Black to play 11.

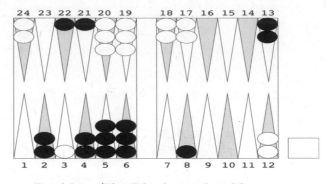

**Problem 72: Black to play 63.**

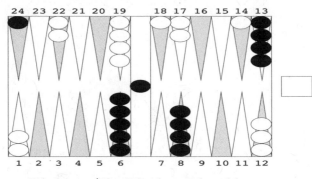

**Problem 73: Black to play 11.**

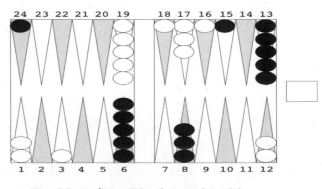

**Problem 74: Black to play 11.**

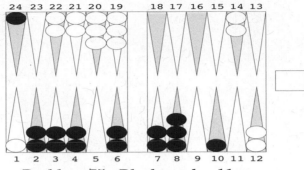

**Problem 75: Black to play 11.**

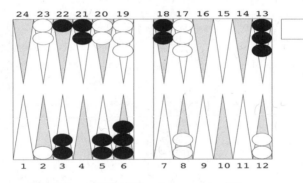

**Problem 76: Black to play 32.**

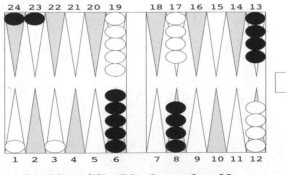

**Problem 77: Black to play 62.**

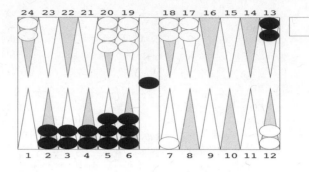

**Problem 78: Black to play 42.**

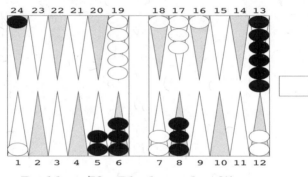

**Problem 79: Black to play 65.**

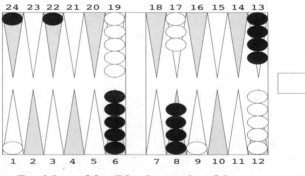

**Problem 80: Black to play 21.**

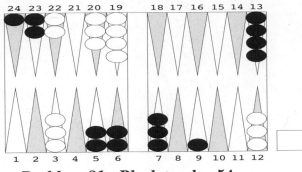

**Problem 81: Black to play 54.**

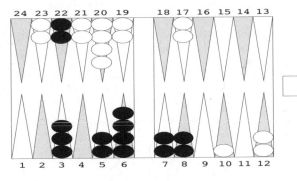

**Problem 82: Black to play 21.**

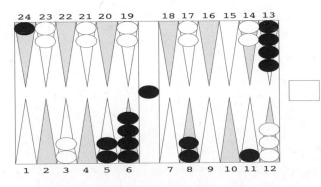

**Problem 83: Black to play 43.**

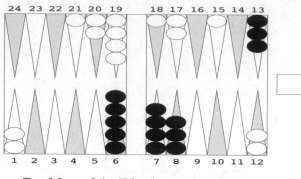

Problem 84:  Black to play 62.

## SOLUTIONS

**Problem 60: Black to play 11.**

Black has two objectives: safety his blot, and create the maximum number of builders for the remaining points in his inner board. Safetying is easy. Black plays 15/13 with his first two aces. With the last two, the right play is 7/5, which leaves Black with three builders for each of the two remaining inner points. If Black makes the blunder of playing 6/4? instead, he only has two active builders for each inner point.

**Problem 61: Black to play 65.**

Diversify your numbers to make key points. Black can cover the 1-point and make a 5-point prime with 13/7 6/1. But his real goal here is to finish White off by actually making the 2-point, and the best way to do that is to play 7/1 13/8, creating three building numbers for the 2-point, rather than just two.

**Problem 62: Black to play 21.**

Points are good, but don't make them automatically. Look around and see if your checkers might be more useful when spread out. Here Black can hit and make a point with 13/11*/10, but the 10-point doesn't really do anything, as Black's checkers are in no danger of being hit. A better play is 13/11* 10/9, diversifying the checkers and giving better chances of making the 7-point.

**Problem 63: Black to play 31.**

When breaking your prime, see if you can do it in a way that puts maximum pressure on your opponent.

Black can play 9/8 9/6. If White then runs off the 3-point, Black can attack him with three numbers: threes, fours, and fives. That's a good situation.

But if Black plays 8/7 8/5, and White runs off the 3-point, Black can attack with *four* numbers: twos, threes, fours, and sixes. That's even better. Keep an eye out for the little plays that can make a difference between winning and losing.

### Problem 64: Black to play 41.

Just because the game's under control is no reason to let up. Squeeze the most out of every position.

Black felt pretty good here and played 13/12*/8. Obvious, but careless. A better play was 13/12* 7/3, getting four builders for the ace-point. Closing the ace-point quickly gives better gammon chances, and the best time to create builders is when your opponent has two men on the bar.

### Problem 65: Black to play 22.

Black could play completely safely with 12/8(2), but there's a better play — 12/4!, getting a fourth builder for the 3-point. Black needs to notice that since White has two blots in his home board, the indirect shots White gets after 12/4 (61, 52, 43, 63) aren't really threats.

### Problem 66: Black to play 53.

The more awkward your distribution, the more points have to give way to flexibility.

Black can make the 3-point, but it leaves him with stripped points and a huge stack. Much better is 13/5, which temporarily passes up a new point but give Black some choices on following turns.

### Problem 67: Black to play 11.

11 is a great shot (Black's best, in fact), but he must play accurately to extract the most from the position.

Three aces are clear: Bar/24* and 2/1*(2). With the last ace, the right play is 7/6!, breaking a good point to get a third builder aiming at the open 2-point. No other play gets three builders for the 2-point.

### Problem 68: Black to play 32.

If you've got a point you need to make, try to get the maximum number of builders bearing on that point.

Here White is on the bar, so Black can proceed with complete safety. His next job is to make the 7-point and 8-point, building a prime. What play gets the maximum builders for each point? The answer is 13/10 11/9! It's an easy play to overlook, but it produces four builders for each point with no risk.

**Problem 69:  Black to play 65.**

Black should attack with this roll, and that's what he did.  He played 8/2* and 9/4.

But his play was wrong on a couple of counts.  The right play was 13/2*.  Here's why:

After 8/2* 9/4, Black has 15 numbers to cover the 2-point next turn if White misses his shot:  all 2s, plus 11, 65, and 66.  After 13/2*, Black can cover next turn with all 6s plus 42, 51, 22, 33, 43, and 52, a total of 21 cover numbers.  That's a big improvement.

If Black plays 13/2* and White enters with a deuce, Black probably won't be able to complete a closeout, so he'll need to build a prime instead.  With a checker still on the 8-point, Black has a good chance to make the 8-point next turn, with a 5-point prime in place.

**Problem 70:  Black to play 32.**

Bar/23 is forced, then Black has a choice of three 3s:  8/5*, 6/3, and 13/10. Hitting is the worst choice in this position.  Of the three plays, it allows the most return hits (21).  Since White has a 5-point board, and another hit could mean the difference between losing a single game and a gammon, that's important.  Also, a hit strips the 8-point, so Black's not as likely to cover successfully next turn as he should be.

Slotting the 3-point is the safest play (only 12 return shots), but the 3-point isn't valuable here, and Black will have trouble next turn covering the 3-point while not leaving another blot somewhere.

The right play is 13/10, which leaves a medium number of shots (18) but does two very good things:  it puts pressure on White's blot on the 5-point, and it unstacks the huge stack on the midpoint.  Big, inflexible stacks lead to sure trouble later on, so getting those checkers into play is a very high priority.

**Problem 71:  Black to play 11.**

Black doesn't want to leave White any game-winning shots from the bar, but he can't safety both blots with this number.  (In fact, he can't safety the blot on the 18-point at all.)  He starts by playing 8/7, picking up one blot.  Then he looks to see if duplication can help him.  He notices that White needs 2s and 3s to enter.  Is there a play that gives him one of those same numbers to hit?  Yes!  Black plays 18/15 with his last three ones, duplicating 3s.

Black could have found this play by ignoring duplication and simply counting White's shots from the bar. The play he made leaves White just three shots — 33 and 23. Any other play would leave more. (Check this yourself.) Over the board, duplication lets you find the right play quickly and easily. To your opponents, your skills may start to look magical.

**Problem 72: Black to play 63.**
Black will certainly hit with 6/3*, then has a choice between playing 22/16 or 21/15 with his six. Noting that White will need ones and threes to enter from the bar, Black correctly plays 21/15, giving Black threes to hit in the outer board, rather than fours.

**Problem 73: Black to play 11.**
If your opponent already has a number which is very strong for him, you can profitably duplicate that number elsewhere on the board.

Here Black's first three ones are pretty much forced: Bar/24 and 6/5(2). Before playing his last ace, Black notices that White's sixes are already very good for him. he can make his bar-point, or, with 61 and 62, make his 5-point. Since six is already a strong number, there's little risk in giving White yet another good six. So Black alertly plays 8/7!, slotting his own bar point. If White hits, he'll have to pass up an already strong point on the other side of the board.

**Problem 74: Black to play 11.**
Three of Black's aces are clear: 6/5(2) and 15/14.
With the last ace Black could play conservatively with 14/13, but that gives him an unwieldy stack of six checkers on the 13-point. Is there a choice? Notice that White needs twos everywhere on the board: twos to anchor on the 3-point, twos to make his own bar-point, and twos to hit. The duplication of twos and the awkwardness of 14/13 argue for a more flexible play: Black should move 6/5! with his last ace.

**Problem 75:  Black to play 11.**

This is a great shot, and three of the aces are very clear:  24/23 (to escape) and 2/1*(2), putting White on the bar.  How about the last ace?

A prosaic player would try either 8/7 or 10/9, both of which leave Black with three builders for the open 5-point, at a cost of one or two shots from the bar.  The ingenious player, however, notices that duplication allows him to play 8/7!  At a cost of three shots (52 and 55) instead of two, Black gets four builders for the 5-point and three builders for the 2-point, with complete diversification of point-making numbers.  A great play.

**Problem 76:  Black to play 32.**

This is an especially awkward roll for Black.  The spare checker on the 13-point can only move half the number, while the checker on the 22-point can't move at all.  6/1 is safe but pathetic.  What to do?

Duplication holds the key.  The right play is 13/10 6/4!, giving White twos everywhere.  If White can't hit, Black's a favorite to fill in a key point in his board.

**Problem 77:  Black to play 62.**

Black has two ways to run into White's outfield with this roll. He can play 23/15 or 24/16.  What's right?

Notice that if he plays 23/15, his checkers on the 15-point and 13-point are two pips apart, just like his checkers on the 8-point and 6-point.  Next turn, the numbers that make outer board points (64, 53, 42) are the very same numbers that make inner points.  Not good.

If he plays 24/16, the 16-point and the 13-point are three pips apart.  As a result, Black has different numbers to make outer board points (63, 52).  That's diversification, and that's the right play.

**Problem 78:  Black to play 42.**

As much as you can, try to give yourself different numbers on the dice for different objectives.

Black will enter with the four, so he'll have a chance of leaping White's prime next turn.  Then he has a seemingly unimportant choice between 6/4 and 5/3 for his deuce.  One play leaves him 4s and 3s to make his 1-point; the other play leaves 5s and 2s. Notice that Black needs 5s to jump White's prime. Therefore he wants to leave himself different numbers to make the 1-point, so he plays 6/4.

**Problem 79: Black to play 65.**

Avoid big stacks of checkers in the middle game.

Black can play totally safe with 24/18*/13, but that leaves a horrible pile on the 13-point, almost surely leading to more blots later. Create some flexibility now by balancing the position. Black should play 24/18* and 13/8!

**Problem 80: Black to play 21.**

An excellent move here, overlooked by most players, is 24/22 6/5! Slotting the 5-point is a good play in most situations, but it's even better when your opponent has escaped a back checker. The reason is simple. If your opponent has two men back, and you slot your 5-point, and he hits you, you've not only lost ground in the race, but he's threatening to establish a powerful advanced anchor. If he has only one man back, and he hits you, there's no possibility of his building an anchor. A point to remember.

**Problem 81: Black to play 54.**

The four is easy enough — Black plays 13/9. What about the five?

Black has three legal fives: 23/18, 13/8, and 7/2. Breaking the anchor with 23/18 is easy to dismiss — that's like a boxer dropping his guard and leading with his chin. But what about 7/2, which looks safe and sound?

It's safe all right, but not too sound. Once Black starts killing checkers behind White's anchor, he's going to find that he doesn't have enough men to continue building blocking points. Slotting points will never look better than it does now, and if Black kills his spares, he'll have to hope that White never rolls a five.

13/8, on the other hand, gives Black a direct path to victory. If Black makes the 8-point before White can hit there, the advantage in the game swings over to Black's side. Reason enough for an aggressive play.

**Problem 82: Black to play 21.**

After your opponent has escaped your home board, your goal is to build your board as quickly as possible, in preparation for a later shot. The right way to accomplish this is to slot the open points, then cover next turn. Black should play 6/4 3/2! Next turn, after covering, he'll have a winning board if he can hit a shot.

**Problem 83: Black, on bar, to play 43.**

In Problem 83, Black has to enter from the bar with his three, playing Bar/22. Then he can consider slotting the bar-point with his four, by playing 11/7. Is this the right play?

No. There are many situations where slotting isn't a good idea. In general, you don't want to slot when your back checkers are split. The reason is that if your opponent misses your slotted checker, he may hit one of the loose checkers in his home board. While you're trying to enter from the bar, you'll have trouble covering your slot. Remember that if you take the risk of slotting, you need to be able to cover your slot when you're missed.

**Problem 84: Black to play 62.**

Once you've escaped your back men, don't play too boldly. Avoid getting a man sent back if possible.

Black could make an aggressive play with 13/5, which would certainly improve his position if he didn't get hit. But with all his back men escaped, he wants to make sure they stay that way. The right move is 13/7 8/6.

# 7

# THE MIDDLE GAME

Once both sides start to make inner points, we're out of the opening and into the middle game. The basic goals remain the same as in the opening: make points, hit blots, and escape your back checkers. But stronger inner boards mean more danger for both sides, and a single bad sequence can allow the doubling cube to make an appearance.

Keep these guidelines in mind when playing the middle game:

- Fight for the key points.
- Remember that inner board points are inherently stronger than outer board points.
- Try to get an advanced anchor before your opponent's game is too strong.
- Be eager to split your back checkers if your opponent has an outside prime, but not yet a strong inner board.
- Be reluctant to split when your opponent's inner board is strong, or he has awkward stacks of checkers that can't form a prime.
- Take chances when your opponent's home board is weak; be cautious when it's strong.
- Prime an anchor; attack a blot.
- Remember that double-hits are always powerful.
- When you escape your back checkers and take a lead in the race, turn cautious.

When you're considering a double, evaluate these factors:

- Are you ahead in the race?
- Is your board better than your opponent's?
- Do you have an advanced anchor, or have you actually escaped your back checkers?
- Does your opponent have loose blots?

If you have an edge in a couple of these areas, and are even in the other two, you probably have a double and your opponent can probably take. If you've taken a lead in all phases of the game, you have a great double and your opponent should probably give up.

**PROBLEMS**

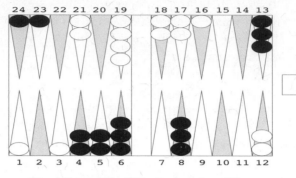

**Problem 85: Black to play 51.**

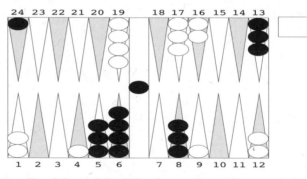

**Problem 86: Black to play 41.**

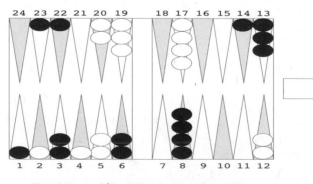

**Problem 87: Black to play 43.**

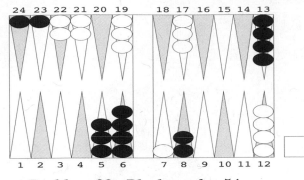

**Problem 88:  Black to play 54.**

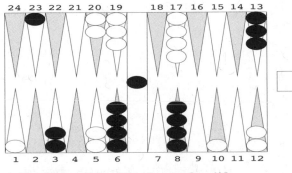

**Problem 89:  Black to play 52.**

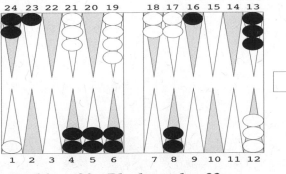

**Problem 90:  Black to play 63.**

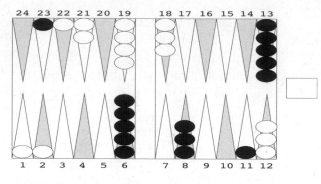

Problem 91: Black to play 42.

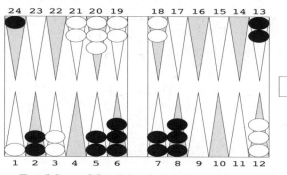

Problem 92: Black to play 22.

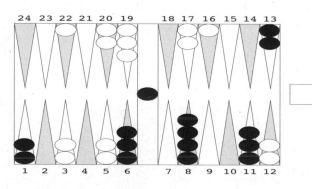

Problem 93: Black to play 22.

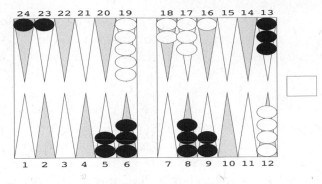

**Problem 94: Black to play 22.**

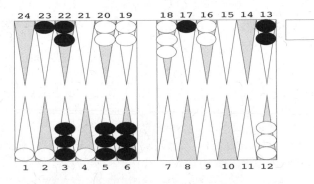

**Problem 95: Black to play 61.**

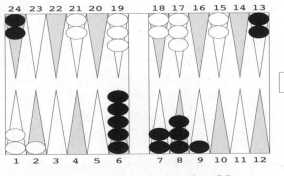

**Problem 96: Black to play 32.**

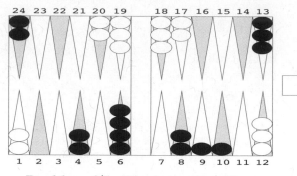

## Problem 97: Black to play 42.

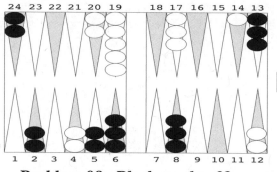

## Problem 98: Black to play 62.

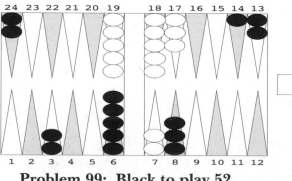

## Problem 99: Black to play 52.

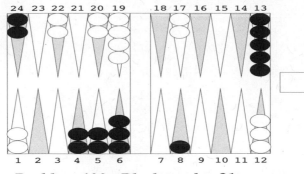

Problem 100: Black to play 21.

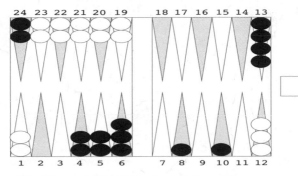

Problem 101: Black to play 65.

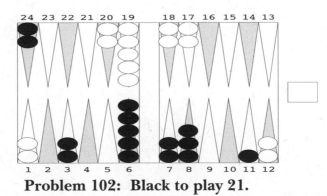

Problem 102: Black to play 21.

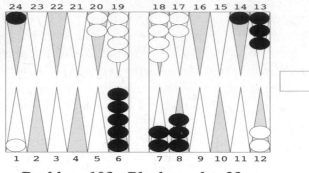

Problem 103: Black to play 33.

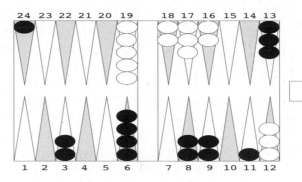

Problem 104: Black to play 33.

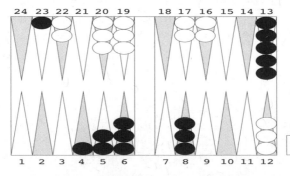

Problem 105: Black to play 42.

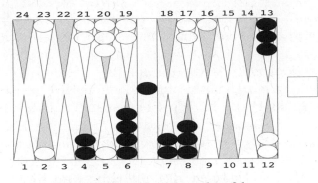

**Problem 106:  Black to play 61.**

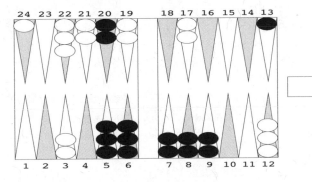

**Problem 107:  Black to play 41.**

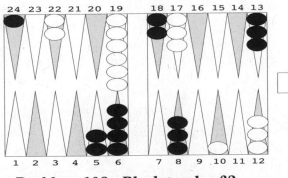

**Problem 108:  Black to play 32.**

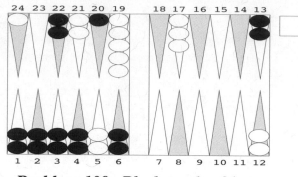

**Problem 109: Black to play 21.**

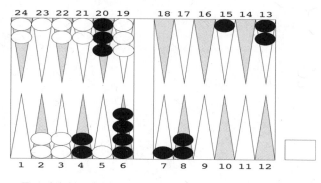

**Problem 110: Black to play 42.**

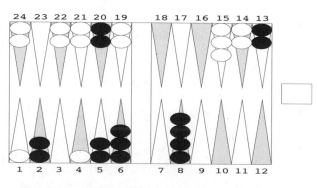

**Problem 111: Black to play 33.**

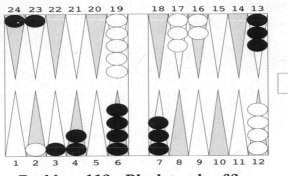

**Problem 112: Black to play 62.**

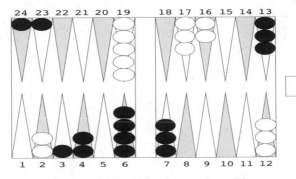

**Problem 113: Black to play 62.**

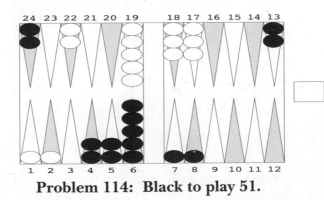

**Problem 114: Black to play 51.**

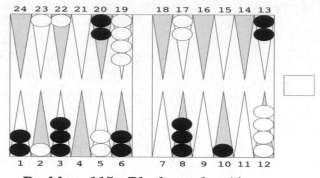

**Problem 115: Black to play 41.**

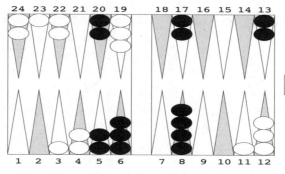

**Problem 116: Black to play 33.**

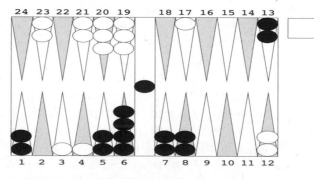

**Problem 117: Black to play 31.**

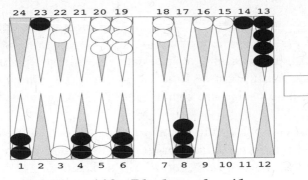

Problem 118: Black to play 41.

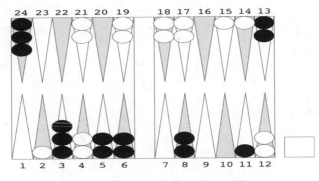

Problem 119: Black to play 41.

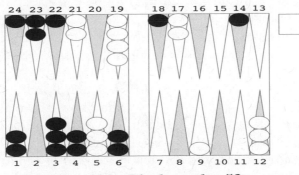

Problem 120: Black to play 52.

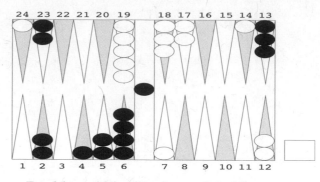

Problem 121:  Black to play 65.

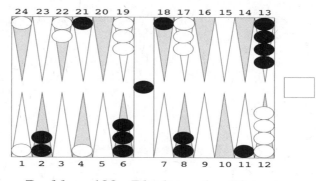

Problem 122:  Black to play 21.

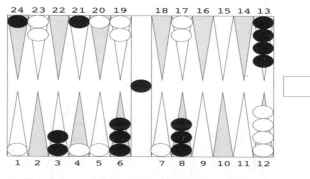

Problem 123:  Black to play 51.

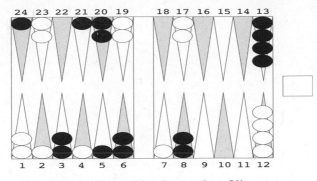

**Problem 124: Black to play 65.**

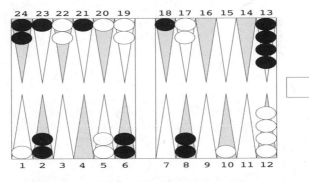

**Problem 125: Black to play 31.**

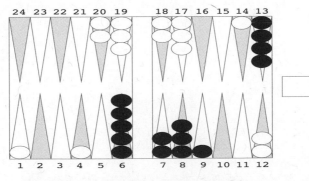

**Problem 126: Black to play 21.**

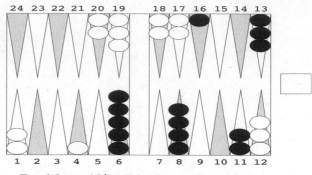

**Problem 127: Black to play 64.**

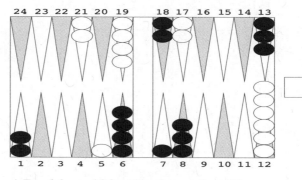

**Problem 128: Black to play 61.**

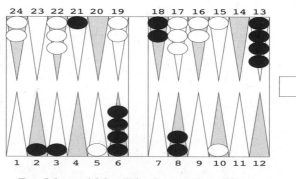

**Problem 129: Black to play 53.**

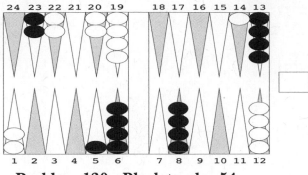

**Problem 130: Black to play 54.**

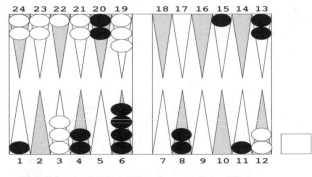

**Problem 131: Black to play 41.**

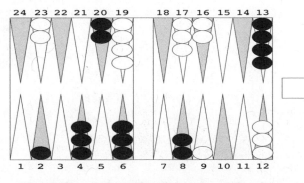

**Problem 132: Black to play 55.**

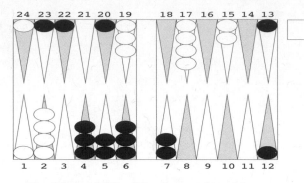

## Problem 133: Black to play 44.

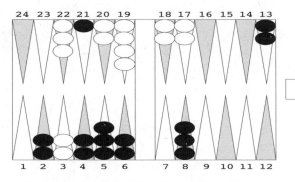

## Problem 134: Black to play 63.

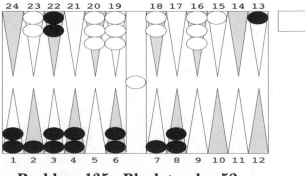

## Problem 135: Black to play 52.

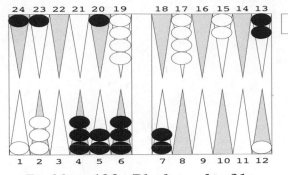

Problem 136: Black to play 21.

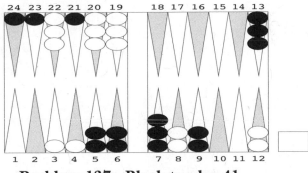

Problem 137: Black to play 41.

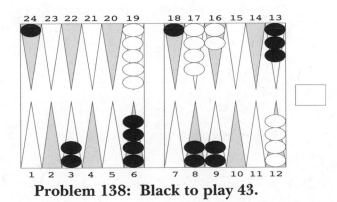

Problem 138: Black to play 43.

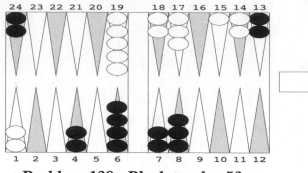

**Problem 139: Black to play 53.**

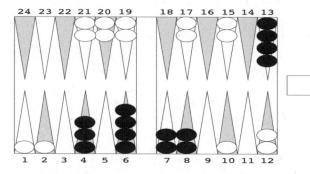

**Problem 140: Should Black double?**
**Should White take if doubled?**

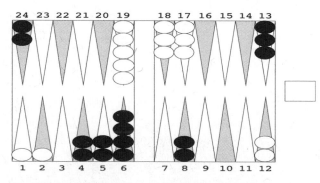

**Problem 141: Should Black double?**
**Should White take if doubled?**

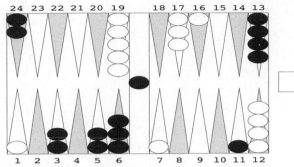

**Problem 142: Should Black double?**
**Should White take if doubled?**

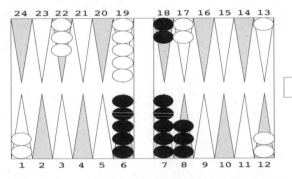

**Problem 143: Should Black double?**
**Should White take if doubled?**

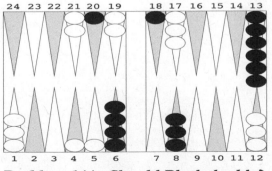

**Problem 144: Should Black double?**
**Should White take if doubled?**

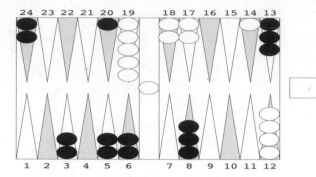

**Problem 145: Should Black double?
Should White take if doubled?**

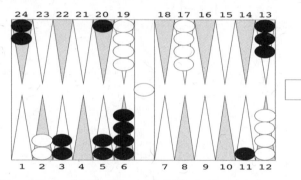

**Problem 146: Should Black double?
Should White take if doubled?**

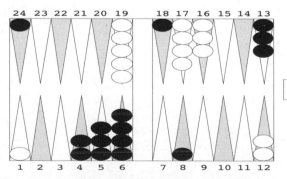

**Problem 147: Should Black double?
Should White take if doubled?**

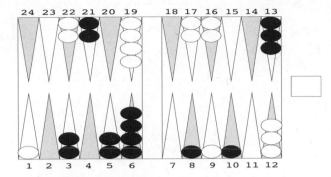

**Problem 148: Should Black double?**
**Should White take if doubled?**

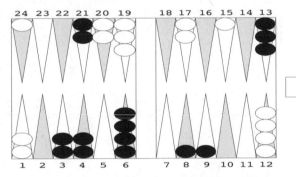

**Problem 149: Should Black double?**
**Should White take if doubled?**

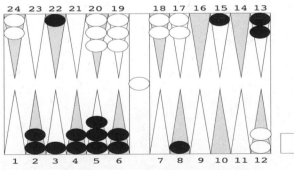

**Problem 150: Should Black double?**
**Should White take if doubled?**

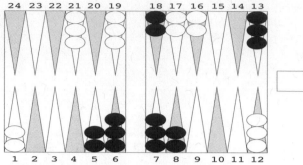

**Problem 151: Should Black double?**
**Should White take if doubled?**

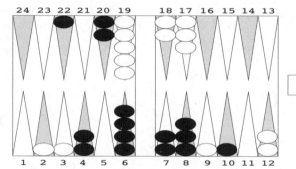

**Problem 152: Should Black double?**
**Should White take if doubled?**

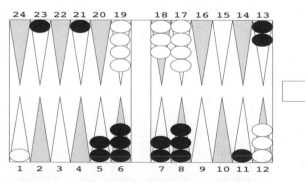

**Problem 153: Should Black double?**
**Should White take if doubled?**

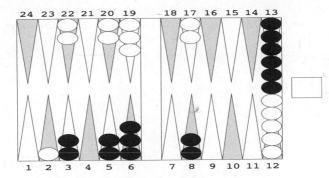

**Problem 154: Should Black double?**
**Should White take if doubled?**

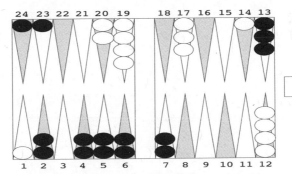

**Problem 155: Should Black double?**
**Should White take if doubled?**

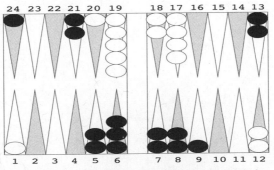

**Problem 156: Should Black double?**
**Should White take if doubled?**

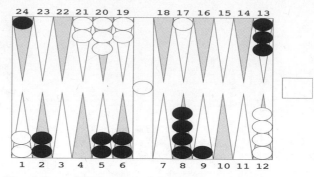

## Problem 157: Should Black double?
## Should White take if doubled?

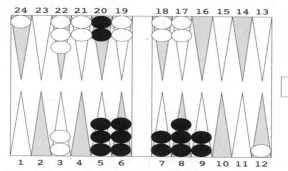

## Problem 158: Should Black double?
## Should White take if doubled?

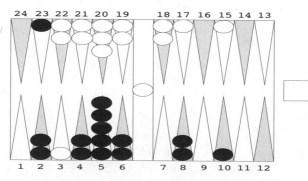

## Problem 159: Should Black double?
## Should White take if doubled?

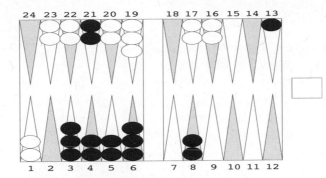

**Problem 160: Should Black double?**
**Should White take if doubled?**

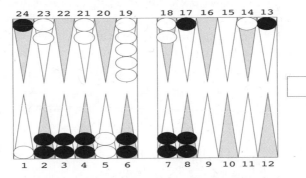

**Problem 161: Should Black double?**
**Should White take if doubled?**

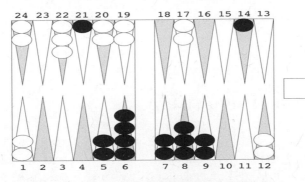

**Problem 162: Should Black double?**
**Should White take if doubled?**

## SOLUTIONS

**Problem 85: Black to play 51.**

In the middle game, players fight for command of key points. Once you've started to build a prime, the point at the front of the prime becomes a key point, which both players very much want to make. Here the key point is Black's 3-point. If Black can make it before White, White will be squeezed into a cramped defensive position. Black should hit with 8/3*, trying to make the point first. The best ace is then 23/22, attacking the White blot on the 16-point.

**Problem 86: Black to play 41.**

Bar/24 13/9* is the safest hit, and might look automatic — but be careful! There are some downsides to this play. The back checkers are stuck back on the 24-point, the midpoint is stripped, and White is ready to anchor on the 21-point if he can't hit back.

A positionally superior play is Bar/21 5/4*. The back checkers get moving, the midpoint keeps a spare, and White is in very hot water if he can't hit back right away. Look at all features of the position before deciding on your move.

**Problem 87: Black to play 43.**

Two basic rules govern hitting on the ace-point.

Rule 1: In general, be reluctant to hit on the ace-point, especially if you have no board, or the position is complicated.

Rule 2: If you have hit on the ace-point, be eager to cover the blot, rather than leaving it around to be hit later. A strong home board is worth having.

Here 14/10 13/10 looks like a good positional play, but the right move is 8/4*/1, per rule 2.

**Problem 88: Black to play 54.**

54 is a poor shot for Black in Problem 88. He was hoping to hit the blot on the 7-point, but missed.

One possible play is making the 1-point with 6/1 5/1, but that should be rejected. Black needs to build a prime in case he eventually hits a checker, so he needs to save his builders to make the vital 4-point and 7-point.

Black could run out a rear checker with something like 23/14 or 24/15, but these plays also have to be rejected. Black trails in the race by 19 pips after the roll, so trying to break contact and enter a running game isn't the right idea.

Black should just play 24/20 13/8! By moving to the 20-point and stopping there, Black covers the area from the 14-point to the 18-point. If the White checker on 7 can't move to safety on his midpoint, Black should be able to get a direct shot next turn. Even if he can't hit a shot, he may be able to anchor on the 20-point with a viable holding game.

**Problem 89: Black to play 52.**

Make your move for an advanced anchor before your opponent's game gets overwhelmingly strong.

Black has to enter with Bar/23, then has a choice of some unappetizing fives. Hitting with 6/1* (the play chosen in the game) risks a big loss in the race for very little potential gain. But 13/8 strips the midpoint, and 8/3 moves a checker essentially out of play.

The right play by far is 23/18!, fighting for a good anchor before White has time to consolidate. Unlike the other plays, the upside here is very big, justifying the apparent risk.

**Problem 90: Black to play 63.**

Don't just make points blindly: Anticipate the flow of the game. In this position, Black could make the 10-point with 16/10 13/10, but a better play is 16/10 23/20. Black has three checkers back, and if White makes the 20-point, those checkers could get trapped. Black should step up and try to make the 20-point himself, while at the same time preventing White from moving builders to the 16, 15, and 14-points.

**Problem 91: Black to play 42.**

Inner points are better than outer points.

Black was feeling a bit nervous because he wasn't able to escape his back checker. He decided to make the 9-point instead of the 4-point, so he wouldn't have an outfield blot to worry about in case he got attacked.

Plausible but flawed thinking. One of the best defenses against an early blitz attack is a strong inner board. As a bonus, the 4-point will play a powerful role for the whole rest of the game. Who knows when you'll be able to make it again? Grab the 4-point, and let the blot on the 11-point fend for itself.

**Problem 92: Black to play 22.**

Strong inner points usually trump outside blocking points.

Here Black played 13/9(2), relying on the power of the outside prime to contain White's checkers. Unfortunately White doesn't have to move his rear checkers for quite a while, since he can play with all the spares on his midpoint. As a result, Black's going to find himself in hot water whenever he can't move his back checker quickly. The right play is just 8/4 6/4 24/22, putting his spares where they belong.

**Problem 93: Black to play 22.**

Inner points beat outer points! — usually. It's a good rule, and this position is typical. Black should play Bar/23 8/4 6/4, grabbing the strong 4-point, instead of Bar/23 11/9(3), grabbing an outer board point. Inner points provide landing spots and can keep your opponent on the bar, while outer points provide blockading power. In most cases, the inner point is more important.

**Problem 94: Black to play 22.**

When your opponent has escaped, concentrate on building your board, rather than outside blocking points.

In the game, Black played 23/21 followed by 9/7(2) 13/11. Moving to the 21-point is a good idea, preparing for an anchor. But with the rest of the roll Black should play 8/4 6/4, building another inner point quickly. The idea is to have a strong board ready as a reception committee if you ever hit a shot. With no opposition, you should build that board as directly as possible.

**Problem 95: Black to play 61.**

When you're attacking, be sure to attack the right point.

Black will certainly play 23/17 with the six, then look for the best ace. He has two ways to attack: 5/4* or 3/2*. Hitting on the 4-point looks good, since that's the more valuable point. But notice — if Black hits on the 4-point, White has 18 return hits, and Black has only 17 covers. If Black instead hits on the 2-point, White has only 14 return hits, and Black has 24 covers. The hit on the 2-point is both much safer and much more likely to later be covered. That's the right play.

**Problem 96: Black to play 32.**

Once your opponent has started to block your back checkers, you must use non-constructive rolls to escape.

Black is starting to feel the pressure as White has built a good blocking position. 32 isn't an especially good shot, since it doesn't make a new point for Black. In this case, he has to make a move to escape. The right deuce is 24/22, preparing to jump next turn with a six. Since Black's back men are now split and exposed, he has to tidy up any loose blots left around, so the awkward-looking 9/6 is the best three.

**Problem 97: Black to play 42.**

Once your opponent has started to prime you in, you must split your back men as soon as possible. Every roll that doesn't build an additional blocking point of your own is a candidate for splitting.

In Problem 97 Black needs to make his move now. The right play is 24/22 13/9. If Black could have made the 5-point or the 7-point, he would have done so, but since he can't form his own prime, he must try to escape White's. This play could easily backfire, but it's still his best chance.

**Problem 98: Black to play 62.**

Once your opponent has an advanced anchor, you can't stay back on the 24-point. You either have to get an anchor yourself, or start to run for home.

An advanced anchor plus a small blockade is usually enough of an edge to double if your back checkers are still in the starting position, so get them moving! Here the right play isn't the safe but passive 13/5, but instead 24/16, heading for home. White can't hit and build his prime, so you're not in too much danger — yet.

**Problem 99:  Black to play 52.**

If your opponent has an awkward structure, don't be in a hurry to split your back men;  it could give him targets for attack.

Here Black could play 14/9 24/22, but splitting would be a mistake.  White's position is awkward, and many rolls force him to dump blots in his home board.  Splitting just gives him an excuse to attack.  Instead Black should play 14/9 6/4, keeping his defensive anchor on the 24-point and building his home board.

**Problem 100:  Black to play 21.**

Don't be in a hurry to split when your opponent has developed a strong board.  If Black plays the natural move 13/11 24/23, White can launch a strong blitzing attack if he can't make new points.  The right play is just 13/10, with minimum risk in the face of White's good board.

**Problem 101:  Black to play 65.**

When your opponent's position is very strong, all alternatives will look dangerous. Seek out a plan that offers some tangible winning chances. Here 24/13 breaks the anchor and leaves several vulnerable blots, while 13/8 10/4 is just a good way to finish second.  The right idea is 13/7 13/8!

If White misses, Black can cover his 7-point and have good chances in a prime versus prime game.

**Problem 102:  Black to play 21.**

The ideal time to split is when your home has a prime combined with a weak home board.  Since 21 can't be used to make a new blocking point, Black has to move up to the edge of his opponent's prime.  The right play is 24/21!

**Problem 103:  Black to play 33.**

If you only have one checker back and your opponent has just a moderately strong blocking position, there's no need to hurry to get your checker to the edge of his formation. Coming up to the edge may just give your opponent the excuse he needs to attack on a critical point.

In Position 103, Black should leave his checker on the 24-point alone and just play 8/5(2) 6/3(2). Creeping up with a play like

24/21 14/11 6/3(2) forces White to attack on the 21-point, which White is eager to do.

## Problem 104: Black to play 33.

If the race is close, don't commit yourself to trying to hit a shot. After Black plays his 3-3, he'll only trail in the race by 1 pip. That's too close to give up on the race, so he should play 24/21, threatening to escape with a six. With his other threes, he can play 11/5 8/5. He won't like it if White points on him, but only White twos will do any real damage.

## Problem 105: Black to play 42.

When you're playing with a straggler, keep out of trouble.

Black played 23/21 8/4, thinking he was getting a better chance to escape. Actually he's walking into a trap. If White makes the 21-point and Black starts dancing, White could close his board before Black got to move again. That could easily lead to a gammon with Black having so many checkers still outside. Avoid this trap by staying back on the 23-point, relatively out of trouble, and playing 13/9 6/4 instead.

## Problem 106: Black to play 61.

Don't provoke a fight when your opponent holds all the cards.

Black played Bar/24/18, but he was asking for trouble. White has a better board and lots of builders ready for a fight. The right idea was just Bar/24 13/7, waiting for a better time to escape.

## Problem 107: Black to play 41.

Beware of making your opponent's good rolls extra strong. It's tempting to try to complete a prime by playing 13/9 5/4. If White then doesn't roll an ace, Black will have many chances to complete his prime. But right now, White's only good rolls are aces, which get him to the edge of the prime, and slotting makes those aces even stronger.

Black should just play 13/8, with a big edge and a safe position, then run off the 20-point next turn.

**Problem 108: Black to play 32.**

If you're well behind in the race, and your opponent has a weak position, you can afford to be very aggressive. If your aggression backfires, your opponent's weak structure won't be able to hurt you.

Black will of course hit with 13/10*, then look for the best two. The right play is 6/4! Black wants to make the 4-point, so he just slots it in the most direct manner. If White hits back, his stacked position isn't very threatening, and if he misses (which happens most of the time) Black is delighted.

Slotting in the face of a checker on the bar is a bit unusual, but in this case all Black's other deuces were clearly worse.

**Problem 109: Black to play 21.**

With a powerful board, don't be afraid to take some chances.

Black actually played 22/20 and 4/3, breaking his board. But right now his board is strong and White's is weak, so this is no time to be cautious. The right play is 13/10!, keeping the board and taking advantage of some duplication of 1s and 5s.

**Problem 110: Black to play 42.**

When your board is weaker, play cautiously.

Black chose 7/5* 15/11. This looks aggressive, and under different circumstances would be the right play. But here White has a stronger home board than Black, so Black should opt for cautious play. The right move was 13/7.

**Problem 111: Black to play 33.**

Be reluctant to blitz if your opponent has the better board.

Black would like to play the aggressive 13/4*/1*, but several factors mitigate against it:

• White has the stronger board now, so a hit from the bar could be fatal.

• Black doesn't have a lot of covers for the one point even if White only enters with one man.

• A simple, safe play puts White under a lot of pressure.

Notice that after the best play, 13/10(2) 20/17(2), White badly needs to anchor to avoid a solid double on Black's part — a double achieved at no risk.

**Problem 112: Black to play 62.**

When you're conducting a blitz or a potential blitz, and your opponent can't anchor, all inner board points are important, even the ones behind a blot. The right play is 7/1 3/1.

**Problem 113: Black to play 62.**

If your opponent has anchored, blocking points are important. Points behind the anchor are pretty useless. Black should keep his formation and hope to make the 3-point turn by playing 23/15.

**Problem 114: Black to play 51.**

Be prepared to switch game plans from move to move, particularly in tactical situations.

Black has been playing a priming game, and he could continue that plan with a move like 13/7. But with this roll, it's time to switch plans entirely. Black should play 7/2*/1*, playing a blitzing game instead. Not only is the blitz powerful in itself, but by keeping White on the bar, Black prevents him from using his active builders on the 19, 18, and 17-points to fill in the 20 and 21-points.

**Problem 115: Black to play 41.**

Don't try to build outside primes once you've made low points in your board. Work on closing the board instead.

Making the outside point with 13/9 10/9 looks fancy, but the right idea is 10/6 3/2*. Outside points and low inner points don't work well together.

**Problem 116: Black to play 33.**

When your opponent has an anchor, concentrate on building blocking points in front of the anchor, not attacking behind the anchor.

Here Black could play 17/11* 6/3* 8/5, hitting two men. But the points behind an anchor aren't worth very much, and the gain isn't enough to justify the risk of being hit. Instead Black should just play 17/11*(2), taking no risk while keeping all checkers in front of White's anchor.

### Problem 117: Black to play 31.

When it's kill or be killed, go for the throat.

Black's in a lot of trouble in Position 117. White owns the cube and is itching to flip it over. A passive play like Bar/22 6/5 is a good way to finish second in a two-player game. Instead, Black should play Bar/24 6/3*, which at least gives him a fighting chance to turn the game around.

### Problem 118: Black to play 41.

When your opponent is ready to land on your head, distract him by attacking first. Here White is well-placed to attack the blot on the 23-point, so Black has to launch a pre-emptive strike. The right play is 8/3*, which prevents White from making any inner-board points.

### Problem 119: Black to play 41.

In a bad position, use tempo hits to maneuver to a playable game.

Black is doing poorly, and a passive play like 11/6 will make things worse. White will make the 20-point or bring down more builders, and Black will have a hard time activating the men on the 24-point before it's too late.

The right idea is 24/20 3/2*! The hit provides a tempo to split to the 20-point in relative safety. The play might backfire, but it gives Black a fighting chance.

### Problem 120: Black to play 52.

When your opponent is on the bar, try to improve your position to the maximum extent possible.

Black will certainly hit with 14/9*. In the game, Black then played his deuce from 24 to 22, grabbing the 22-point. The 22-point has some value, but White is sitting on the bar right now and can't do much. This is the time to go for the best anchor around. Black should have played 22/20! with his deuce.

### Problem 121: Black to play 65.

65 is a super shot in position 121. Black can enter and hit. But which hit is right?

The correct hit is Bar/20/14*. It's right for three reasons:
- It gains more ground in the race.
- White's unhit blot is much harder to safety.
- Black avoids a huge downswing on White's two best numbers, 11 and 33.

## Problem 122: Black to play 21.

Attacking on the valuable high points in your board loses much of its power if you have to attack with your very last spare.

Here Black will enter and hit with his ace, Bar/24*. Hitting on the 4-point with the other half of his roll would normally be a routine play. But here he has to hit with his last builder, which would leave him with a stripped and weak 6-point. Accordingly, the simple building play, 13/11, moves up in value and now becomes a well-balanced top choice.

## Problem 123: Black to play 51.

Black will certainly enter with the five, Bar/20*. He then has a choice of three different aces. Playing 21/20 is safe but ultra-passive. With all White's blots scattered around, a more aggressive play is called for. Playing 6/5* fights for the best point, but strips away an active builder and leaves a weak formation behind. The right ace is 8/7*, which leaves a good distribution of builders and attackers, as well as no direct return shots.

## Problem 124: Black to play 65.

Don't overlook the double-hit plays. Even when they seem to involve a lot of risk, they can put tremendous pressure on your opponent.

Here 65 is a relatively poor shot, but Black can still apply maximum pressure with 13/7*/2*! Although many players wouldn't consider this move because it leaves two blots in the home board, in fact it's the play that gives Black the best chance of winning the game quickly.

## Problem 125: Black to play 31.

The double-hit is such a powerful play that it can even outweigh making key defensive points.

Here Black will play 21/20* with his ace, then look around for the best three. A conservative player might opt for 23/20, nailing down the key 20-point anchor. But an even better move is the double-hit with 13/10*, which gains ground in the race and leaves Black very likely to grab the 20-point next turn.

### Problem 126: Black to play 21.

Once you've escaped your back checkers, fighting for key points goes way down in priority.

Here Black has his back checkers home and he's got a comfortable 19-pip lead in the race (129-148). The game is pretty much won unless he gets hit, so his game plan changes from building a prime to maneuvering home safely. The right play is the super-quiet 9/7 8/7, leaving nothing to be hit. Even 9/8 13/11 represents too much risk under the circumstances.

### Problem 127: Black to play 64.

Escaping your back checkers is a worthy goal. Don't lose sight of it.

Here Black could get distracted by plays like 13/7 11/7 or 8/2 6/2, both of which are constructive. But simply 16/6 is the right play, safetying and escaping all blots. Black's distribution is good enough so that he should be able to continue to make points in the future.

### Problem 128: Black to play 61.

Use a little caution when leading in the race.

If Black were trailing or even in the race, the obvious play here would be 13/7 6/5*, hitting to gain some ground. But with a 21-pip lead after the roll, some prudence is in order. Black should protect his racing advantage with the better play, 13/7 8/7.

### Problem 129: Black to play 53.

When in doubt, play to win.

Black can hit two checkers here with 18/15*/10*, but it's a risky play, leaving five blots strung around the board, including two in his home board. Alternatively, he can play safe with 21/18 13/8, waiting for a better chance later.

The problem with the safe play is that later may never come. White, if left alone, might just make his 10-point and move his rear checker into the outfield. In that case, Black still wouldn't be ready to hit, and would probably never get another chance. Black has to make his move now, while there's still possibility for contact in the game. (Note that he trails in the race by 44 pips before the roll.) The right play is hitting two.

**Problem 130: Black to play 54.**

Don't get stuck in an ace-point or deuce-point game without a fight.

The obvious play here is 23/14*, but on a quick glance it looks pretty risky. White will have 5s, 4s, and 2s to hit somewhere, and Black will have lost his anchor.

The problem here is that Black will have a bad game in any event. Whether he plays 13/4 or 13/8 13/9, he has to leave a couple of blots around, and his game is very vulnerable. The merit of 23/14 is that it gives Black a chance to become a favorite, which the other plays don't. That makes it worth a try.

**Problem 131: Black to play 41.**

Sometimes a direct shot is the safest play of all.

When you're trying to balance risk and reward, sometimes it helps to actually count shots, rather than estimate shots. Black played 15/10 here. His thinking was that he wanted to make the 5-point soon, and he thought he could do it by leaving indirect shots, which were less likely to be hit than a direct shot.

But is that right? Had he actually counted shots, he would have found that 15/11 6/5 represents 11 shots and one blot, while 15/10 is 10 shots but two blots! In addition, Black is a lot more likely to make the 5-point after slotting it than after any other play. 15/11 6/5 wins for both risk and reward.

**Problem 132: Black to play 55.**

Before you make what you think is an obvious play — stop and look! 55 is a great shot for Black. He catches up and takes a small lead in the race (120-125 after the roll). In the actual game, Black instantly played 20/10(2), which is normally the right way to handle 55 in this sort of position.

But the presence of the White blot on Black's 9-point changes the position a bit. The position isn't only about disengaging and entering a slightly favorable race — Black would also like to take a big advantage by hitting White's last blot.

After 20/10(2), only a few rolls leave White's blot in jeopardy — 11, 22, 44, and 41, a total of 5 numbers. But after 20/15(2) 8/3(2), White has problems after 22, 44, 66, 64, 42, 51, and 41 — a total of 11 numbers. Since a hit is such a big swing, Black should stop on the 15-point.

### Problem 133: Black to play 44.

When you throw a double, make sure you see **all** the plays. There's nothing worse than throwing away the game because you threw a great shot and didn't see it.

Did you see the right play here? It's 20/8 12/8. Overpowering — if you see it.

### Problem 134: Black to play 63.

"Safety matters." All other things being equal, you should always factor in safety when deciding on a play. Of course Black will escape White's board by playing 21/15 with his six. With the three, he can choose to keep the same checker moving, 15/12, or play 8/5. To see which is best, take a look at the number of shots White has after either play.

After 21/15/12, White can hit with 63 or 54. That's four shots. After 21/15 8/5, White can only hit with 66 or 44. That's just two shots. No other factor enters into this decision, so Black should play 21/15 8/5, which is twice as safe as the other play.

### Problem 135: Black to play 52.

If you have a choice of two good things to do, do the hard thing first.

Black would like to cover his 2-point, but he'd also like to hit White's exposed blot on the 15-point. It's easy to cover the 2-point (most numbers do that), but very hard to hit (only four numbers hit), so the best move is 22/15*.

**Problem 136: Black to play 21.**

The time to worry about your opponent's miracle throws is when you gave the game well under control, and there's very little else to worry about.

Black will of course hit with the ace, 13/12*, then look around for the best deuce. He has plenty of choices, and from an offensive point of view they don't matter much: 24/22, 23/21, or 13/11 all give Black excellent chances after a normal sequence.

But suppose White throws one of his best two shots from the bar — either 11 or 33? In that case, one deuce stands out above all the others — 20/18, preventing White from making the 20-point on Black's head. That's the right play, but only because Black's game is so strong that he can afford to worry about the long shots.

By the way, some players might be scared to hit here, for fear of letting White get a back game. Don't fall into this trap! Back games are losing propositions, hard to time under the best of circumstances. Let your opponents play the back games if they want, while you score the gammons and backgammons.

**Problem 137: Black to play 41.**

Move in front of stripped points; stay away from heavy points. The ace here is pretty easy. Black plays 24/23, securing an anchor. How about the four? Black has a few choices: 7/3* hitting, 13/9, or 21/17.

There's nothing terrible about either hitting on the 3-point or putting a builder on the 9-point. But 21/17 cries out to be made. Why? On the 17-point, the checker is vulnerable to being hit by 5s from the midpoint. But those hits involve a big concession on White's part. He has to give up the midpoint to hit. If Black stays on the 21-point, White gets to hit with spares, keeping all key points. Moving vulnerable checkers in front of stripped points carries much less risk.

**Problem 138: Black to play 43.**

Don't abandon your rear checker unless you have to. In the actual game, Black played 18/11, leaving the checker on the 24-point to White's mercies. A better plan was just 9/5 8/5, incidentally making the 5-point but remaining on the 18-point to try and form an anchor there. If White hits, he won't make an inner point, and Black may get plenty of return shots.

**Problem 139: Black to play 53.**

Making a new blocking point will usually trump simply escaping a back checker. But be careful! If escaping serves other functions, it may be the better play.

Here the obvious play is to make the 3-point. But take another look at running with 24/16. Not only does it try to escape a checker, but it also throws a wrench in White's plan of making his 5-point next turn. If White hits he can't make the 5-point and vice-versa. This double duty makes 24/16 the better play.

**Problem 140: Should Black double?**
**Should White take if doubled?**

This is a strong double for Black and a clear pass for White. If you didn't want to double this position, your doubling strategy is much too conservative. You're probably waiting to double until you reach positions that are completely **gin** (virtually certain winners), rather than doubling when you're 70% to 75% to win, which is the optimal doubling area. If you took this, on the other hand, your taking strategy is much to optimistic: You need to tighten up a bit.

Black leads in every phase of the game. He's ahead in the pip count by 36 pips, 118-154. That means White hardly ever wins a race from this position — if he wins the game, he's going to have to hit a shot. Black has escaped all his back checkers, while White still has two men trapped. Most importantly, White hasn't made a defensive anchor, so there's still a possibility that his back checkers could get blitzed and closed out, a variation which mostly leads to a gammon for Black. White should concede a point rather than risking 4 points on a very long shot.

**Problem 141: Should Black double?**
**Should White take if doubled?**

Black's off to a good start, but he doesn't have a double yet. His board is stronger, and he's three pips ahead in the race (145-148), but he's very short on decisive threats. While he's trying to escape his back checkers, White may be able to build strong points of his own. Black shouldn't double, and White has an easy take if doubled.

**Problem 142: Should Black double?**
**Should White take if doubled?**

Doubling from the bar requires much more in the way of powerful threats than doubling with the whole roll available. If Black's checker on the bar were somewhere in White's home board, he'd have a good double with many threats. As is, his only threat is to enter and hit the blot on the 7-point. That's not enough for a double, and White has an easy take.

**Problem 143: Should Black double?**
**Should White take if doubled?**

Black has a 16-pip lead in the race (125-141), a good anchor on the 18-point, and a solid front position. He also has some strong threats – not threats to hit White's blot, which doesn't help him very much, but a lot of rolls that start to fill in his board. In addition, White's position is fairly weak, with his rear checkers still back, a weak board, and a stripped midpoint.

The combination of White's weak position and Black's good distribution and racing lead give Black a small double. White has a pretty easy take.

**Problem 144: Should Black double?**
**Should White take if doubled?**

A lead in the race isn't enough to double unless you have some structure to go with it.

Black is off to a good start with a racing lead of 32 pips (164-196). Some players might get excited and offer a quick double. Don't fall into this trap! Black's a favorite with the cube in the middle, but if White owns the cube Black is actually an underdog. It's not a double and White should beaver if doubled! Leave the cube alone for now.

**Problem 145: Should Black double?**
**Should White take if doubled?**

Black has some threats in position 145, and many players would be tempted to double. But what happens if Black doesn't hit the blot on the 14-point? White will reenter pretty easily, safety the blot on the 14, and the game goes on. Black's trailing in the race to start (159-155), and he won't be closing his board anytime soon. The time to think about doubling is after Black hits the second checker, and White reenters with perhaps only one man. That might be a good double. As is, it's no double and easy take.

## Problem 146: Should Black double?
## Should White take if doubled?

A good double and a sound take.

The double is pretty obvious. Black is ahead in the race, he's got a 3-point board, and White is still on the bar. The take might be less clear, but it illustrates the power of a defensive anchor. No matter what happens, White will always have a 2-point game, which is close to a take all by itself. Throw in White's other possibilities — he's not that far down in the race, and his checkers are all in play with plenty of spares, and the take is quite reasonable.

## Problem 147: Should Black double?
## Should White take if doubled?

Black's off to a good start. He's made two strong inner points, and he's slightly ahead in the race (136-139). Should he double?

Not yet. He's got an advantage, but it's not threatening to become overwhelming. His real goal this turn is to consolidate, which is not a reason for doubling. White has a good distribution — he can make inner points with small numbers, and run with 6s. He's got nothing much to fear right now. No double, and easy take.

## Problem 148: Should Black double?
## Should White take if doubled?

Position 148 shows a good early-game double. Black is slightly ahead in several key areas: he has a small lead in the race (139-143), his home board is slightly stronger than White's (three points vs two), and he has a defensive anchor, while White doesn't. Those are all small, permanent advantages. He also has the chance of gaining a lot of ground on the next roll, if he can hit White's blot. He's got a lot of hitting rolls: all 4s and 1s, plus 66 and 22. In addition, 55 is a strong roll, making the 1-point. With a very good sequence (Black hits and White stays out) Black's game will be so strong that White won't take a double. So Black should double now, and White can still take.

**Problem 149: Should Black double?**
**Should White take if doubled?**

Black has a nice edge. He's got a stronger board than White, and an advanced anchor. He also has some immediate threats to improve his game: sixes hit, 41, 31, and 43 make the 5-point, 21 makes the bar-point, and 51 hits. That's enough to give Black a good double.

Can White take? Yes. He's anchored and has no checkers on the bar. Black's 5-point and 7-point aren't made yet, and may not be anytime soon. White has his 5-point, and just enough wiggle room to venture a take.

**Problem 150: Should Black double?**
**Should White take if doubled?**

White's chance of turning this game around quickly hinges on Black's failing to cover the 3-point, followed by a White hit. What are the chances of that? Black covers with 27 numbers: all 5s and 2s, 41 and 11, plus 64, 66, and 44. That leaves 9 misses (25%). White then hits with 13 numbers from the bar (all 3s plus 21) — about a 1/3 chances. The chance of these two events occurring one after the other is 1/4 * 1/3, or about 1/12. Not very good odds — 11 to 1 against. Black should double and White should pass. If you like to take these positions, you'd better be a very lucky player!

**Problem 151: Should Black double?**
**Should White take if doubled?**

The combination of a budding prime and an advanced anchor, if the opponent hasn't moved his back men, constitutes a good double. Since Black only has a 4-point prime, and White is still even in the race, White can just squeeze out a take.

**Problem 152: Should Black double?**
**Should White take if doubled?**

Black has a nice double. He's ahead in every phase of the game. He has an anchor, White doesn't. He's ahead in the race, 142-155. He has two points in his inner board, White has only one. Most important, he has some immediate priming and attacking threats, while White's still trying to consolidate. None of these advantages are enormous, but the total gives him a nice double. Since it's still early in the game and White has plenty of chances to wiggle loose, he has a take.

**Problem 153: Should Black double?**
**Should White take if doubled?**

If you're doubling positions like this, you're probably watching a lot of cubes coming back to you at the four level, and saying "Why me?"

Black has a very slight advantage — he has a 4-point prime instead of a 3-point prime. Other than that, things aren't going too well. White is ahead in the race, all White's checkers are active and ready to make points, and Black's own numbers are duplicated (all his twos play well in different ways.) Optimism is good, but too much optimism can lead to sudden bouts of pessimism. No double, and almost a beaver!

**Problem 154: Should Black double?**
**Should White take if doubled?**

Black has escaped both back men, while White still has one checker back. Positions like this are very common, and need to be handled accurately.

Here are a couple of basic rules:

(1) If the race is close, the straggler can usually take, unless the other side has a pretty good prime.

(2) If the straggler is well behind in the race (more than 10%), he should pass a cube unless the leader's structure is really awkward.

This one is an easy call. White trails by 10 pips (138 to 128) which is about 8% of the leader's count. Black also has a huge stack on his midpoint, so he can't threaten White's checker anytime soon. Easy double, easy take.

**Problem 155: Should Black double?**
**Should White take if doubled?**

If you have a very strong position and your opponent doesn't have an anchor, you may be able to double even without a lot of strong threats. Here Black has a better position (five points out of six and a strong home board), a lead in the race, and a few very strong rolls—6-4 and 5-4 to hit in the outfield and 6-6, 5-5, and 3-3 to hit and make a prime. It's a good double for Black, but also an easy take for White.

**Problem 156: Should Black double?**
**Should White take if doubled?**

A big lead in the race can compensate for a lot of positional disadvantages.

Here Black has a better prime, an advanced anchor, and a double shot at a second checker. Pretty impressive, right? Not so fast. White has one advantage, and it's a big one — he leads in the race by 28 pips. If Black doesn't hit this shot, he's trailing in the race and White's game will start to come together. Even if he does hit the shot, the race will just be even. Don't jump the gun here — no double and take.

**Problem 157: Should Black double?**
**Should White take if doubled?**

Black has a good collection of advantages which add up to a double — he's ahead in the race, White's on the bar, and about half of Black's numbers make a good new point or hit a blot. White can squeeze out a take, based on Black's slightly awkward distribution, White's good board, and his 1-point anchor, which will give him chances right up to the end.

**Problem 158: Should Black double?**
**Should White take if doubled?**

Black has a good double. He has two checkers caught behind a prime, and his own checkers on the 20-point should get away without too much trouble. If he gets really lucky and rolls an 8, he can send a third checker back.

Many players would take in White's position because they have an anchor. That's a good rule in many positions, but here White has too many hurdles to overcome and he should give the game up. White's behind a full prime and he's not even at the edge, so he lacks the chance to throw a big double and get back in the game. He'll have to wait for Black to dismantle his prime and then hope to race, but he'll be a long shot to pull that game out. Better to pass now.

**Problem 159: Should Black double?**
**Should White take if doubled?**

Beware of taking a double if there's a strong chance you will be gammoned when your opponent executes his threats. Here Black has a checker behind a 5-prime, but White has a checker on the bar and three other exposed blots. Black can hit with 6s, 2s, 5s, and 41 or 43 or 11. That's a lot of shots. White is in big danger of having three or four checkers on the bar shortly, with a huge threat of losing a gammon. Black should double, and White should drop.

### Problem 160: Should Black double?
### Should White take if doubled?

Black has a good shot of pinning White in an ace-point game, and he has an advanced anchor himself. Those two factors are enough to give him a good double. White has enough of a prime himself to cause Black some trouble, and his board is as strong as Black's. Those two factors give White a reasonable take.

### Problem 161: Should Black double?
### Should White take if doubled?

Black should double and White should take. Black has three edges: a better inner board, a lead in the race (114-131), and shots at another loose checker. The combination of solid positional advantages coupled with some immediate crushing shots gives him a good double.

White, however, has an anchor and isn't out of the game yet. If Black misses his shot, White will have indirect shots in the outfield plus some chances to harass Black's remaining checker. A good take on his part.

### Problem 162: Should Black double?
### Should White take if doubled?

Black has a nice 5-prime, and depending on where his checker on the 14-point ends up, he'll have several active builders for extending his prime. White's only game plan is to attack on the 21-point, then use the time while Black enters to slither up to the 4-point with his back men. This might work or not, but even if it succeeds as planned, White will remain a solid underdog. Double and pass.

# THE 5-POINT

In the early game, the most important point to make on your side of the board is your 5-point. This comes as a surprise to many players, who like the bar-point because it blocks enemy sixes. But make no mistake; the 5-point is better. It's not only a blocking point but also an inner-board point.

Despite its importance, there are times when it's best to pass on the 5-point for other considerations. Take a look at the examples in this chapter to get a feel for when to grab the 5-point and when not to.

**PROBLEMS**

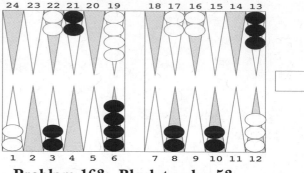

Problem 163:  Black to play 53.

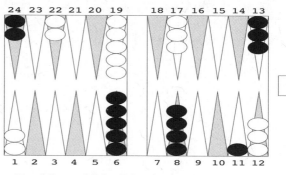

Problem 164:  Black to play 61.

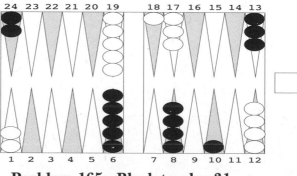

Problem 165:  Black to play 31.

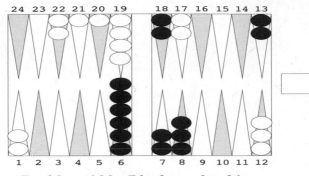

Problem 166: Black to play 21.

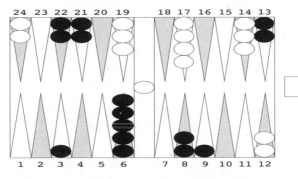

Problem 167: Black to play 11.

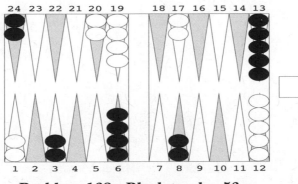

Problem 168: Black to play 53.

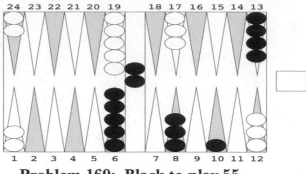

Problem 169: Black to play 55.

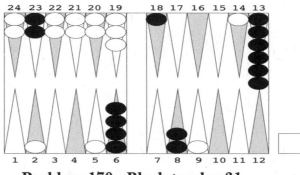

Problem 170: Black to play 31.

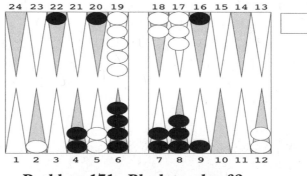

Problem 171: Black to play 62.

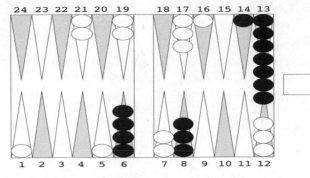

**Problem 172: Black to play 33.**

## SOLUTIONS

**Problem 163: Black to play 53.**

The key point in the early stages of the game is your own 5-point. It helps make a strong board, blocks in your opponent, and prevents him from moving up to an advanced anchor. It's worth taking a few risks to make the 5-point quickly. Black should just play 8/5 10/5, giving himself a strong home board, despite the two blots in the outfield. It would be a mistake to play either 13/8 6/3 (safe but too passive) or 21/13 (allowing White to attack the checker left behind).

**Problem 164: Black to play 61.**

If you have a choice between making the 5-point and making some other point, make the 5-point.

Here Black can make either his 5-point or his bar-point. The bar-point is only a blocking point. The 5-point is both a blocking point and an inner-board point. It's more valuable by far, so make the 5-point.

**Problem 165: Black to play 31.**

Another example of the same theme. Make the 5-point instead of the bar-point.

**Problem 166: Black to play 21.**

Two blots in your opponent's inner board should be like a red flag — play aggressively! Even if you get hit, you'll get one or two return shots.

With White blots on the 20-point and 21-point, Black can make the play he wants to make — 7/5 6/5, smoothing out his stack and making the key 5-point. If White rolls a six, he'll have to figure out if he even wants to hit.

**Problem 167: Black to play 11.**

Black could play 6/3, then look around for the best last ace, but this is much too good a roll to waste covering an unimportant blot on an unimportant point. Black should instead grab two great points: 6/5(2) 21/20(2)! With both 5-points secured, Black is in good shape for anything that comes later.

**Problem 168: Black to play 53.**

Once your opponent makes his 5-point, you're under extra pressure to make an advanced anchor before the opponent develops an even more threatening position. Splitting at the first opportunity is usually the best strategy, so Black should play 24/21 with his three.

How about the five? There's no particular advantage to playing 21/16, especially since Black would like to anchor on the 21-point. The best five is 13/8, which unstacks the midpoint and adds a spare to the stripped 8-point.

**Problem 169: Black to play 55.**

The 5-point is a key point, but sometimes you must give it up to keep the rest of your game in balance.

Black will enter with his first two fives: Bar/20(2). Having made the enemy 5-point, he now has to find two more good fives. The choices, however, aren't that appetizing. Playing 8/3(2) makes an inner point but leaves a big stack on the 6-point plus two outfield blots. Playing 13/8(2) leaves an ugly combination of stacked and stripped points. Playing 20/10 breaks the strong 20-point to make the weaker 10-point.

The right play is to abandon the 20-point now with 20/15(2)! This keeps a compact position with good coordination between Black's checkers. With plenty of spares on all points, Black will have lots to rolls to make good points next turn.

**Problem 170: Black to play 31.**

If survival is key, even the 5-point will have to wait.

White has a 5-point board, so Black has to tread lightly. Making the 5-point is great if it works, but 8/5* 6/5 leaves White 18 shots from the bar (44, 22, 46, 34, 35, 36, 24, 26, 14, 16). The more prudent 18/14*, by contrast, just leaves 9 shots. If White's board were weaker, Black could grab the 5-point, but here the best course is to hit in the outfield and cut down on exposure.

**Problem 171: Black to play 62.**

You might have to pass on the 5-point if making it leaves you too vulnerable or disjointed.

Black can play 22/20, making his opponent's 5-point, but his choice of sixes is then reduced to 16/10 or 9/3, either one of which leaves a double shot. Since Black is 28 pips ahead in the race after he plays, he'd like to keep that advantage if possible.

The right play is 22/16 9/7, which cleans things up nicely and leaves just one checker to scramble home.

**Problem 172: Black to play 33.**

What could be easier? Black can play 14/8 8/5*(2), making the 5-point and putting White on the bar at the same time. How could this be bad?

Learn to look at all features of the position before you make your play. Don't get in the habit of rolling and quickly grabbing your checkers. You may think you're impressing your opponent by playing quickly, but I guarantee you he won't be impressed if he's taking your money at the same time.

Mostly making the 5-point is a good play, but here's an exception. The problem is Black's big stack on the midpoint. It's more important to get some of those checkers into play and develop some flexibility than to grab the 5-point right now. The right play, which a calm, deliberate player would spot, is 14/8 13/10(2), with a nice, balanced distribution.

# 9

# THE BLITZ

The early blitz is one of the most exciting game plans in backgammon. Your opponent splits his back men and tries to run for home. You roll a double (55 is the most common blitzing double) and attack, making a couple of inner points and putting your opponent on the bar. He stays out! Now a blitz is in full swing.

Blitzes are characterized by quick doubles, big swings of fortune, and plenty of gammons. Here are some of the salient features you'll need to consider when evaluating a blitz:

• How many home board points does the attacker have?. Doubling with just a 2-point board is unusual. 3-point boards often yield strong doubles but clear takes. 4-point boards are the sign of a likely pass.

• How many checkers on the bar? One checker is typical. Two checkers on the bar usually means a pass.

• How many vulnerable blots does the defender have? One is tolerable. More than that usually points to a pass.

• How many builders does the attacker have? More is better.

• Does the defender have points made in his home board? Even one extra home board point enhances the defender's chances enormously.

You'll need to develop a feel for these double-edged positions to play the game well. Here are some examples to guide you.

**PROBLEMS**

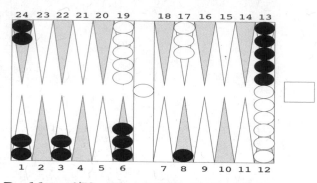

### Problem 173: Should Black double?
### Should White take if doubled?

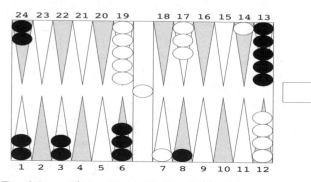

### Problem 174: Should Black double?
### Should White take if doubled?

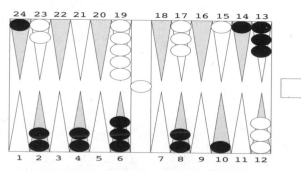

### Problem 175: Should Black double?
### Should White take if doubled?

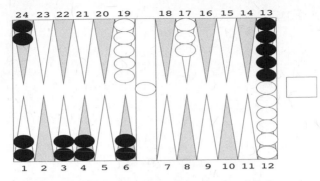

**Problem 176: Should Black double?
Should White take if doubled?**

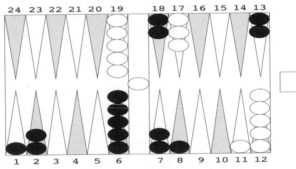

**Problem 177: Should Black double?
Should White take if doubled?**

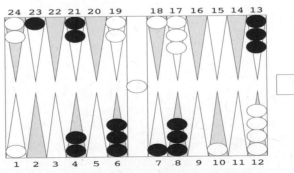

**Problem 178: Should Black double?
Should White take if doubled?**

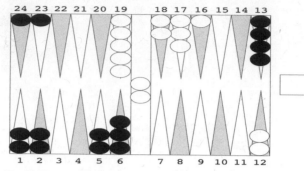

**Problem 179: Should Black double?**
**Should White take if doubled?**

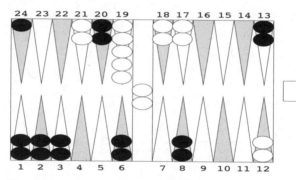

**Problem 180: Should Black double?**
**Should White take if doubled?**

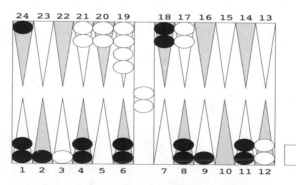

**Problem 181: Should Black double?**
**Should White take if doubled?**

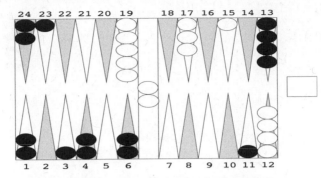

**Problem 182: Should Black double?
Should White take if doubled?**

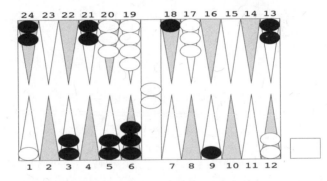

**Problem 183: Should Black double?
Should White take if doubled?**

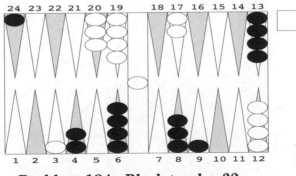

**Problem 184: Black to play 32.**

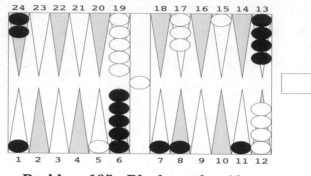

Problem 185: Black to play 41.

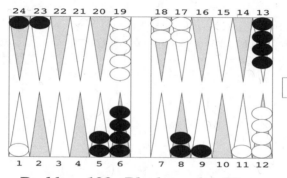

Problem 186: Black to play 66.

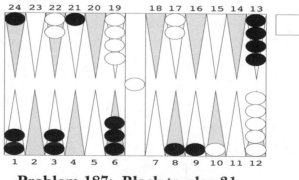

Problem 187: Black to play 31.

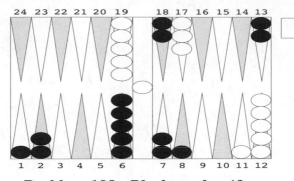

Problem 188: Black to play 43.

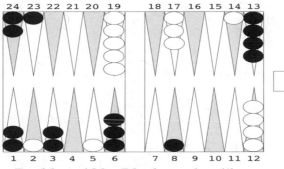

Problem 189: Black to play 11.

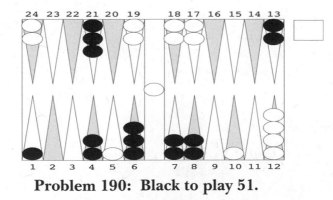

Problem 190: Black to play 51.

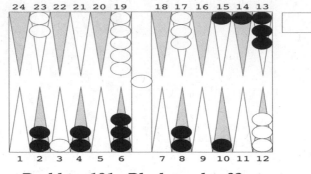

Problem 191: Black to play 62.

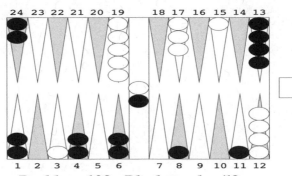

Problem 192: Black to play 52.

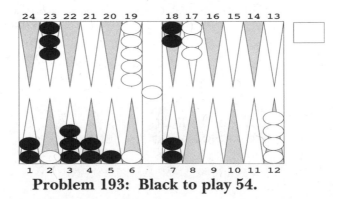

Problem 193: Black to play 54.

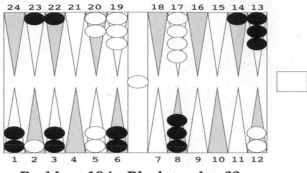

**Problem 194: Black to play 62.**

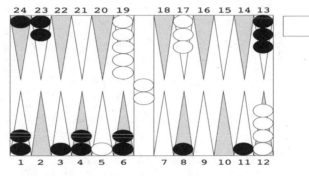

**Problem 195: Black to play 21.**

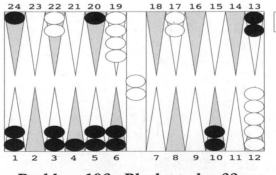

**Problem 196: Black to play 32.**

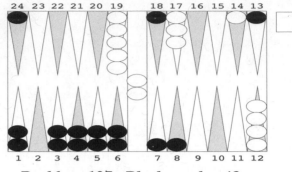

Problem 197: Black to play 42.

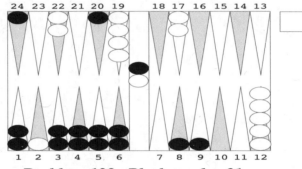

Problem 198: Black to play 31.

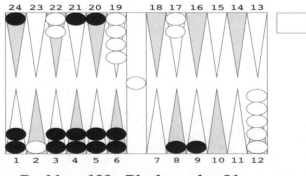

Problem 199: Black to play 21.

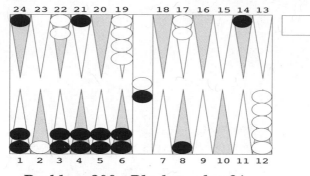

Problem 200:  Black to play 64.

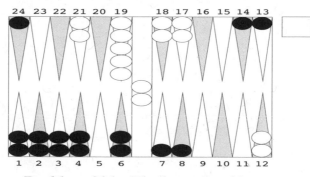

Problem 201:  Black to play 62.

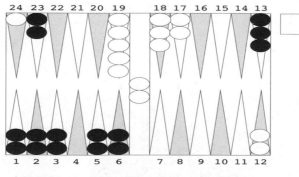

Problem 202:  Black to play 52.

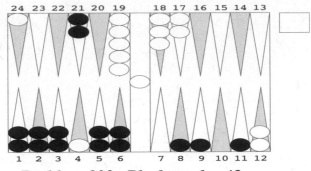

**Problem 203: Black to play 43.**

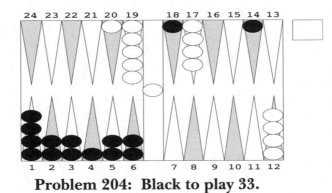

**Problem 204: Black to play 33.**

**Problem 205: Black to play 53.**

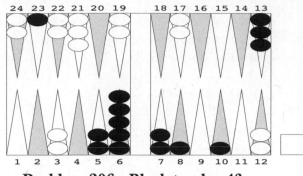

**Problem 206: Black to play 43.**

## SOLUTIONS

**Problem 173: Should Black double?**
**Should White take if doubled?**

Here's the position after an opening 65, followed by 55 and fan. Without a second blot to shoot at, Black doesn't have a double and White has an easy take. If White had an outfield blot (say on the 11-point, if he had run with a 64), then Black would have a clear double, and White a clear take.

**Problem 174: Should Black double?**
**Should White take if doubled?**

In this early blitz, White's exposed checker on the bar is threatened by a double shot (24 numbers). That's too much danger for White. Black should double, and White should pass.

**Problem 175: Should Black double?**
**Should White take if doubled?**

Black has a 3-point board and White is on the bar. Those are normally the conditions for an opening blitz double and a take. Before making a decision, however, you need to take any unusual features of the position into account. Black's double is stronger in two ways: he's escaped a back checker and he has a couple of more builders bearing on his inner board. But White's take is also stronger: he has a second point made in his board, and he doesn't have a second checker vulnerable to a direct shot. The net is a wash, and the position is still double and take.

**Problem 176: Should Black double?**
**Should White take if doubled?**

This is similar to Position 173, but now Black has a four-point board—a big improvement. The verdict is now double and pass.

**Problem 177: Should Black double?**
**Should White take if doubled?**

Black has only a two-point board in position 177, but don't be fooled. There's more to evaluating a blitz than just a count of inner board points. Notice also how much ammunition Black has immediately available to make new points (six builders on the 6, 7, and 8-points, plus a slotted ace-point). Then notice Black's huge lead in the race (39 pips, 119-158), and Black's possession of an advanced anchor. This is a double and a big pass.

**Problem 178: Should Black double?**
**Should White take if doubled?**

Even a two-point board can lead to a winning blitz if the opponent's position is weak enough.

Here Black has a great double and White should pass in a shot. It's not that Black's position is so crushing, but that White's game is so weak. He's got a checker on the bar, three other blots floating around, and no anchor, plus two checkers out of play on his own 1-point. White may wake up in a turn or two to find himself with four checkers back in some gruesome holding game. Better to let this one go.

**Problem 179: Should Black double?**
**Should White take if doubled?**

Two checkers on the bar against a four-point board is a tremendously strong blitz. The fact that White has made his bar-point doesn't count for much. Black doubles, and White has a huge pass.

**Problem 180: Should Black double?**
**Should White take if doubled?**

Once again, two checkers on the bar against a 4-point board equals double and pass. Black will bring two builders down next turn, giving him four builders operating against the two open points. White has a little compensation in terms of a modest blockade, but Black will have plenty of time to escape. Clear pass.

**Problem 181: Should Black double?**
**Should White take if doubled?**

Black has a three-point board with another point already started. White has two checkers on the bar and another blot in a vulnerable position. Two checkers on the bar in a blitz generally means double and pass, and this position is no exception. Many players would be fooled into taking by White's apparently strong home board, but this asset is neutralized by Black's advanced anchor. White's in big trouble here, and he must pass.

**Problem 182: Should Black double?**
**Should White take if doubled?**

Two men up on the bar against a 3-point board is a good double even if other conditions are unfavorable.

Here Black has a third man back, and no direct cover numbers for the 3-point, but he has a good double nonetheless. White's take is correct.

**Problem 183: Should Black double?**
**Should White take if doubled?**

Here's a case where two men on the bar isn't so bad. Here Black got carried away and redoubled, but he shouldn't have. Although White has two men up, those men will be reentering pretty soon. Meanwhile Black doesn't have enough men in position to finish White off. He'll be lucky to make another point before White is in and moving. No double, almost a beaver.

**Problem 184: Black to play 32.**

White has been caught with a checker on the bar, and Black is ready to launch a powerful blitz attack. If successful, he'll win a gammon and four points. The first step is to keep White from anchoring, so Black hits with 6/3*. The final step is to figure out the best two.

Moving up with the back checker, 24/22, is craven. If the attack works, that checker will be able to escape at any time. Shifting from 9/7 doesn't really do much. The shift move leaves Black with three builders aimed at the 5-point and three aimed at the 3-point, which is exactly what Black had before.

The only play which brings new ammunition to bear is 13/11! After that move, Black has four builders aimed at the 5-point and three aimed at the 3-point, a slight improvement. When your opponent's on the bar, pile on the pressure.

**Problem 185: Black to play 41.**

Once a blitz starts to materialize, go for it. It's liable to be a stronger game plan than any positional alternative.

Here Black should just play 6/5*/1, putting two men on the bar against a 2-point board. With a good distribution of builders, Black is already a solid favorite.

## Problem 186: Black to play 66.

We normally think of an early 55 as a blitzing move and 66 as a blocking move, but under the right circumstance (especially if the back men are split) 66 may be a blitzing roll as well.

Here Black can prime with 13/7(4), but it leaves White in complete control of the outfield. Much better is 13/1*(2), which leads to a powerful double if White fans.

## Problem 187: Black to play 31.

The three is clear: Black should put a second man up with 13/10*. The ace isn't so obvious. Slotting is the wrong idea when two of your opponent's men are on the bar, so 6/5 is out. Playing 8/7 does nothing. Both 10/9 and 9/8 actually reduce Black's chances of making an inner point next turn. We're reduced to looking at 21/20 or 24/23. Is there any difference between the two plays? Actually, yes. 24/23 doesn't do anything, but 21/20 creates a new point-making number (55, making Black's 5-point). 21/20 is the other half of this subtle play.

## Problem 188: Black to play 43.

In conducting a successful blitz, the really tough plays are those which give a choice between making another inner-board point or hitting a second (or third) checker. Position 188 is a typical example.

Black can hit a second checker with 18/11* while at the same time bringing another builder to bear on his 5-point. Alternatively, he can make a third inner-board point in a variety of ways. He can make the 4-point with 8/4 7/4, grab the 3-point with 7/3 6/3, or even the lowly ace-point with 8/1. What's right?

There are two key ideas to remember when conducting a blitz. The first is that you really need to cover blots in your board, because getting hit on a slotted point is a very big swing. You lose ground in the race, you lose half of your next roll, and you lose the opportunity to make the slotted point with a single number. The second idea is that low points in your board may be just as valuable, if not more valuable, than high points. Your high points are closer to your builders on the midpoint and thus easier to make; your low points are further away from your builders and harder to make.

Put these factors together and 8/1 becomes the clear choice. It covers a slotted inner point, makes a three-point board, and leaves no blots lying around, with Black in good position to continue blitzing whether White enters or not, with no risk. That's a lot for one play.

**Problem 189: Black to play 11.**

Making points quickly is the key to a successful blitz. Given a choice between hitting two men, or hitting just one man but making another point, make the point.

The right play is 8/5* 6/5, not the double hit of 3/2*(2) 6/5* 23/22. The double hit could backfire in any number of ways: White could throw a five from the bar, or White could fail to cover for awhile, etc. Once you make the extra point, you'll have that asset for the rest of the game, and it will exert its power every single move.

**Problem 190: Black to play 51.**

Blitzes frequently involve a choice between closing another point in the home board, or hitting a second checker. Often closing the point is more important.

Here Black should play 6/1 21/20, making a 3-point board and preparing to attack with renewed vigor if White fails to anchor. That's much better than 6/5* 21/16, which gives White plenty of opportunities to reenter and hit before Black consolidates.

**Problem 191: Black to play 62.**

Once your back checkers have escaped, you don't need to over-play a blitz. Minimize risk while keeping blitzing potential.

Black actually played 15/9 13/11, on the theory that he wanted to go all out for attack. White reentered and hit a fly shot, turning the game around.

Black's bold play wasn't necessary. Black can play safely since the race is now secure, and switch back to a blitz later if the dice allow it. The right play is just 14/8 15/13.

**Problem 192: Black to play 52.**

When a blitz starts to lose steam, revert to positional mode before overextending yourself.

Here Black could play Bar/23 8/3*, trying to keep the blitz going, but he doesn't have any covers for the 3-point, and his position is getting disjointed. If White enters quickly, with or without a hit, he'll be in real trouble.

The right idea is Bar/20 13/11, rebuilding his game and starting the 20-point while White is on the bar.

### Problem 193: Black to play 54.

When the blitz starts to run out of gas, pull back and look to establish a viable holding game. Falling farther behind in the race is counter-productive at this point.

Black can continue blitzing with 7/2* 18/14, but he's running out of ammo and this play could completely backfire. A better idea is to realize that Black's going to have to win this much later from a holding position, keep the valuable 7-point and 18-point, and bide time. The right idea is just 23/14, awaiting developments.

### Problem 194: Black to play 62.

Once your opponent has survived the blitz and anchored, there's very little value in continuing the attack on deep points. You should revert to normal positional play, concentrating on getting your checkers around the board.

Here Black played 8/2* 8/6, an all-out blitzing play which would be worth the risk if White didn't have an anchor. But with White solidly anchored, the upside of this play is much less, while the down-side is still large. Black should just play 22/14, consolidating.

### Problem 195: Black to play 21.

In a full-fledged blitz, the order of points in your inner board doesn't matter much. When you're committed to blitzing, all points are valuable as long as you keep your opponent in the air.

Here many players would play 8/5*, putting the third White checker in the air but leaving two blots in their board. The right play is 6/5*/3!, achieving the same goal with just one inner-board blot.

### Problem 196: Black to play 32.

Black wanted to cover the 4-point, but he didn't. Now he wants to make the play that gives himself the best chance to make a fifth inner point next turn. What might that play be?

The obvious choice is 13/8, bringing down a second cover number while keeping the 10-point. Let's see how many cover numbers that play yields. All 4s and 6s, of course, which is 20. In addition, 51 and 31 work, making 24, and then three small doubles – 11, 22, and 33. The total looks like 27.

Now let's look at breaking the 10-point: 10/7 10/8. Now Black has 3s and 4s to cover, which is 20 numbers. He picks up 4 more covers with 21, 22, and 11. We can cover from the 13-point with 63, 54, and 33, but we've counted those numbers already.

Are we done? No! Black can also make a 5-point board by filling in the 2-point, and there are several more numbers that work to do that: 62, 52, 65, and even 66 (remember the checker on the 20-point!) That adds 7 more numbers, bringing the total to 31 point-makers! Playing 10/7 10/8 wins handily, by bringing spares to bear on both open inner points.

### Problem 197: Black to play 42.

In a blitz, picking up loose checkers outweighs bringing more builders into play. The extra checkers delay the time when your opponent gets in from the bar, minimize the effect of a miracle double, and pick up some extra backgammons on the tail end.

Here Black should play 18/14* 13/11.

### Problem 198: Black to play 31.

Black will play Bar/24 with the ace, of course, then look for his best three. There are two choices: 9/6 and 24/21.

In the later stages of a blitz, it's important not to go wrong by overplaying the attack. Here's a good example. The move 9/6, getting fours to hit on the 2-point, is a good play if White fails to enter and if Black then rolls a 4 (other than 42, 43, or 46, which would have hit anyway). If White does enter, the checker is out of play, and Black's rear checkers have to scramble to make an anchor.

A much better move is 24/21 with the three. It may seem counter-intuitive to make a defensive play in the middle of an attack, but in backgammon you're always striving to balance your game between competing priorities. 24/21 does a lot for Black's defense if the attack fails, while 9/6 abandons defense for only a marginal attacking improvement.

### Problem 199: Black to play 21.

The more checkers you have to bring around the board, the more important the immediate closeout becomes and the more aggressively you have to play. The safest play here is 9/8 20/18, which tries to lock White behind a 5-prime while moving the back checkers.

Once White enters, however, he'll have plenty of counterplay while Black hobbles around the board. In the process of getting home, the gammon will often slip away.

A better plan is 9/7 21/20, giving Black the maximum attacking chances when White fails to enter. It gives Black about the same winning chances as the safer play while substantially increasing his gammons.

**Problem 200: Black to play 64.**

Don't carry the idea of balance in a blitz to an extreme. The slightly cautious play was right in the previous examples because Black couldn't hit. If hitting is possible, it's so strong that it trumps all defensive ideas. Here Black has to reject Bar/21 14/8, building a prime, and just put two men up with Bar/21 8/2*.

**Problem 201: Black to play 62.**

Repair the weakest parts of your position first.

Black is in complete control with a very likely closeout brewing. He could strengthen his attack even more with 14/6 or 14/8 13/11, giving himself three builders for the 5-point. But right now the biggest danger to his position is that he might throw an awkward double like 66 or 55 which would force him to bury checkers while leaving his back man stranded. The right play is to ensure that the back checker gets out with 24/16.

**Problem 202: Black to play 52.**

At the tail end of a successful blitz, you need to balance attacking and escaping.

Black has three plays in position 202: all escape with 23/16, all attack with 13/8 13/11, and some of each, with 13/8 23/21. The right play balances the two goals. Playing the five from 13 to 8 gives a direct shot at the 4-point; that's very good for the attack. Playing the deuce from 13 to 11 only gives a couple of extra indirect numbers to attack the 4-point; that's not a powerful attacking play. On the other side, playing 23/21 is great for escaping. Now 66, 55, and 65 are great shots rather than mini-disasters. The balanced play of 13/8 and 23/21 is top choice.

**Problem 203: Black to play 43.**

Hit and stay or pick and pass? The answer depends on the race.

Black has a choice between picking and passing with 8/4*/1, or hitting and staying with 8/4* 11/8. The right play depends on the position of the back men. If the two checkers on the 21-point were home or almost home (say on the 5-point and 6-point), then pick and pass would be a strong, almost risk-free play. But with the checkers way back and needing many rolls to get around the board, Black needs to shut down counterplay quickly. He should hit and stay, and aim to snuff out resistance by closing his board.

**Problem 204: Black to play 33.**

When you're almost home, extra risks only muck up the works. Look for safety from accidents.

Black could play 14/5 18/15, trying to make a closed board. But a four from the bar for White could cost him the game, and even if White dances, Black is a favorite not to cover. Instead, Black should cut down on the hassle and just play 18/15 14/8 4/1.

**Problem 205: Black to play 53.**

When you're being blitzed, don't panic; normal building plays might still be in order.

Black played Bar/22/17. He was scared of the blitz, and wanted to get his back checker home as quickly as possible. While it's okay to be scared of a blitz (nobody likes losing 4 points), you still have to keep a cool head. Black's checker is just as likely to be hit on the 17-point as on the 22-point, but notice that if Black gets hit in the outfield, he'll only have an indirect shot at White's blot. If he gets hit on the 22-point, he'll have a direct return shot from the bar. That's a big improvement. Black should play Bar/22, then balance his game with 13/8.

**Problem 206: Black to play 43.**

When you're vulnerable and under attack, button up any loose blots. You don't want to get stuck on the bar and have other blots lying around to be picked up. Black should prepare for the coming storm by playing 8/5 10/6.

# 10

# ONE MAN BACK

At the start of the game, you've got two men located on your 24-point. We call those the back men, and one of your first objectives is to get those men to the safety of the midpoint or your own outer board.

Once one of those checkers has escaped, we're in a zone known as "one man back." In this situation, strategy changes subtly for both sides. A single man can't form an anchor. Hence, the opponent has more incentive to attack the lone checker, and you have a strong incentive not to put this checker into a vulnerable position until it has a chance to run all the way home.

## PROBLEMS

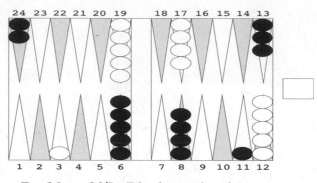

**Problem 207: Black to play 64.**

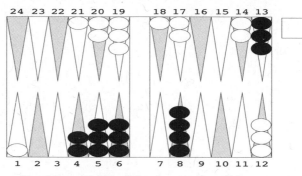

**Problem 208: Black to play 54.**

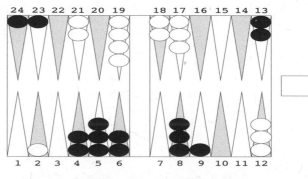

**Problem 209: Black to play 64.**

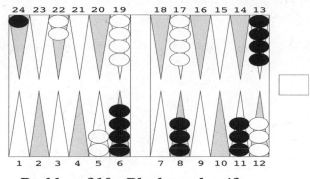

**Problem 210: Black to play 43.**

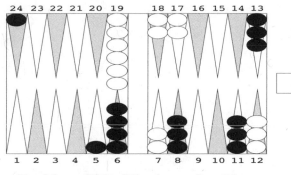

**Problem 211: Black to play 52.**

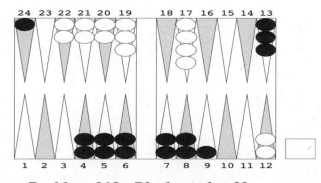

**Problem 212: Black to play 62.**

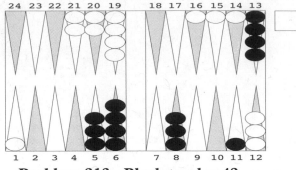

Problem 213: Black to play 42.

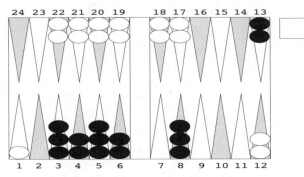

Problem 214: Black to play 55.

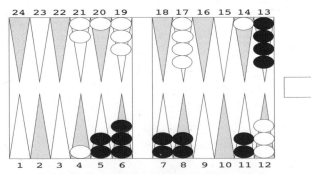

Problem 215: Should Black double?
Should White take if doubled?

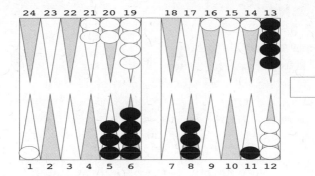

**Problem 216: Should Black double?**
**Should White take if doubled?**

## SOLUTIONS

**Problem 207: Black to play 64.**

Block two checkers; attack one checker.

One checker is most vulnerable to being attacked, since it can never form an anchor. Two checkers are more vulnerable to being primed, since they can't escape as quickly as one.

Here 13/7 11/7 is a pretty blocking play, but the block isn't so effective and the resulting distribution is poor. A better plan is 8/2 6/2!, building the board, smoothing the distribution, and preparing to hit next turn.

**Problem 208: Black to play 54.**

Here Black played 13/4. It's a nice positional play, leaving a good distribution of builders, but ...

The way you exploit a single checker back is to put it on the bar and keep it there while you fill in your board. A single checker can't form an anchor, so it's highly vulnerable to being attacked and closed out. The right play was 6/1* 5/1.

**Problem 209: Black to play 64.**

With nothing very strong to do with this roll, Black should take advantage of the weakness of a single checker and attack. The right play is 8/2* 24/20!

**Problem 210: Black to play 43.**

With one checker back, stay out of the "danger zone" — the area between the 22 and 18-points. White is eager to hit in this area, while he's reluctant to hit if you remain safely tucked away on the 24-point. Don't move up until you can make a run for safety — at least out to White's outfield. Here Black should play 11/4, and not 24/20 11/8.

**Problem 211: Black to play 52.**

Here's another example. A play like 13/8 24/22 puts Black into White's attacking zone. Instead, stay back until you can leap right into the outer board. Black should just make his 3-point with 8/3 5/3.

## Problem 212:  Black to play 62.

When you're in danger of being primed or closed out, it's easy to panic and make a run for it, but watch out!  It may not be the right play.

Black saw that White was closing in on him, so he ran for home with 24/16.  It was a blunder on two counts:

1)  Black is in bad shape even if White misses the shot.  After running, he still trails by 24 pips in the race, 124-100.  In a straight race, he has almost no chance.

2)  If he gets hit and spends any time on the bar, he may get gammoned as a result.

Black should just play 13/5.  The more checkers he can get into his inner board before he gets closed out, the less likely he'll be gammoned.  And staying back just might result in a lucky winning shot.

## Problem 213:  Black to play 42.

Weigh risks carefully.

Black can play 8/4 6/4, or 13/9 11/9.  The 4-point is a better point than the 9-point, without doubt.  But it comes at a price — allowing White a 17-1 shot at Black's loose blot.  Is it worth it?

No.  A 17-1 shot means giving your opponent an extra 5.5% chance to win the game right on the spot.  Making a better point picks up some winning chances, but not nearly that much.  Play completely safe here by making the 9-point.

## Problem 214:  Black to play 55.

Use a timely switch to get your opponent out of your hair.

Here Black played 13/3(2) and got into trouble because his game was so awkward.  The right idea was 13/8(2) 6/1*(2), pushing White forward and out of the way.

## Problem 215:  Should Black double?
## Should White take if doubled?

The race here is very close (Black 132, White 134).  Despite the closeness of the race, Black has a good double.  The reason is that some upcoming sequences are very strong for him.

If Black makes the 4-point next turn, and White doesn't respond with a very good number, Black will become a huge favorite.

If Black hits loose on the 4-point, and White fails to hit back, Black will be a big favorite.

If Black does nothing and White can't escape, the same threats repeat next turn.

Double when you have a solid edge and something very good is about to happen. That's the case here. White still has a take, but he might not next turn.

**Problem 216: Should Black double?**
**Should White take if doubled?**

Here's a perfect double for Black against one checker back. He has a modest lead in the race (126-135), coupled with a good distribution of all his men, and chances of making another key point next turn. White has a good take: he has some chances of hitting a lucky shot, which would probably win immediately, and he retains some slim racing chances if he can ever get his last checker out.

# HOLDING GAMES

Holding games are the bread-and-butter positions of backgammon. Between two strong players, a majority of games turn into holding games of some sort.

A one-way holding game is most common. One side escapes his back men to his midpoint and beyond. The other side makes an advanced anchor, usually on the 20-point or the 18-point. The side with the anchor is said to be "holding" the other, keeping the anchor while waiting to hit a shot.

A mutual holding game means that both sides have anchors. The play is pretty even, with each side waiting to roll a double or hit a shot.

Here are some guidelines for these very important positions:

• When ahead in the race, break contact; when behind, keep contact.

• If you're ahead, try to clear points when your opponent's home board is vulnerable.

• Keep a strong home board as long as possible.

• Don't double without a solid racing lead.

## PROBLEMS

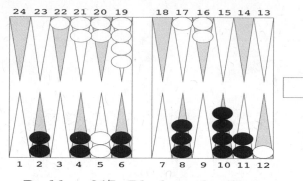

Problem 217: Black to play 51.

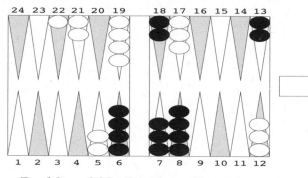

Problem 218: Black to play 44.

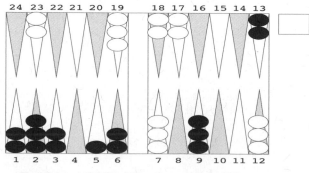

Problem 219: Black to play 62.

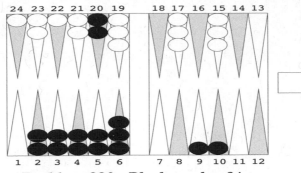

Problem 220: Black to play 64.

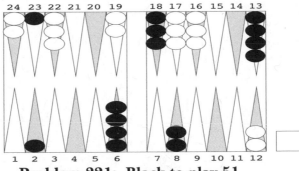

Problem 221: Black to play 51.

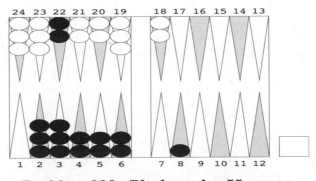

Problem 222: Black to play 55.

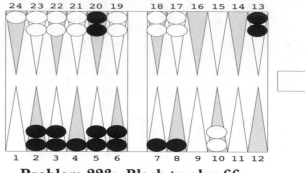

Problem 223: Black to play 66.

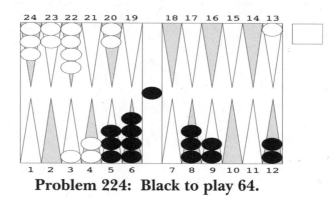

Problem 224: Black to play 64.

Problem 225: Black to play 42.

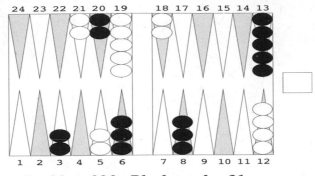

**Problem 226: Black to play 21.**

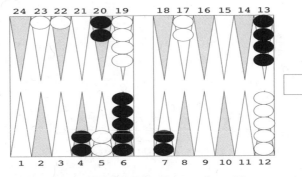

**Problem 227: Black to play 41.**

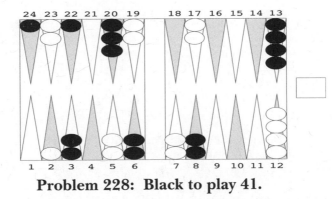

**Problem 228: Black to play 41.**

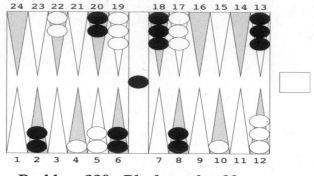

**Problem 229: Black to play 22.**

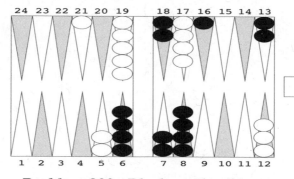

**Problem 230: Black to play 54.**

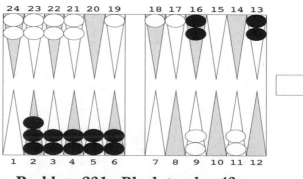

**Problem 231: Black to play 43.**

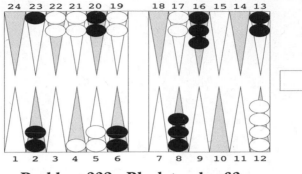

**Problem 232: Black to play 63.**

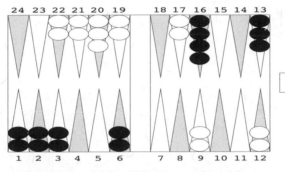

**Problem 233: Black to play 22.**

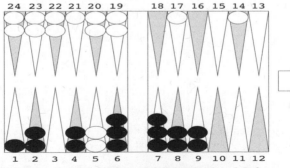

**Problem 234: Should Black double?**
**Should White take if doubled?**

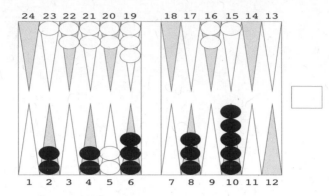

**Problem 235: Should Black double?**
**Should White take if doubled?**

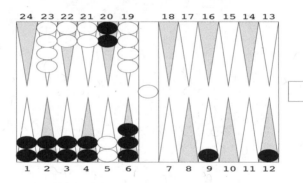

**Problem 236: Should Black double?**
**Should White take if doubled?**

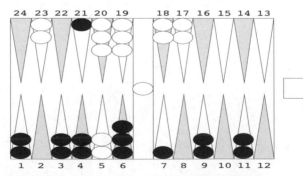

**Problem 237: Should Black double?**
**Should White take if doubled?**

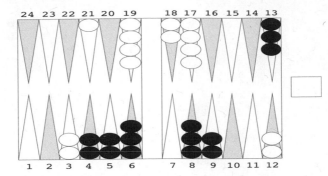

**Problem 238: Should Black double?**
**Should White take if doubled?**

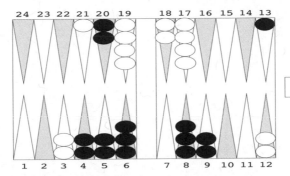

**Problem 239: Should Black double?**
**Should White take if doubled?**

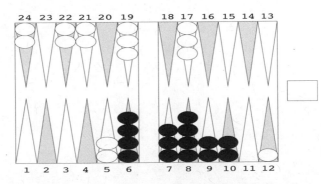

**Problem 240: Should Black double?**
**Should White take if doubled?**

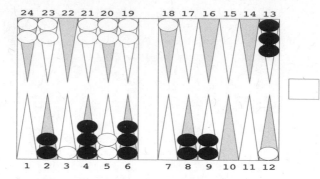

**Problem 241: Should Black double?**
**Should White take if doubled?**

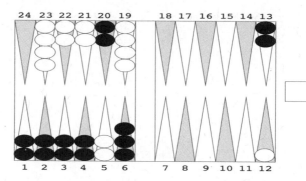

**Problem 242: Should Black double?**
**Should White take if doubled?**

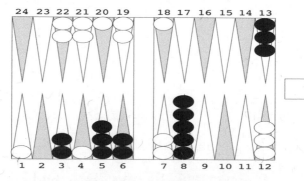

**Problem 243: Should Black double?**
**Should White take if doubled?**

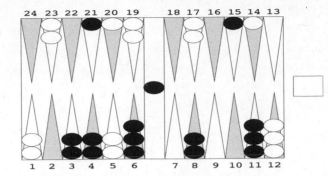

**Problem 244:  Should Black double?**
**Should White take if doubled?**

## SOLUTIONS

**Problem 217: Black to play 51.**

Black has a couple of choices with his 51. He can keep his block-ade by playing 10/4, or he can dismantle the 11-point by playing 11/10 11/6. What's right?

The race tells us the answer. After Black plays his 51, he'll be leading in the race by 20 pips (104-124). With a big racing lead, his goal is to avoid contact and get all his men home safely. In this position, he's not holding White; White is holding him! Breaking the 11-point is the right move.

**Problem 218: Black to play 44.**

Throwing a big double in a close mutual holding game almost always means you disengage your back anchor. Before the roll, the race was 138-139 in favor of White. The 44 roll will put Black 15 pips ahead, so now is a good time to turn the game into a one-way holding game. Black should play 18/10(2).

**Problem 219: Black to play 62.**

When you're way ahead in a holding game, look for a good time to break contact.

Black leads by 61 pips before the roll. He can play 62 safely with 9/1. The trouble is that from that point on, his position steadily deteriorates. If he's forced to leave a shot later, which is very likely, his board will be weak while White's will probably have improved.

Instead, Black should take a great opportunity and play 13/5!! Although he leaves a double shot, it comes at a time when White's board is weak while Black's is very strong. White, if he hits, will have a hard time containing the checker without leaving a series of dangerous, potentially gammon-losing shots. It's a bold play, but that's what winning backgammon looks like.

**Problem 220: Black to play 64.**

Black has just rolled a good number for leaving his opponent's home board. Should he play 20/14 20/16, leaving White just an ace shot to hit, or stay put and play something like 10/4 6/2?

The answer: Black should definitely stay put on the 20-point. Right now the pip count is 88 for White and 105 for Black. Black's losing the race, so he doesn't want to disengage. He needs to stay put and hope for a later shot. Running just gives White the tasty option of hitting with a few small numbers (numbers which would be bad in a racing game) or racing if he doesn't hit. Play 10/4 6/2 instead.

**Problem 221: Black to play 51.**

In a really bad holding game, play to maintain as much contact as possible.

Here Black trails by 70 (!) pips before the roll. He has to hit a shot to win. (In fact, he may have to hit a shot to save the gammon!) Playing safe with 23/18 6/5 isn't an option. Although the checker on the 23-point might get attacked at an embarrassing moment, Black needs the extra contact to get the shots he must have to turn the game around. The right idea is to try to build his board as quickly as possible, with 13/8 and 6/5.

**Problem 222: Black to play 55.**

Don't run just because you can.

Black's 55 looks like a pretty good racing roll, and in fact Black bolted for home with 22/12(2). Big mistake. Before the roll, Black is trailing in the pip count by 97-59, or 38 pips. After the roll, he'll still trail by 18 pips. He has to keep some contact — hitting a shot is still his best way to win. The right play is 22/7 8/3.

**Problem 223: Black to play 66.**

If you're leading in the race, minimize contact; if you're trailing, maximize contact.

Black has thrown a great racing number. He starts with 20/14(2), then has to decide whether to keep the 14-point (maximum contact) or the 13-point (minimum contact). The race gives the answer. After Black plays, he will still trail, 93-91. If he's trailing he needs to maximize contact, so the right play is to keep the 14-point and play 13/7(2).

**Problem 224: Black to play 64.**

Blocking points in front of an anchor are powerful restraints. Don't be in a hurry to break them to hit loose behind the anchor.

In the actual game, Black played Bar/21 9/3*. While hitting blots is usually good, here it's a serious mistake. In this position it's White, not Black, that has the stronger board, so Black should be leery of starting a blot-hitting contest. A better play was Bar/19 6/2, keeping the block and looking to prime the White checkers.

**Problem 225: Black to play 42.**

If you're going to have a difficult bearin against an anchor, watch your opponent's home board position. If it becomes vulnerable, that's the time for a bold play to improve your game.

Black could play safe here with 10/6 10/8, which certainly doesn't ruin his game. But with the 5-point and 7-point open, his chances of getting home without leaving a shot are very slim.

Notice, however, that while White's home board is liable to be quite strong in a move or two, it's vulnerable now. Accordingly, Black played 10/6 13/11!, exposing two blots to indirect shots. White has 10 hitting numbers, but they leave him with five(!) blots around the board, and facing a disaster if Black rolls a three from the bar. If White doesn't hit, which is most likely, Black should be able to fill in one of the open points, with a much easier time getting home.

**Problem 226: Black to play 21.**

The normal rule when both sides are playing a holding game is to play safe, wait for a double, and let the other guy take the chances. But there are exceptions to this approach, and they occur when the alternatives are very awkward. Here Black's only safe plays, moves like 8/6 3/2 or 6/3, are either very awkward or leave plenty of blots and stacks. The only play to keep a fluid position is 13/10!, which unstacks the midpoint and keeps spares on all key points. It's the right play, although Black certainly won't be happy if he gets hit.

**Problem 227: Black to play 41.**

Problem 227 shows the other exception to the rule of playing safely and waiting in mutual holding games. The normal play here would just be 6/1. But Black notices the two blots in White's home board, and realizes that he can make a more natural and constructive play. He correctly moves 13/8!, preparing to make the 8-point or perhaps the 3-point next turn. White's board is too weak for him to hit this blot unless he rolls a perfecta like 31.

**Problem 228: Black to play 41.**

In holding games with many men back on each side, avoid big stacks of checkers. Keep your men flexible and moving freely.

Here Black played 24/20 22/21, but the big stack he created on the 20-point didn't play well in the next few turns. Instead he should have tried 20/16 22/21, keeping his checkers flexible and connected, for maximum future possibilities.

**Problem 229: Black to play 22.**

Spread your anchors.

In a long holding game where you have many men back, you don't want your anchors close together. Anchors that are too close to each other waste the energy of your position, because they tie up a lot of checkers controlling the same points.

Here Black's anchors on the 20-point and the 18-point are too close together. The 22 roll gives him a great chance to rectify the situation. The right play is Bar/23 18/16(3)!

**Problem 230: Black to play 54.**

Leave blots because you must, not because you can.

Black notices that White's home board is weak, with a blot, so he flirts with the idea of 16/11 8/4. Why not? White could get in trouble if he hits.

The trouble with this line of thinking is that it has a downside but no upside. White will only hit if he can do so with safety. He'll hit with 62, 64, and 66 — nothing else. So there's no way Black can gain from leaving a blot, although the play looks clever. The right play is the simple 16/7.

**Problem 231: Black to play 43.**

Breaking up a good home board is a last resort in holding games; try to avoid it as long as possible.

Here Black could play safely with 6/2 6/3, but a much better move is 16/13 16/12!, leaving a voluntary double shot. If Black gets hit, he's likely to have some winning return shots. If he's missed, he'll be able to hold his remaining point for a long time. If White's board were flawless, Black couldn't make this play, but White's weaknesses enable Black to play more aggressively.

## Problem 232: Black to play 63.

In a mutual holding game, try to keep moving from the back.

When you're in a holding game and your opponent has made a few blocking points, it's the status of your rearmost checker that helps determine how well you're doing. If that checker gets stuck and can't move for awhile, you'll have to move the checkers on other, more vital points instead. When you have a choice, it's a good idea to keep that back checker moving while holding your other checkers in reserve.

Here Black could get distracted by looking at plays like hitting on the 4-point or making the 10-point, but the right idea is to get the checker on the 23-point into the game. Black correctly played 23/14!

## Problem 233: Black to play 22.

In mutual holding games, try to create plenty of spares, so you can hold key points safely.

Black played 16/14(2) 6/4(2), which gave him several points but only one true spare, on the 13-point. After he plays this spare, he may have to volunteer shots at really bad times.

A much better play was 13/11(3) 6/4! Now Black has three spares to move (two on the 16-point, one on the 11-point), while he only has to hold two points. His chances of not leaving a blot at a key time are much improved.

## Problem 234: Should Black double?
## Should White take if doubled?

Black leads in the race by 11 pips, 86 to 97. That would be a double and a take in a straight race with no contact. With a 5-point holding game, the proper cube action is just the same as in a race; it's also a double and a take.

There's more going on in this position than in a race. Each side has some additional advantages and disadvantages. Black might leave a shot while he comes home, which could cost him the game. Or he might never fill in the 5-point, which could cost him time in the race later on. White's back checkers might get stuck, so he might not get full value for his small doubles. Or White might have to run off the anchor with one checker, leaving the other checker behind to be attacked. In practice, these advantages for both sides tend to cancel out, leaving the race as the overriding consideration.

**Problem 235: Should Black double?**
**Should White take if doubled?**
No, Black shouldn't double. Black only leads in the pip count by 104-112, about 8%. In a straight race, with no contact left, that would be enough to offer a minimal double. But here, Black still has to clear his 10-point and his 8-point, and he could leave a shot clearing either point. That means White has substantially better defensive chances than in a straight race, so Black should hold off on doubling until he gets a bigger racing lead.

**Problem 236: Should Black double?**
**Should White take if doubled?**
Here's a basic position in holding games that needs to be understood. Black leads in the race by 12 pips (99-111), and White is on the bar against a 5-point board. Although Black may leave some indirect and direct shots as he lumbers around the board, there will be other variations where White stays on the bar a long time. Black doubles and White has a clear pass.

**Problem 237: Should Black double?**
**Should White take if doubled?**
A 30-pip lead in the race is worth a double in most holding games.
Here Black leads by 30 (102-132) and White is on the bar. In most holding games these advantages would translate into double and pass. Here Black has just enough problems (a checker to leap from the 21-point, some outfield points to disassemble later) that White can venture a take.

### Problem 238:  Should Black double?
### Should White take if doubled?

Here White is playing a 3-point anchor game.  He's trapped behind a 5-point prime.  Without even knowing the race, we know that White has a pass.  It's too difficult for him to extricate his checkers for the race, and he won't win enough games by hitting a shot to compensate.  Black should double, and White passes.

### Problem 239:  Should Black double?
### Should White take if doubled?

An asset that can't be maintained may actually be a big liability. Problem 239 looks like the previous problem, and many players get confused evaluating it.  They see Black's anchor on the 20-point, and think that in addition to Black's strengths in the previous situation, he has the added advantage of a strong anchor.  Thus they evaluate the position as an even bigger double and an even more convincing pass.

Actually the anchor on the 20-point is a big liability for Black, so the position is no double and take.  The reason the anchor is a liability is that Black must leave it almost immediately.  This will give White many extra chances as he tries to attack or prime the checker that remains behind.

### Problem 240:  Should Black double?
### Should White take if doubled?

Black has a solid 5-point prime in front of White's anchor.  Is this good enough for a double?  Can White take?

It's actually not a double and an easy take.  A prime doesn't mean much against a 5-point anchor, since Black can't hold it very long.  While White moves his outside checkers home, Black will first move his spares, then break down his prime and move further checkers into the board.  In order to double against the 5-point anchor, Black must have a solid racing advantage to go with his prime. Here Black trails in the race by 115-111.  No double.

### Problem 241:  Should Black double?
### Should White take if doubled?

White's playing a 5-point holding game, and Black's ahead in the count by 107 to 118, an 11-pip lead.  With several outside points to clear, that normally wouldn't be enough to double in a holding game. But here Black caught a break because White's last roll (63) forced him to expose a blot on the midpoint. The extra gammon chances from being able to hit one or possibly two more blots give Black enough chances for a healthy double. White still has a solid take based on his strong home board coupled with both racing chances and (eventual) hitting chances.

### Problem 242: Should Black double?
### Should White take if doubled?

When a close holding game leads to a direct shot, pay attention; it may be time to double.

Here Black trails slightly in the race (104-99), but he's now got a direct shot at the blot on the 12-point, with a total of 17 numbers to hit (all ones plus six 8s). A hit followed by a dance for White will leave White unable to take a double next turn. That's a good enough reason to turn the cube right now. Black has solid market-losing chances, and he'll still be in the game even if he rolls poorly.

### Problem 243: Should Black double?
### Should White take if doubled?

This is a good double for Black. He's far ahead in the race, and he has some attacking chances against White's loose blots in his home board. There could be a big swing on the next roll if Black hits one or two blots and White rolls poorly.

White has just enough chances to take. Black rates to leave one or two blots somewhere as he tries to come home, and if White hits, he could build a prime of his own and turn the game around. Good double, sound take.

### Problem 244: Should Black double?
### Should White take if doubled?

The ace-five game is a difficult game to play. It's not quite a holding game and not quite a back game, but combines some aspects of both. Diagram 244 shows a possible doubling situation against an ace-five game. Black's threatening to hit White with all fives and some ones. An optimistic player might double, but the problem is that Black still has several men to get around the board and some difficult points to clear, so hitting isn't the same as winning. No double and easy take.

# PRIMING GAMES

When one or both sides have primes, the game becomes quite fascinating and complex. These games require the utmost skill on both sides to handle properly. Each play requires balancing the need to extend one's own prime with the need to escape the opponent's prime.

Here are a few guidelines for these positions:

• The overriding goal is to build a full 6-point prime. A full prime will win the game, unless opposed by another prime.

• Once you've built a prime, roll it forward by slotting (or attacking) at the front of the prime.

• Given a choice in priming games, do what is hardest first.

• Be alert for chances to convert a winning prime into a gammonish blitz.

## PROBLEMS

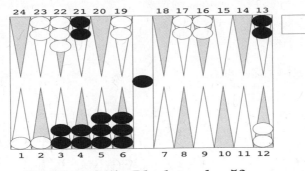

Problem 245:  Black to play 53.

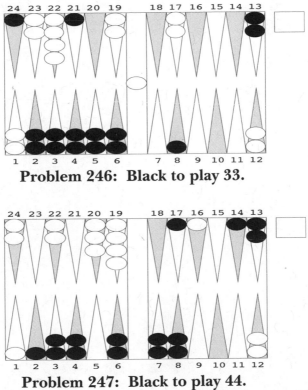

Problem 246:  Black to play 33.

Problem 247:  Black to play 44.

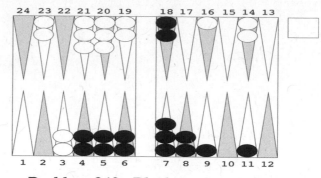

**Problem 248: Black to play 62.**

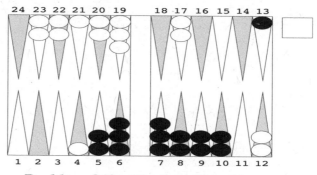

**Problem 249: Black to play 54.**

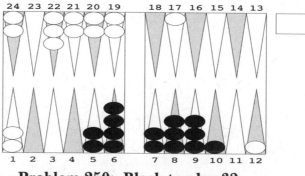

**Problem 250: Black to play 32.**

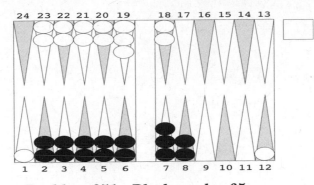

Problem 251: Black to play 65.

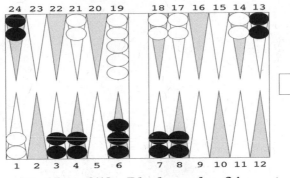

Problem 252: Black to play 64.

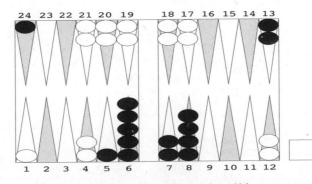

Problem 253: Black to play 51.

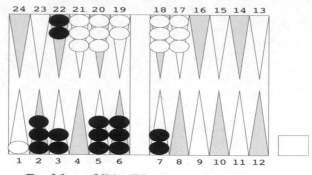

**Problem 254: Black to play 65.**

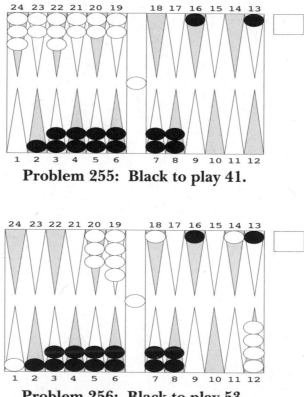

**Problem 255: Black to play 41.**

**Problem 256: Black to play 53.**

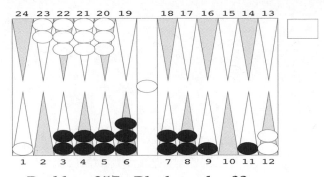

Problem 257:  Black to play 32.

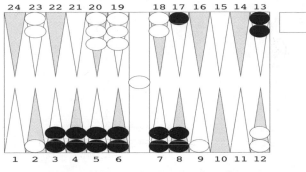

Problem 258:  Black to play 53.

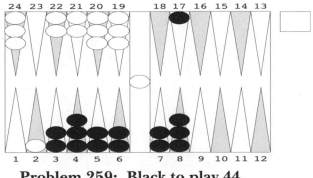

Problem 259:  Black to play 44.

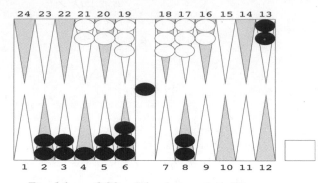

**Problem 260: Black to play 21.**

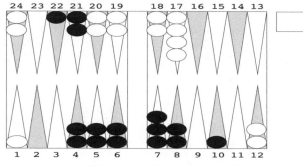

**Problem 261: Black to play 11.**

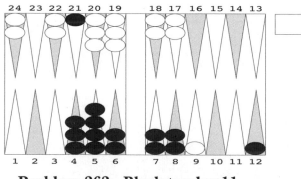

**Problem 262: Black to play 11.**

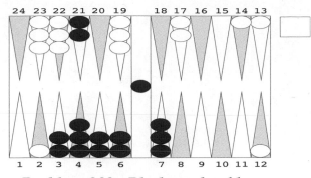

Problem 263: Black to play 11.

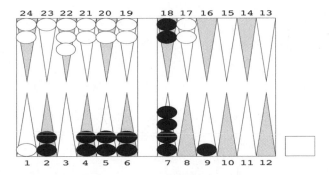

Problem 264: Should Black double?
Should White take if doubled?

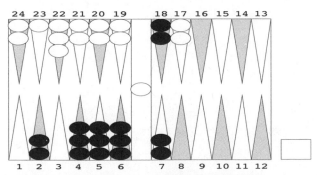

Problem 265: Should Black double?
Should White take if doubled?

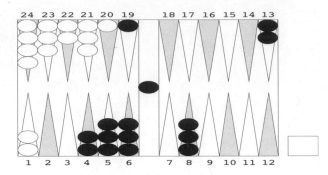

**Problem 266: Should Black double?
Should White take if doubled?**

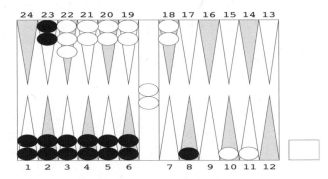

**Problem 267: Should Black double?
Should White take if doubled?**

## SOLUTIONS

**Problem 245: Black to play 53.**

*Attack at the edge of the prime* is a great principle that applies in hundreds of key situations. The point at the front edge of a growing prime is the key point in the position. Whoever gets control of that point first will make a big improvement in their situation. Black should play the aggressive Bar/20 5/2*!, rather than the passive Bar/20 6/3.

**Problem 246: Black to play 33.**

*Build your prime first, then escape.* A full 6-point prime is the most powerful blocking formation in backgammon. It's rarely right to pass on a chance to build a full prime. Although Black could use this roll to escape his back checkers, he should just play 13/7(2)!

**Problem 247: Black to play 44.**

A full 6-point prime is so strong that it's right to make some serious concessions to obtain one. Here Black has the option of a perfectly safe play, 14/2 17/13, which leaves him in a favorable position. But a much better play is 13/5(2), which leaves three blots (!) but builds a full prime. No matter how many blots White hits, he can only win by forcing Black to break his prime, which is quite unlikely.

**Problem 248: Black to play 62.**

A 6-point prime is a tremendously strong formation. Don't let distractions prevent you from making one.

Here Black can hit with 18/16* 18/12, sending a third checker behind his 5-prime. That might be enough to win, but it leaves White some strong returns from the bar, for instance 16, 26. 36, 32, 22, 12, or 11, any one of which might turn the game around.

A better play is 18/12 11/9! creating a full 6-point prime. Now the White checkers can't escape until Black breaks the prime. That's a surer way of winning.

### Problem 249: Black to play 54.

Once you have a 6-point prime, rolling it home is a straightforward procedure; just hit (or slot) at the front of the prime, then cover, then repeat the process.

Black should play 13/4*, then cover next turn (keeping six in a row), then slot the 3-point, and so on. Don't worry about getting hit and trapped. Most likely, getting hit will just give you a chance to pick up a second checker.

### Problem 250: Black to play 32.

When rolling a prime home, pay attention to how strong your opponent's board is.

White could play safely with 10/5, which gives him four builders for the 4-point, the next point he needs to make. He could play a little more aggressively with 8/5 9/7, which gives him five builders for the 4-point (he'd be willing to break the 9-point to make the 4-point) but at the cost of leaving a 17-1 shot (63). What's right?

The answer lies in White's home board. Since White's board is so strong, Black should play safe with 10/5. If White's board were weak, Black could make the bolder play.

### Problem 251: Black to play 65.

Black's had a 6-point prime for awhile, but now he's run into some awkwardness. He can play this roll safely (8/2 8/3), but that opens up the possibility of some really bad rolls next turn. (Any two large numbers will open up a shot.)

Alternatively, he can try to rectify things right now, by hitting: 7/1* 8/3. This could lose, but it requires a pretty big parlay: White has to immediately roll an ace, then Black has to enter quickly, then Black has to break his 6-prime before White does, then White has to escape. This sequence could happen, but it's less likely than the trouble Black could get into in the other variation. Hitting is the right approach.

### Problem 252: Black to play 64.

Black could play 8/2 6/2, and many players would make that play instinctively. But the 2-point doesn't address Black's two main goals: escaping his back men and making his 5-point. A much better play is 24/20 13/7! The checker on the 7-point adds another builder for the 5-point. Splitting with 24/20 might look dangerous, but it's the right time to split. Note that White's 7, 8, and 11-points are all stripped, so it's hard for White to make the 5-point without leaving a bunch of return shots. Black needs to split and he might not get a chance next turn, so he should go now.

**Problem 253: Black to play 51.**

The ace is easy: 6/5. What's the right five, 8/3 or 6/1*?

If White had some immediate threats, 6/1* might be right, to take away half of White's roll. But White's not threatening anything here, so positional play is called for. The right five is 8/3, aiming to make a better blocking point.

**Problem 254: Black to play 65.**

A good rule in priming games is this: "Do what's difficult for you to do. Make your opponent do what's difficult for him to do." It's hard for White to enter with an ace from the bar, so hit him with 6/1*. After you've hit, your choices are covering with 7/1, or jumping with 22/16. It's easy to cover; it's hard to jump. So jump now and leave the covering for later. The right play is 22/16 6/1*.

**Problem 255: Black to play 41.**

Problem 255 shows a trap that a few players will stumble into, especially when moving quickly. Don't make the mistake of playing 7/2??, covering the 2-point. This gives White a winning shot, 16 from the bar. Instead just play 16/11. As long as you keep your full 6-point prime, there's no danger in White's entering and hitting.

**Problem 256: Black to play 53.**

This looks very similar to the previous problem but it's actually quite different. Black can keep his full prime by playing 16/11 13/10, but now that's an error. Instead he should play 7/2 16/13, building his 2-point! The reason is that Black has significant gammon chances in this position, and his best chance to win a gammon is to close his board quickly and attack on the 1-point. The extra gammon chances are worth taking the small chance that White enters with a 16, hitting, and wins the game from that point.

### Problem 257: Black to play 32.

Don't be so concerned with rolling your prime that you overlook a chance to convert to a blitz.

Here the best play to advance Black's 6-point prime is 11/8 9/7, aiming three spares at the 2-point. But a better play is to keep the prime and hit loose with 6/1*. That play might lead to a close-out with a little luck, which would result in a sure gammon. The methodical priming play is more likely to just win a single game. Maximize, maximize, maximize.

### Problem 258: Black to play 53.

The obvious play of 17/9* is certainly tempting. It sends a third checker behind Black's solid 6-point prime. However, if White simply throws a deuce, he'll have reasonably good chances in a 2-point game.

The right idea is to break the prime and go directly for a close-out with 7/2* 17/14. This has two merits over the routine 17/9*: better gammon chances, since closing out two men on the bar will lead to an almost certain gammon; and fewer losing chances, since the chance of losing to two men on the bar is much less than the chance of losing to a 2-point game.

### Problem 259: Black to play 44.

Be prepared to desert the priming game if a blitz is possible.

Here Black can play consistently to keep his prime with 17/5 8/4. But this play may not be good enough to win a gammon, and could even lose if White enters with a deuce next turn and then gets a shot. Instead Black should switch into blitz mode with 6/2*(2)!, followed by 17/9. This pretty much eliminates White's chances of anchoring and considerably improves Black's gammon chances.

### Problem 260: Black to play 21.

Playing Bar/22, getting to the edge of the prime, would be an automatic play if White had a 4-prime or a 5-prime, but it doesn't work here. The problem is that since White has a full 6-prime, Black isn't threatening to escape. He can't get out unless White rolls poorly, breaking up his prime. (Rolls like 44 or 55 for White force him to break the full prime.)

The right play is Bar/24 6/4. This has two objectives. By filling in his board, Black threatens to contain any checker he might hit. By staying back on the 24-point, Black eliminates the variations where he gets hit as White rolls forward, stays on the bar awhile, and eventually gets gammoned because he couldn't move his outfield checkers home. That's actually a fairly common variation, and it's worth preventing.

### Problem 261: Black to play 11.

In priming positions with the issue in doubt, give maximum attention to variations that make the full 6-point prime.

Black could play safely with 22/21 10/8 7/6. But a better play is 22/21 10/9 7/5. By staying on the 9-point, Black creates possibilities of eventually making the 9-point, completing a full prime, and he'll also have four builders aiming at the 3-point, rather than just three. This will matter if White rolls a deuce anytime soon.

### Problem 262: Black to play 11.

In contrast to the previous game, here the right play is 12/9*/8, rather than staying on the 9-point with 12/9* 5/4.

What's the difference? Now Black has a blot on the 21-point, rather than an anchor. That means there will be plenty of variations where White enters and hits on the 21-point, and Black stays on the bar. In these variations, Black can't use the 9-point checker as a builder, and he doesn't need another blot around for White to shoot at.

### Problem 263: Black to play 11.

A strong position with no risk is to be preferred to a potentially gin position with considerable risk.

Black should play Bar/24 3/2*(2) 7/6. The switch gives Black an excellent position with no chance of being hit next turn.

Black could play Bar/24 4/2* 7/6, which opens up the possibility of making a full 6-point prime, locking up the game. But there's a risk of being hit with a deuce from the bar, which could put the whole game in jeopardy. With White's blots floating around, Black needs to be sure that he's not on the bar next turn.

## Problem 264: Should Black double?
## Should White take if doubled?

You should always consider the race in assessing priming positions.

Most players would double Black's position, and many would consider passing as White. Black has five points out of six and some builders in position to fight for the missing 3-point. White only has a good board. Time for a new game?

Not quite. White's ace in the hole is his huge 24-pip lead in the race. If he can get to the outfield and not be hit, he'll win with a redouble. If White moves to the 3-point and Black hits him loose there (the most likely scenario) White's strong home board turns return hits into likely winners. White is 50% to throw a deuce in the next two turns, and he'll win many of those games. Good double and close take.

## Problem 265: Should Black double?
## Should White take if doubled?

Notice the difference between this position and the last one. Now Black is even money to make the 3-point next turn, and every turn after that. Once he makes it, White's racing lead plays no roll. Double and pass.

## Problem 266: Should Black double?
## Should White take if doubled?

Black has a very strong redouble and White has a huge pass. An immediate 5 for Black is crushing, of course, but any 6 also leaves White in dire straits. The chance that White can escape both rear checkers and run all the way around the board while Black flounders on the bar is pretty slim. Only a desperate player would take this.

## Problem 267: Should Black double?
## Should White take if doubled?

Be alert to doubling possibilities when there is a great chance of winning a gammon. Black jumps White's prime with any 6; that happens in 11 rolls out of 36. In 15 rolls out of 36, Black rolls a small number which keeps his closed board; in 1/3 of those games (5 games), Black then rolls a six. That's a total of 16 games where Black hops the prime before his board breaks. In almost all of these games, Black wins a gammon. Since he still has reasonable winning chances even when his board breaks before he jumps, his advantage is huge. Black should double, and White should pass.

# CONNECTIVITY

In backgammon, it's a good idea to have all 15 of your checkers working together as a group. Checkers that are cut off and isolated from the main body of your army are a weakness, one that you should repair whenever possible.

Some apparently risky plays are made to enhance the chances of keeping your army connected. Learn these positions, and you'll cut down on the losses that come when a straggler gets trapped and primed.

## PROBLEMS

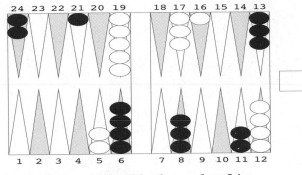

Problem 268: Black to play 64.

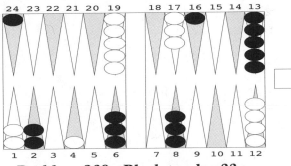

Problem 269: Black to play 33.

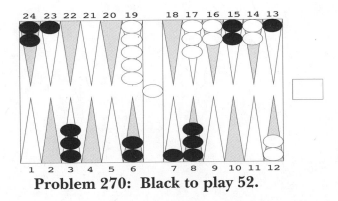

Problem 270: Black to play 52.

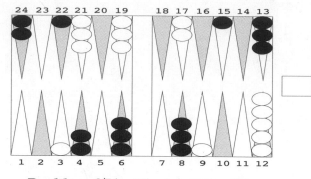

Problem 271: Black to play 52.

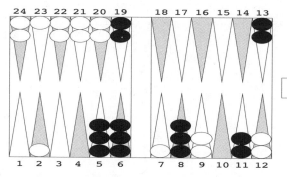

Problem 272: Should Black double?
Should White take if doubled?

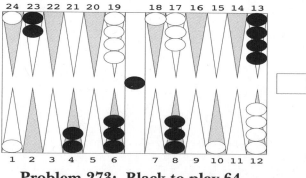

Problem 273: Black to play 64.

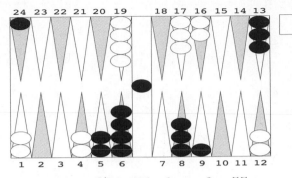

**Problem 274: Black to play 55.**

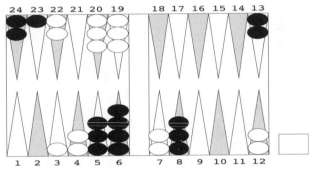

**Problem 275: Black to play 43.**

## SOLUTIONS

**Problem 268: Black to play 64.**

Black could play safely with 21/11. While that play looks neat, it has a serious problem: Black's trailers on the 24-point are completely cut off from the rest of Black's army. With White ready to build blocking points, Black could find himself in some trouble in a couple of turns.

To play backgammon at the highest level, you need to develop a sense for problems before they occur. As the great Chinese general and philosopher Sun Tsu once said, "Every battle is won before it is ever fought." Spying future trouble, Black made the right play: 24/14! He duplicates twos, and his checkers stay connected. Unless White gets very lucky, Black may be able to make an anchor next turn, solving the problem of keeping his army together.

**Problem 269: Black to play 33.**

Black has a sizeable advantage, and he now needs to consolidate. One candidate play is 8/5(3) 16/13, which makes the 5-point but leaves Black without any landing spots in his outfield. Another is 16/4*, which looks good when it works but leaves Black with nothing if White hits back.

The right play is 13/10(2) 16/10, which consolidates Black's lead in the race and leaves him with a nice compact position that will generate new points in the future.

**Problem 270: Black to play 52.**

Black has a lot of plays here, but to find the right one, he has to understand the biggest problem with his position. After a play like 15/10 15/13, his rear checkers are in danger of being cut off from his front checkers. Even a more balanced play like 13/6 leaves the back checkers in difficulty. The best play is to start building a connection while White is on the bar. Black should move 23/18 8/6, preparing to make the 18-point next turn, connecting his rear checkers to his front checkers.

**Problem 271: Black to play 52.**

Black can play safely with 22/15, but this leaves his rear checkers disconnected from the bulk of his army. A better play is 8/3* 24/22. Hitting is always useful, and the 22-point anchor helps keep his men working together.

**Problem 272: Should Black double?**
**Should White take if doubled?**

A good double based on the vulnerability of White's lines of communication. If Black makes the bar-point, White may enter and break apart in the outfield. The anchor on the 19-point gives Black good chances even if he can't execute his main threat. Double and take.

**Problem 273: Black to play 64.**

Three checkers back often function well as a unit, providing good board coverage as well as offering chances to move a deep anchor forward.

Black could operate with just one blot by playing Bar/21/15. However, that play leaves the rear checkers on the 23-point isolated from the rest of Black's army, while Black loses the chance to anchor on the 21-point.

Instead, Black should play Bar/21 13/7! This gives Black a lot of offensive potential. He might anchor on the 21-point, make his 7-point, or hit checkers in White's outfield. White's weak board gives Black the chance to keep his checkers communicating while making a good, aggressive play.

**Problem 274: Black to play 55.**

Black will enter with his first five and then has a choice of two plays: making the 3-point with 13/3 8/3, or swinging around the board with 20/5.

Making the 3-point looks constructive, but it leaves Black's game a little fragile and strung out. The blots on the 9-point and 20-point are vulnerable, and the 13-point and 8-point are stripped. Since the 3-point isn't all that valuable right now (it's behind White's forward anchor), Black should consolidate his game instead with 20/5. Then he has only one vulnerable blot and a great collection of spares — a solid position with good prospects for the future.

**Problem 275: Black to play 43.**

There's an obvious and easy play here: 6/2 5/2, exposing no new blots and making another inner point, if not a great one.

But it's quite wrong. Points behind your opponent's anchors aren't much good, so the 2-point isn't really an asset. More important, Black has a real connection problem in this position. His midpoint is stripped and his three back men are far away, while White's position is just formidable enough to cause Black problems. (Note that the checker Black really wants to move this turn, the one on the 23-point, can't budge.)

Right now White has some problems too. His midpoint is also stripped, and his five back men are well away from the scene of the action. That situation may not last long, so the time to move is now. Black should play 24/17!, trying to make the 17-point or at least cause White some problems in the outfield. White can try to attack, but he doesn't quite have enough ammo on the scene yet.

Repair your connection problems early; don't wait for your game to deteriorate.

# 14

# HIT OR NOT?

Many tactical questions revolve around the question of hitting or not hitting an enemy blot. What if you can make an inner board point instead of hitting? Or improve your distribution? Or hop a prime?

In general, if hitting an opposing blot is an option, you probably want to hit. But there are plenty of exceptions, and you'll need to know about them. Here are the main cases:

• If you can hit a blot in the outfield or make a key inner board point (like the 5-point), the inner point may take precedence.

• If hitting leaves you with lots of blots, and your opponent with lots of return shots, you will probably pass up the hit.

• If your position is stacked and awkward, a developing play may be better.

• If you can hit or fill in a key point of a prime, especially a point that's hard to make otherwise, the prime is probably better.

Here are some concrete examples to test yourself on.

**PROBLEMS**

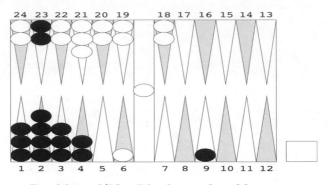

Problem 276: Black to play 63.

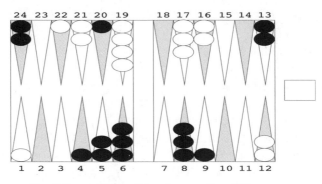

Problem 277: Black to play 62.

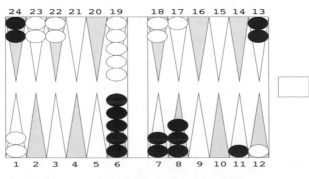

Problem 278: Black to play 61.

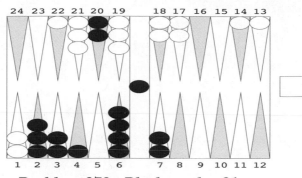

Problem 279: Black to play 21.

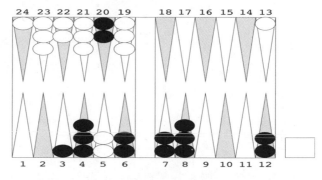

Problem 280: Black to play 52.

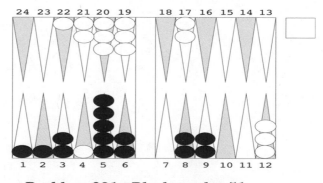

Problem 281: Black to play 51.

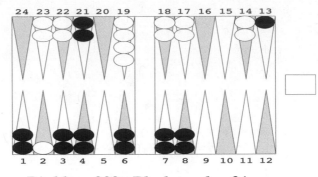

Problem 282:  Black to play 64.

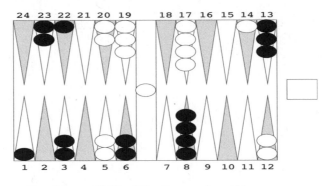

Problem 283:  Black to play 54.

## SOLUTIONS

**Problem 276: Black to play 63.**

Don't be afraid to hit loose if you're liable to lose the game even if you play "safe." Here Black obviously has to jump out with 23/17, then consider his best three, either 9/6* or 17/14. A cautious player might decline to hit, on the theory that he's more likely to be hit back next turn. But the right way to think about the position is to realize that if White enters next turn, Black is highly likely to lose whether he hits or not. The hit with 9/6* is really a free shot, which works very well when White stays out with both men.

**Problem 277: Black to play 62.**

When your position is loose, with many exposed blots, hitting is likely to be less important than consolidating. Here Black can choose between hitting with 24/22* 20/14, and building points in various ways. After hitting, he has five blots scattered around the board, and any return hit by White leaves him in very bad shape. He needs to consolidate, and the best building play is 6/4 20/14, making a good board while giving White only deuces to hit.

**Problem 278: Black to play 61.**

White is well ahead in the race, but his position is awkward and too advanced. If Black can build a prime, White won't be able to simultaneously escape his back men and fill in the gaps in his board. The right play is to eschew the hit and just make the 5-point, 11/5 6/5.

**Problem 279: Black to play 21.**

In a battle or primes, it's often more important to strengthen your own prime than to send another checker back. In this position, hitting with Bar/22* turns the game into a slugfest where White has reasonable chances, but locking White in with Bar/24 6/4 just about wraps up the game.

### Problem 280: Black to play 52.

Although Black trails in the race, hitting is way too dangerous in this position. White has the stronger board, and after hitting Black would have three blots exposed to a total of 17 immediate shots. Black already owns the cube, which argues for prudence. The right idea is to bide time with 8/3 4/2. More (and safer) opportunities to hit will soon arise.

### Problem 281: Black to play 51.

Pay me now or pay me later? That's the question here. The only safe play is 6/1 6/5, but with the 6-point and 7-point open, Black is likely to leave a shot later as he tries to clear his outer points. Or Black could play 9/4* 2/1, gambling it all on this roll. If he gets away with the hit, he's pretty much home free.

To make the right decision, consider two factors: Black is massively ahead in the race (74 to 120 is he makes the safe play) and White's board is already strong enough to win after most hitting sequences. Those two considerations make playing safe almost certainly correct. Notice also that while hitting might win a gammon for Black, he might also lose a gammon if White hits back. Just clear the 6-point and see what happens next.

### Problem 282: Black to play 64.

Don't hit if your opponent's position is deteriorating.

Black has two plays: 13/3, waiting, and 8/2* 8/4, hitting. The two plays look like a tough choice at first glance. To find the right play, look at White's position.

White's position is a little awkward, and it could get worse quickly. With White's stripped points and Black's firm anchor, any roll not containing a three is likely to cause White some problems. Hold the prime and see if White cracks. The right move is 13/3.

### Problem 283: Black to play 54.

Beware of hitting when you create a position where it's very hard to consolidate your racing lead. Here Black can consider hitting with 23/14*, which would leave him with a 27-pip lead in the race. But his position would then have four blots plus very little in the way of useful points or structure. Instead he needs to consolidate with 22/18 23/18, after which he has a solid position that can gradually improve.

# 15

# BREAKING ANCHOR

A strong anchor in your opponent's home board, or on his bar point, is a powerful asset. It is so powerful, in fact, that the decision to eventually run off the anchor is usually a critical one. Here are some of the issues to consider when you're deciding whether to leave the anchor or not.

• A lead in the race argues for running off the anchor before you get squeezed. Trailing in the race argues for holding the anchor and waiting for a shot.

• If you still have constructive plays to make, stay on the anchor. If your position would break up otherwise, leave the anchor.

• If your checker can run to a safe place, you're more likely to break the anchor.

• If you have one or two stragglers behind the anchor, keep the point until you can move the stragglers forward.

## PROBLEMS

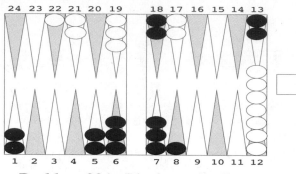

Problem 284: Black to play 54.

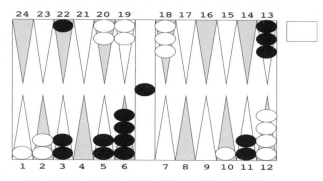

Problem 285: Black to play 63.

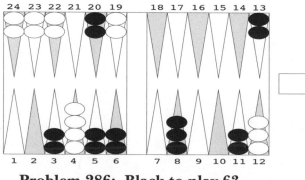

Problem 286: Black to play 63.

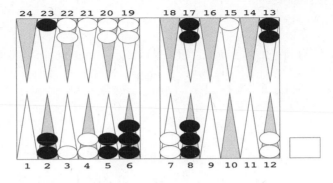

Problem 287:  Black to play 43.

## SOLUTIONS

**Problem 284: Black to play 54.**

All the preconditions for a successful anchor-breaking play are here: a healthy racing lead (24 pips after the roll), minimal shots (only 11 if he plays 18/13 18/14), and a weak enemy board with a blot. White's game will improve from roll to roll, so Black should bolt from the 18-point with both men.

**Problem 285: Black to play 63.**

When you're ahead in the race, anchors aren't so valuable.

Once Black enters with Bar/22, he looks around and notices that after he plays, he'll be up 41 pips in the race. That means White can hold his key points for as long as he wants, while Black needs to look for a good time to scramble home. There's no time like the present, so he correctly plays 22/16.

**Problem 286: Black to play 63.**

You can break anchor more readily if there's no pressure on the point.

Here Black can play safely with 11/8 11/5, but at the cost of forfeiting the potential to make new blocking points in front of White. Instead Black should leave the anchor with 20/11. White's unlikely to be able to attack the checker left behind, while Black's now in a good position to make the 7, 9, or 10-points in upcoming turns.

**Problem 287: Black to play 43.**

Part of connectivity is building links to keep your checkers together. Another part is keeping those links until your rear checkers get out.

Black can make a clever-looking anchor breaking play, 17/13 17/14, breaking anchor at a time when White's board is a little vulnerable. If there wasn't anyone back on the 23-point, this would be a great move. But the straggler on the 23 needs the 17-point as a landing spot. Without it, he's stuck, reduced to relying on the kindness of strangers. A better move is the simple 8/1, preserving all links for the next move.

# 16

# CRUNCH POSITIONS

A "crunch" position is one where your home board has collapsed before you've been able to bring your back men around a home. (Usually a crunch position results when you've thrown an awkward double that can only be played by your front men.) Crunch positions are extremely dangerous. Once your front position is gone, you'll need to race your back men home as quickly as possible.

A good rule of thumb is to double as soon as your opponent's front game has collapsed. Even if the double is technically incorrect, you'll pick up a lot of passes.

## PROBLEMS

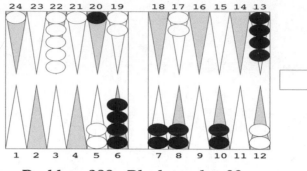

Problem 288: Black to play 66.

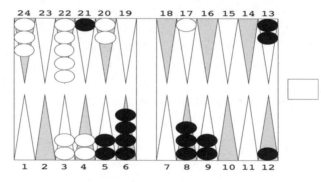

Problem 289: Should Black double?
Should White take if doubled?

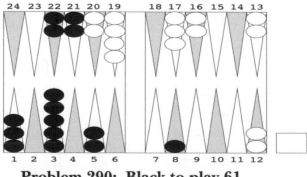

Problem 290: Black to play 61.

## SOLUTIONS

**Problem 288: Black to play 66.**

When your opponent is under pressure, don't let him off the hook. Keep contact!

Here White's game is weak and crumbling. A hasty play like 20/8 13/7(2) or 20/8 10/4(2) relieves all the pressure on the White checkers on the 17-point and the 12-point. Now these checkers are free to move, and White has a good chance of rebuilding his board. Instead Black should play 13/1(2)! forcing White to move and expose more blots, while his board is weak.

**Problem 289: Should Black double?**
**Should White take if doubled?**

Beware of taking cubes if your front position has collapsed and the game has a ways to go. Here White is actually ahead in the race, but eight of his 15 checkers are out of play on the 24-point and the 22-point. There's only a slim chance that his checkers on the 3-point and 4-point will make the race to home without being hit and losing a lot of ground. Black should double and White should pass.

**Problem 290: Black to play 61.**

Don't leap at the first play you see. Sit on your hands and consider your choices.

Black can make his 2-point with 8/2 3/2, and most players would grab the point without hesitation. But there's a better move available. Black needs to think about just how he plans to win this game. He can't win a back game, since his front checkers are too far forward. His best chance is to convert into a 4-point holding game, where he'd have good chances in a relatively even race. This roll is a good shot to break the back anchor now, while White's board is still weaker than Black's. He should play 22/15!

# ACTION DOUBLES

An action double is a double based on the possibility of getting a big advantage by hitting a shot. You don't need to be a favorite to hit a shot, as long as the hit will give you good winning and/or gammoning chances, while you'll still be in the game even if you miss the shot.

Giving a good action double can be a brutal psychological weapon when it works and leads to a gammon. Your opponent will probably think that you offered a bad double and just got lucky — the ideal situation for putting him on tilt, as the poker players say.

**PROBLEMS**

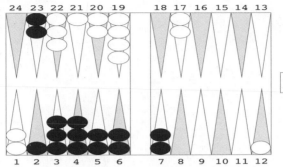

**Problem 291: Should Black double?**
**Should White take if doubled?**

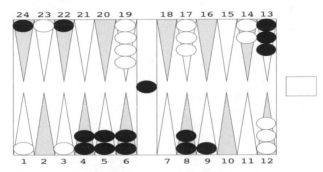

**Problem 292: Should Black double?**
**Should White take if doubled?**

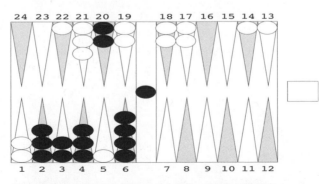

**Problem 293: Should Black double?**
**Should White take if doubled?**

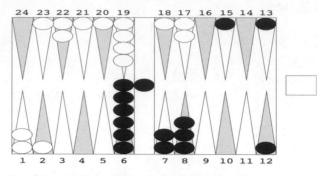

**Problem 294: Should Black double?**
**Should White take if doubled?**

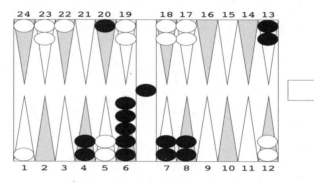

**Problem 295: Should Black double?**
**Should White take if doubled?**

## SOLUTIONS

### Problem 291:  Should Black double?
### Should White take if doubled?

Black has some powerful threats in this double-edged position. Any deuce will send a third man back with substantial gammon possibilities.  A five enables Black to jump a checker, in which case his priming advantage will probably hold up.  Black has a couple of other good rolls:  61 can only be played 3/2, while 66 holds the position.  If Black doesn't roll one of these numbers, his prime will break and the advantage which switch to White.  It's a good double because of the strengths of Black's threats, and the fact he has more good rolls than bad;  it's a good take since White can turn the game around quickly if Black doesn't throw one of his good numbers.

### Problem 292:  Should Black double?
### Should White take if doubled?

A great action double.  Black has 18 shots at the blot on the 23-point, his strongest 3-point board, and the beginnings of a good prime or a potential blitz.  White can squeeze out a thin take, since he rates to enter pretty easily after being hit, and his outside checkers are all in play.

### Problem 293:  Should Black double?
### Should White take if doubled?

The more solid your opponent's position, the more threats you need to justify an action double. Here Black has 22 hitting numbers, but White already has an anchor and will be favored to reenter. In addition, White has a good structure in place and some of Black's entering numbers (2-2, 3-3) are disasters. Black should wait with the cube and see how the position looks next turn.

### Problem 294:  Should Black double?
### Should White take if doubled?

Now here's a real action position!  Black has 32 hits from the bar — only the four dancing numbers miss.  He's ahead in the race anyway, and some very good things could happen here, so he doubles.

Although it looks scary, White can take. Black still only has a 1-point board, and that big stack on the 6-point could prove awkward. White could get a wide variety of holding game or back game formations. The game could go a lot of different ways, and it's too soon to give up.

**Problem 295: Should Black double?**
**Should White take if doubled?**

Just because you're shooting at a couple of blots doesn't mean you have a double. Here Black has a good position with a chance to hit White's blots on the 24-point and 22-point. The trouble is that White already has a strong defensive position, and getting hit won't destroy his position. Black has threats, but they aren't strong enough to double.

## 18

# LATE-GAME BLITZ

A late blitz occurs when one side gets caught without an anchor later in the middle game. Late blitzes are harder to evaluate than early blitzes; typically the defender has a developed position, and play can get very double-edged. Escaping the back men is probably more important than in a typical early blitz. Be on the alert for possible switch plays, which might buy time to get your rear checkers home.

**PROBLEMS**

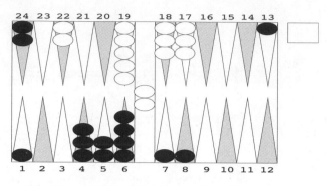

Problem 296:  Black to play 53.

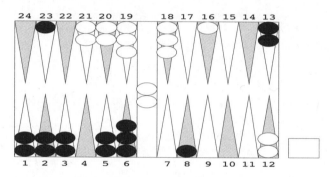

Problem 297:  Should Black double?
Should White take if doubled?

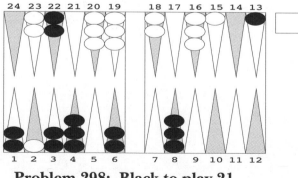

Problem 298:  Black to play 21.

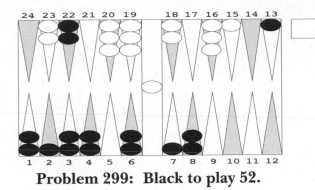

Problem 299: Black to play 52.

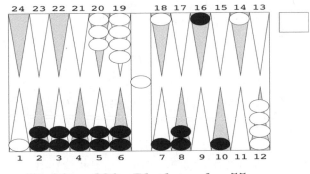

Problem 300: Black to play 55.

## SOLUTIONS

### Problem 296:  Black to play 53.

In any blitz, low points may be more valuable than high points.

We normally learn to make our inner board points in order, from high points (6, 5, 4) to low (3, 2, 1).  But in a blitz, this order doesn't really apply.  Low points are just as good as high points for keeping the opponent on the bar, while open high points are closer to our remaining builders than open low points, thus easier to fill in later.

The right play here is not the stereotyped 8/3 6/3, but instead 6/1 24/21!  (Splitting to the 21-point makes it less likely that our back checkers get stuck after the blitz has done its job — an important consideration in later blitzes.)

### Problem 297:  Should Black double?
### Should White take if doubled?

Black took an early cube and defended for a long time.  Now a sudden swing has left him in control, with two White checkers on the bar.  Should he redouble?

The answer is no!  He's much too good to redouble.  Instead of doubling and winning just two points, he should play on and try to win a gammon and four points!  If Black makes the mistake of doubling, White should of course pass.

Late blizes can occur very suddenly;  be alert for situations which are too strong to turn the cube.

### Problem 298:  Black to play 21.

When the game is on the line, don't be afraid to play to win.  White is in the process of building a prime to contain Black's rear checkers, and this is Black's last chance to strike.  He should play 4/2* 8/7, which could wrap up the game if White dances.

### Problem 299:  Black to play 52.

When given a choice between two plays with two different goals, make the play that achieves the more difficult goal first.  Here Black can hit on the 15-point with 22/15*, or cover the 2-point with 7/2 13/11.  Which should he pick?

To choose, ask yourself "Which goal is easier?" The 2-point can be covered with all 5s and 6s, a total of 28 rolls. The blot can only be hit with 4 rolls: 52 and 61. Hit the blot first, and cover the point later.

**Problem 300: Black to play 55.**

When finishing off a blitz, don't overlook the tactic of switching points. Here Black could play 16/1* 10/5, which will likely result in a closeout; however, this allows White the chance of entering with an ace followed by another ace and securing an ace-point game, which could win in the end. Instead Black should play 6/1*(2) 16/11 8/3, which wipes out White's chances for a low anchor and brings four builders to bear on the 6-point.

# POST-BLITZ
# TURNAROUND GAMES

A post-blitz turnaround is a position where you've survived a blitz, either by anchoring or escaping, and now you're in the process of priming your opponent's last few checkers.

Beware — these positions are very deceptive and treacherous for both sides! The blitzing side usually has two advantages: a strong home board, left over from the failed blitz, and a solid racing lead. The survivor has the potential of building a winning prime. Judging just when the priming threats are strong enough to redouble is a tricky business, one that often confounds even the strongest masters. Study these positions carefully.

**PROBLEMS**

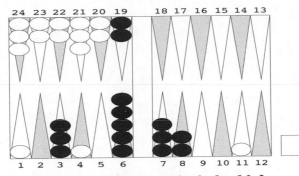

**Problem 301: Should Black double?**
**Should White take if doubled?**

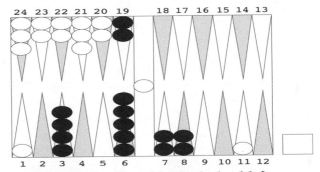

**Problem 302: Should Black double?**
**Should White take if doubled?**

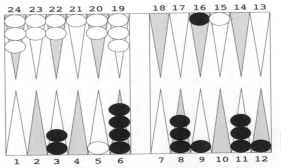

**Problem 303: Should Black double?**
**Should White take if doubled?**

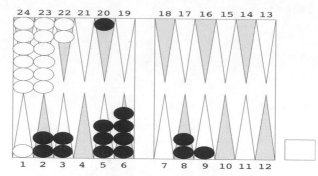

**Problem 304: Should Black double?
Should White take if doubled?**

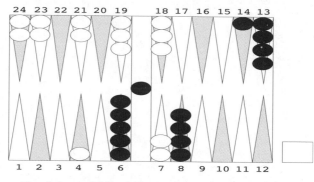

**Problem 305: Black to play 32.**

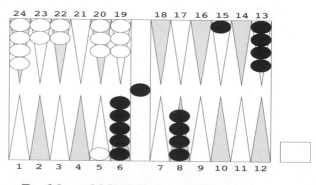

**Problem 306: Black to play 41.**

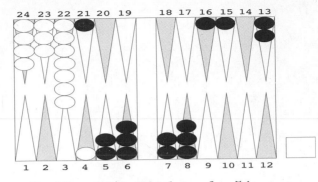

Problem 307: Black to play 54.

## SOLUTIONS

**Problem 301: Should Black double?**
**Should White take if doubled?**

Black has survived a blitz and started to turn the game around, but it's too soon to give up the cube. Black has a 2-point board, White has a 5-point board. That's going to cause Black big problems if he ever has to hit loose. In addition, White leads by 20 pips in the race, a big asset. No double and take.

**Problem 302: Should Black double?**
**Should White take if doubled?**

With White caught on the bar, it's a whole different story. Now Black can look forward to making the ace-point on White's head, hitting loose on the 11-point, or just improving his structure gradually. Catching your opponent on the bar is usually a good time to double, and this position is no exception. Double and take.

**Problem 303: Should Black double?**
**Should White take if doubled?**

Surviving a blitz can give some players an itchy trigger finger. Black has done well to survive a closeout, and White has just entered from the bar with an awkward 56, forcing him to expose a second blot on the 15-point. Black felt cocky and redoubled, which was a big mistake. He's still far behind in the race, and only has a 2-point board compared to White's 5-point board. White correctly beavered Black's double to 8, and won a really big game.

**Problem 304: Should Black double?**
**Should White take if doubled?**

Black has turned the game around and now stands at an excellent doubling point. He has threats to make the 4-point and attack on the 1-point. If Black makes the 4-point or the 7-point and White doesn't leap out, Black would have an easy cash next turn. The time to double is now, when White still has a bare take.

**Problem 305: Black to play 32.**

When you're in trouble after any play, attack! Here Black can play "safe" with Bar/22/20, but his blots can be hit with any one, any two, sevens, and tens. That's 25 numbers out of 36. He has nothing to lose by trying to take the initiative, so he should hit with Bar/22 6/4*!

**Problem 306: Black to play 41.**

Here's an even scarier variation of the same principle. Despite White's 5-point board, Black should fight for survival with the aggressive Bar/21 6/5*.

**Problem 307: Black to play 54.**

Remember that your roll comes in two parts. Don't be in a hurry to play the whole roll. Look at both parts separately. You may spot a play you would otherwise miss.

In the game from which this position was taken, Black rolled a 54 and immediately grabbed a checker on the 13-point and played 13/4*. Mistake!

Why? Note that although hitting on the 4-point is clear, Black doesn't need to use his whole roll to do it. He should just play 8/4*, then calmly look for his best five. It certainly won't be 13/8, which does nothing. Instead, he should play 16/11, creating three builders each for the critical 9-point and 10-point.

# TOO GOOD TO DOUBLE?

In most backgammon clubs, the Jacoby rule is considered to always be in force for money games and chouettes. The Jacoby rule simply states that no gammon can be scored unless the cube has already been turned. This is an excellent rule (as one might expect, given the brilliance of its inventor, Oswald Jacoby, who was probably the best player in the world during the 1940s, 50s, and 60s), which has the effect of speeding up play by forcing a player who gets a quick, early advantage to double and cash the game.

If the cube has already been turned, however, the possibility of playing for a gammon rather than doubling your opponent out is always a real one. Keep these general rules in mind:

• If you can't lose, play on. If your opponent is trapped behind a full 6-prime, he's not going to take your cube next time, so take a free roll and see what happens. As long as you can always win by doubling later, keep playing.

• If your game is strong, but you could lose it, be careful. Evaluate just how likely the sequences are that could cost you the game on the next exchange. If you think your losing chances are under 10%, it's usually right to play on. Losing chances in the 20% range generally mean it's right to cash the game.

• If you own the cube and you're playing for the gammon, try to keep the win in hand. Stay away from risky checker plays which, if they backfire, could prevent you from doubling.

**PROBLEMS**

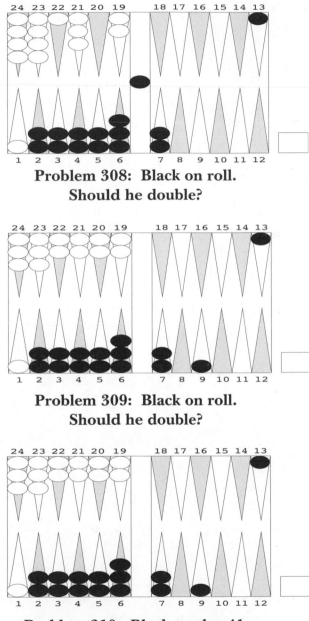

**Problem 308: Black on roll.
Should he double?**

**Problem 309: Black on roll.
Should he double?**

**Problem 310: Black to play 41.**

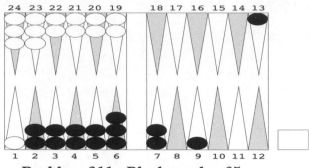

Problem 311: Black to play 65.

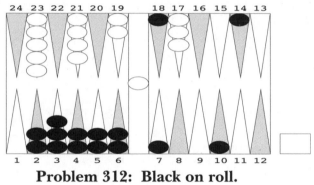

Problem 312: Black on roll.
Should he double?

## SOLUTIONS

### Problem 308: Black on roll.
### Should he double?

Black had been doubled earlier in the game, but now he's turned matters around. Although Black is on the bar, he's shooting at a 3-shot to hit a second checker. Even more important, White's checker on the 1-point is trapped behind a full six-point prime and can never escape until Black lifts his blockade.

Clearly, if Black doubles White should pass. But Black mustn't give him that chance! Instead of doubling, Black must play on, hoping to win a gammon (worth four points) rather than doubling and collecting a mere two points. Is Black favored to win a gammon? Not at all. But as long as he keeps his six-point prime, his losing chances are zero, since he can double White out at any point. Black's correct strategy is to play on, doubling only when his gammon chances are completely exhausted.

### Problem 309: Black on roll.
### Should he double?

This looks worse for Black than the previous position. He's not shooting at a second checker, and now White has a closed board. Should he double and collect his two points? (Obviously White will pass.)

Again the answer is no! Although Black's gammon chances aren't as good as in the previous example, his losing chances are still zero. (After any sequence, Black could double next turn and White would have to pass.) For Black's correct checker strategy, see the next problem.

### Problem 310: Black to play 41.

In the previous position, Black decided to play on, and rolled a 41. He should hit with 6/1*!

Hit against a closed board? Yes indeed! Look what happens if White rolls an ace.

• If White rolls 11, he plays Bar/1*, 23/24, 19/20(2). Now Black simply rolls until he throws a 6. Meanwhile White can't escape from his prison on the 1-point, and has to continue destroying his board.

• If White rolls 16, he plays just Bar/1*, but then (since Black can't move), he has to keep rolling and destroy his board.

• If White rolls 12, 13, 14, or 15, he has to enter, hitting, then break a point (his 19-point is his best chance), immediately exposing another blot. If Black hits this blot, he's well on his way to a gammon.

## Problem 311: Black to play 65.

Black could make the 1-point, locking up the win, but leaving him with very few gammon chances. (He's only about 3% to win a gammon with one enemy checker closed out.) Instead, he should apply the same strategy we just learned: the right play is 13/7 6/1*, hoping to get hit and pick up a second checker.

## Problem 312: Black on roll. Should he double?

Black should play on, trying the same plan as in the last few problems. His first job is to make his 7-point (20 rolls make it on his first throw.) After making the 7-point, he will stick a checker on the 1-point, hoping to get hit and recirculated, perhaps picking up a White checker along the way. This plan will only backfire if White throws a 16 on his first or second shake, but that's a small risk, well worth taking.

# ACE-POINT GAMES

Ace-point games are one of the bread-and-butter positions of backgammon. You'll have to play many ace-point games, from both sides of the board, and you'll need to know how to play them well.

An ace-point game means you've held onto your opponent's ace-point while he built a prime in front of you and escaped his back checkers. You're holding on desperately, hoping to hit a shot as he bears off his checkers.

There aren't any doubling positions in this chapter, since almost all normal ace-point games are passes. The exceptions are positions where the side bearing home has left some gaps in his board. In this case, the chance of getting and hitting a shot can be high enough so that the game is actually a take.

For the side bearing in against an ace-point game, the main question is "How best to bear off my checkers?" The basic idea is to clear your points from the back, but there are a few exceptions. We'll show you plenty of examples in this chapter.

For the side playing the ace-point game, the key questions are "How do I build my prime?" and "When do I run with my last checker?" Again, take a look at the examples.

Incidentally, if you play an ace-point game and you hit a shot, you're not in an ace-point game anymore. Those positions are called "Containment Games," and we'll look at some of them in Chapter 23. If you hit a shot, contain it, and close your board, you're in a "Post-Ace-Point Game," covered in Chapter 24.

**PROBLEMS**

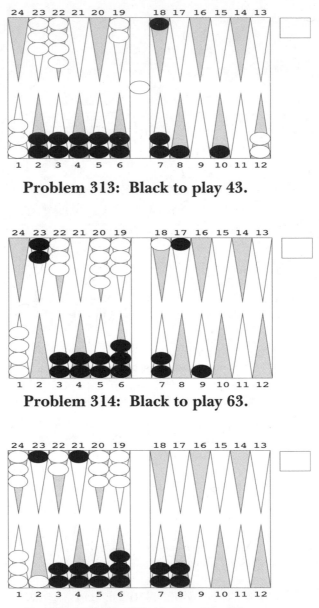

Problem 313:  Black to play 43.

Problem 314:  Black to play 63.

Problem 315:  Black to play 51.

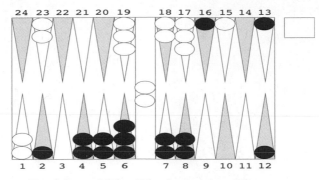

Problem 316: Black to play 61.

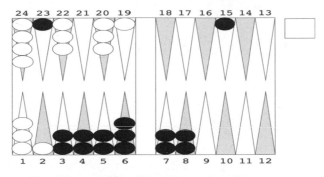

Problem 317: Black to play 54.

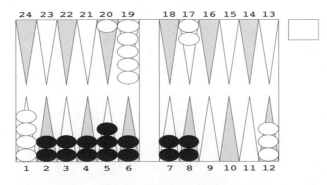

Problem 318: Black to play 43.

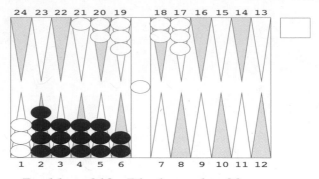

Problem 319: Black to play 22.

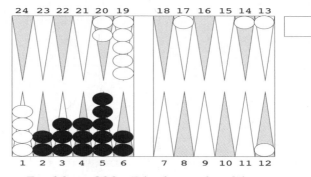

Problem 320: Black to play 21.

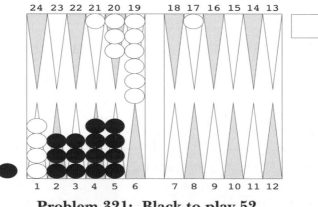

Problem 321: Black to play 52.

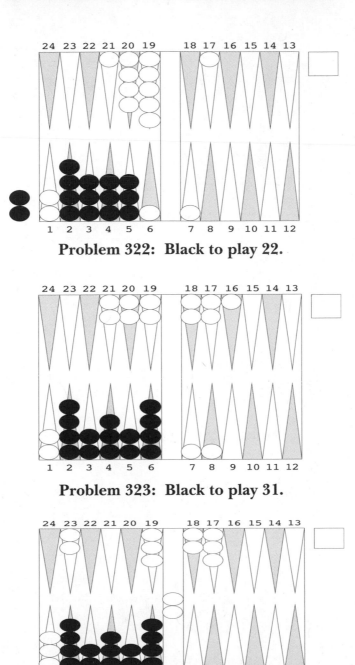

Problem 322: Black to play 22.

Problem 323: Black to play 31.

Problem 324: Black to play 31.

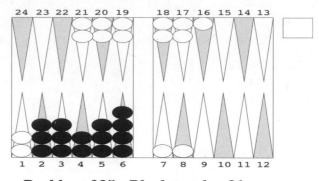

Problem 325: Black to play 21.

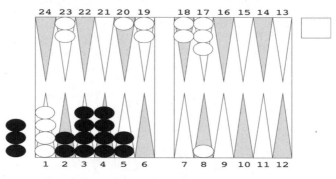

Problem 326: Black to play 41.

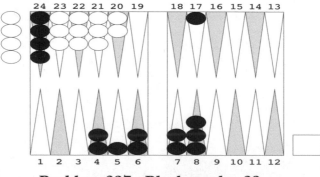

Problem 327: Black to play 32.

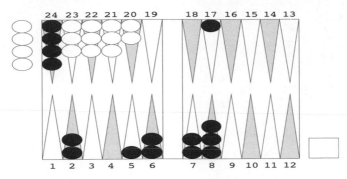

**Problem 328: Black to play 32.**

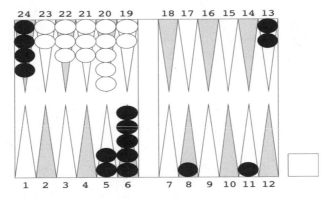

**Problem 329: Black to play 21.**

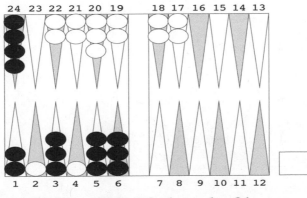

**Problem 330: Black to play 21.**

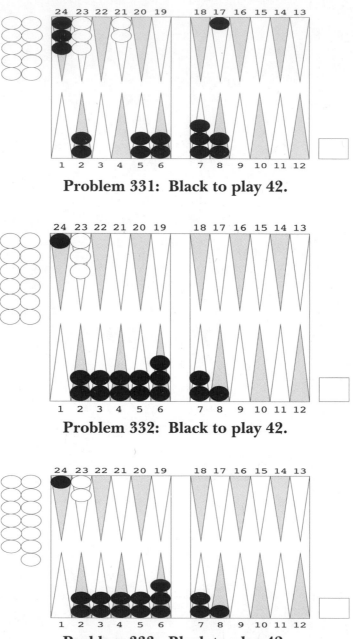

Problem 331: Black to play 42.

Problem 332: Black to play 42.

Problem 333: Black to play 42.

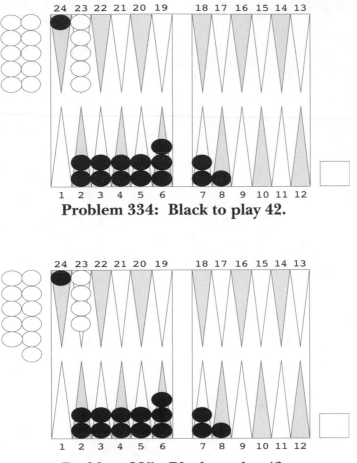

Problem 334: Black to play 42.

Problem 335: Black to play 42.

## SOLUTIONS

**Problem 313: Black to play 43.**

*When your opponent's on the ropes, hit him again!* Backgammon's not a game for the squeamish or the merciful. When you have a big edge, try for even more. Your opponent will when it's his turn.

Black can break contact in the outer boards by playing 18/11. A conservative player might try this, hoping to get home safely. But look what happens if you leave your back checker where it is and play 10/6 8/5. Now if White enters with a 16, he has to expose two more blots. If he enters with any other ace, he'll break his 6-point rather than move one of the checkers on the 12. That's good for you. Keep up the pressure, and try to win a gammon or a backgammon!

**Problem 314: Black to play 63.**

When the game's under control, make sure you maximize your gammon chances.

Black has a good shot at winning a gammon in position 314. In the actual game, however, he let his chances slip away. Afraid that his back men might get trapped, he played 23/17 9/6.

What happened then wasn't hard to foresee. White made the 23-point. Black stayed on the bar for a few turns, while White rolled a couple of aces and crept up to the 2-point. Because White had a few turns to play while Black was on the bar, White ended up in a 2-point game and was able to save the gammon.

The right idea for Black is 17/8!, keeping the 23-point anchor. Now White will have to bury checkers down to the 24-point, destroying his board. Meanwhile Black's in position to attack if White tries to move up to the 2-point. This play gives Black a great chance of both destroying White's board and keeping four checkers pinned back on the 1-point.

**Problem 315: Black to play 51.**

When playing for a gammon, keep the pressure on.

Playing 23/17 takes the pressure off White by allowing him to play checkers down to the 24, 23, and 22-points without leaving a shot. Running off the 21-point keeps up the pressure, since it's harder for White to play safely as long as Black stays on the 23-point.

**Problem 316: Black to play 61.**

When your opponent's stuck in an ace-point game, hit all the blots you can.

Here the right play is 8/2 16/15*. Some players are reluctant to hit in this situation for fear of improving their opponent's timing. While that might happen, the extra gammons and backgammons you'll win are more than sufficient compensation.

**Problem 317: Black to play 54.**

Black is playing for the gammon, and the ideal position he can reach from here is to pin five of White's men back on the ace-point. The play that gives him the best chance to bring this about is the double-hit: 23/19* 7/2*. There's a very small chance this will backfire, but that tiny risk is worth taking to jack up the gammon chances to their maximum.

**Problem 318: Black to play 43.**

When bearing in against an ace-point game, don't automatically clear points from the back. Look and see if breaking a contact point might be better.

If Black plays 8/4 8/5, he leaves a direct shot next turn with either 65 or 64. If instead he clears the 7-point now with 7/3 7/4, only 55 will leave a direct shot next. That's a 300% increase in safety with the alert play.

**Problem 319: Black to play 22.**

The normal way to handle an ace-point game, as Kit Woolsey has often said, is to "clear from the back, and ask no questions." Here's a typical play. Black should move 6/4(2) — clearing the back point, then 5/3 — preparing to clear the new back point, and finally 2/off — bearing off a checker when there's no more clearing to be done.

**Problem 320: Black to play 21.**

The basic rule of bearing off against ace-point games is "Clear from the back." Every point you clear is a point you can't be hit on. Clear all the points safely, and you win.

Black, with a gammon well in hand as long as he isn't hit, should play 6/4 6/5.

**Problem 321: Black to play 52.**

The second rule of bearing off against ace-point games is "Prepare to clear the back point." The sooner you clear points, the less long-term risk you run.

Black should play 5/off 5/3.

**Problem 322: Black to play 22.**

Here Black can both clear the back point and prepare to clear the next point, all in one swoop. The right play is 5/3(3) 4/2.

**Problem 323: Black to play 31.**

Black's only concern in Problem 323 is safety. If he doesn't get hit while bearing off, he'll win a gammon. In this case, the safest play is the paradoxical-looking 5/2 5/4! Although Black leaves a gap, he succeeds in clearing one of his five remaining points, and each point cleared represents a big jump in safety. Remember this position — if you can't actually clear the 6-point, but you can clear the 5-point, then clearing the 5-point is probably right.

**Problem 324: Black to play 31.**

This position is subtly different from the previous one. Black can still clear the 5-point, but now it's not the right play. Do you see why?

There are actually two reasons. If Black clears the 5-point, White might actually enter and make the point before Black can clear the 6-point. That would put Black in extra jeopardy. The other reason is that the longer White stays on the bar, the less likely he is to have a strong home board when and if he hits a shot. If White hits a shot with a weak home board, Black will have extra chances to scramble home.

Black's proper play here is 6/3 6/5.

**Problem 325: Black to play 21.**

Leaving a gap on the 5-point is a special case. Don't go leaving deeper gaps — those are very dangerous, because there are more points to clear above them.

Here Black can clear the 4-point, but that's a mistake. Just play 6/4 6/5 instead, preparing to clear from the rear.

**Problem 326: Black to play 41.**

Don't let the desire to be even-ended force you into awkward positions. Here Black could play 4/off 4/3, which leaves him with two checkers each on the 4-point and 5-point. The downside is that all his spares are bunched on the 3-point, reducing his future choices.

A better play is 4/off 3/2, staying even on the highest point, but keeping spares on three different points, leading to flexibility down the road.

**Problem 327: Black to play 32.**

The choice here is pretty easy. Black plays 8/5 17/15, building his 5-point prime and getting ready to contain a checker.

**Problem 328: Black to play 32.**

The choice here isn't so easy. If Black plays 8/5 17/15, as in the last problem, his two checkers on the 2-point don't work as part of his prime. The gaps on the 3-point and 4-point will cause big problems if Black ever hits a shot.

The only way to bring the 2-point into Black's prime is to build a prime from the 2-point to the 6-point, filling in the 3-point and 4-point as quickly as possible. With that in mind, the right play is 7/5 7/4, starting the 4-point now.

**Problem 329: Black to play 21.**

Don't try to save the gammon if it can't be saved.

In the game, Black remembered that the best way to save a gammon was to bring all your men to the 6-point by an exact count, and get crossovers when possible. So he played 8/6 13/12, getting a man to the 6-point and two crossovers.

The problem: Black's too far behind. He won't save the gammon unless he actually hits a shot, so he has to give himself the best chance to win if that happens. The right play is 6/4 6/5, starting to build a prime for the variations where he does hit the shot.

By the way, hitting a shot isn't a real long shot from this position. A well-timed ace-point game will leave at least one shot about 90% (!) of the time.

### Problem 330: Black to play 21.

In a hopeless position, concentrate on saving the gammon.

Turning a gammon loss into a single loss saves you two points (with the cube on two). That's worth some effort. In position 330, making the 4-point (5/4* 6/4) looks automatic, but it doesn't help Black win the game, since his back checkers can't get out. The best play is 24/23 (making the 23-point will cut down on gammons considerably) and 3/1 (getting hit will increase gammons considerably). Stay alert, and try to save what's savable.

### Problem 331: Black to play 42.

At the end of an ace-point game, make sure you get all the shots you're entitled to.

In the actual game, Black panicked and played 24/20 24/22, spreading out his blots. White rolled 63 and played 4/off 4/1*, leaving a shot. Black missed with 54, and that was the end.

A better play would have been to keep the 24-point, playing 24/22 7/3. Now White's 63 would be played 4/off, leaving a double shot. Even if Black missed the shot, he might get another shot later as White tries to clear the 23-point. Keeping an anchor instead of breaking it can give you extra shots at the end of the game.

### Problem 332: Black to play 42.

Black has a choice between running, 24/18, which saves the backgammon but concedes the gammon, or 8/2, sticking around in the hopes of hitting a shot and perhaps even winning! What's right?

When White has three checkers left, the right play is to stay. If White's next roll is 21, 31, 41, 51, or 61 (10 rolls), White will actually have to leave two blots, and if Black can pick them both up, he'll be a favorite in the game. (This particular disaster happens more than you might think. It even has a name — "coup classique"!)

Any other non-double will leave a single blot, and hitting it means saving the gammon, at least. Staying on the 24-point is a good percentage play.

**Problem 333: Black to play 42.**
With only two White checkers left, there's no chance for a "coup classique," and White is a favorite to win a backgammon if Black sticks around. The right play is to run, 24/18.

**Problem 334: Black to play 42.**
With five checkers left, Black can't be backgammoned on the next roll, and he has a good chance of transposing to the "coup classique" position. It's right to stay on the 24-point.

**Problem 335: Black to play 42.**
With four checkers, no coup classique position can arise. Black should run with 24/18.

# BACK GAMES

You're in a back game when you've made two (or more) points in your opponent's home board, and you've fallen so far behind in the race that the only way to win the game is to hit a shot. If you miss your shots, you'll certainly lose, and you may well be gammoned or backgammoned.

Back games are the goal line stands of backgammon. They're exciting and complicated, and they're a style of game that you need to know how to play from either side.

Some players enjoy winning from back games so much that they try to play back games when they don't have to. They slot points wildly and look for opportunities to fall far behind in the race, confident they can pull the game out at the last minute. Don't fall into this trap. Well-timed back games can give you a chance to save a bad game, but that's all. Don't seek them out.

Here are some tips to guide you when playing back games. First, some tips for when your opponent has the back game:

  • Once your opponent has a back game, concentrate on building a prime in front of him.

  • Back games with three points are very strong. Stop your opponent from making the third point at all cost.

  • When bearing in, clear your points from the back.

Second, some tips for the times when you are playing a back game:

• Look for opportunities to break out of the back game by hitting shots. Remember that the back game is the last alternative, when other plans have failed.

• When you've made two or three back game points, and your opponent hasn't built a prime, slot freely. Don't be afraid to have other men sent back.

• If you have spare checkers on your back game points, your top priority is releasing them to the outfield.

If you play a successful back game and actually hit a shot, you're in what I call a containment game. As I mentioned earlier, see Chapter 23 for these positions.

**PROBLEMS**

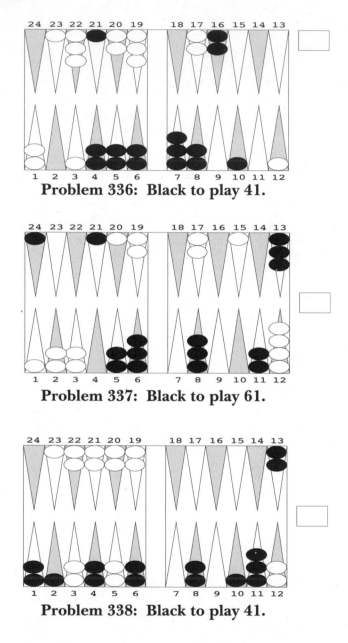

Problem 336: Black to play 41.

Problem 337: Black to play 61.

Problem 338: Black to play 41.

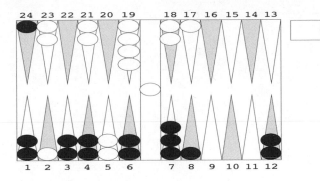

Problem 339: Black to play 62.

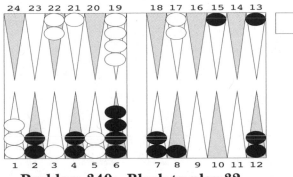

Problem 340: Black to play 32.

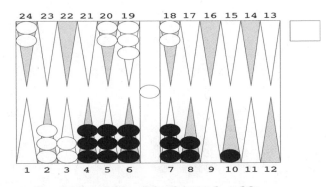

Problem 341: Black to play 32.

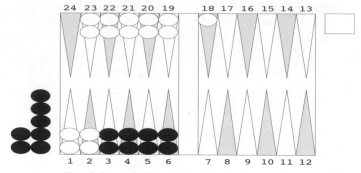

Problem 342: Black to play 11.

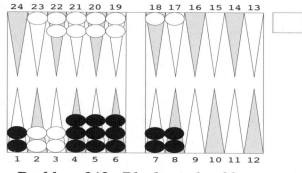

Problem 343: Black to play 32.

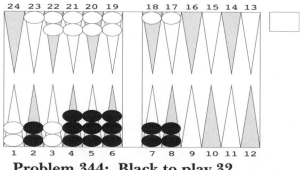

Problem 344: Black to play 32.

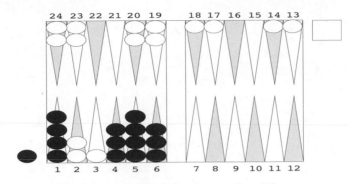

Problem 345: Black to play 51.

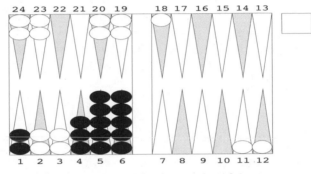

Problem 346: Black to play 64.

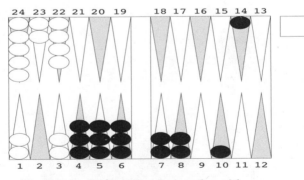

Problem 347: Black to play 41.

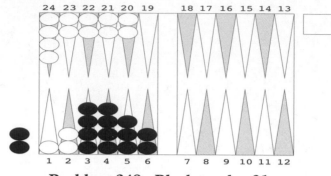

Problem 348: Black to play 31.

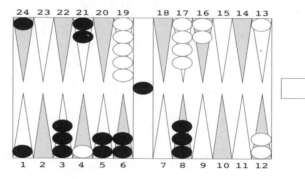

Problem 349: Black to play 32.

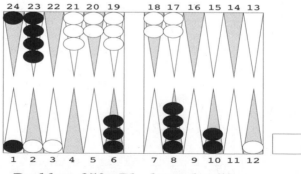

Problem 350: Black to play 52.

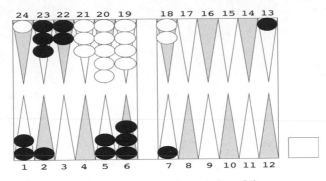

Problem 351: Black to play 31.

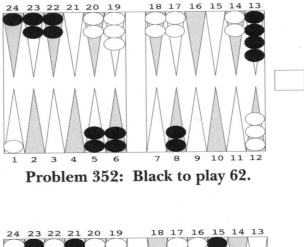

Problem 352: Black to play 62.

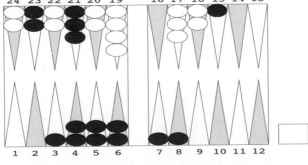

Problem 353: Black to play 63.

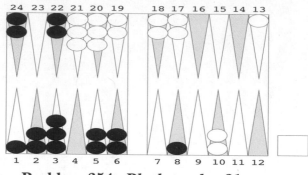

### Problem 354: Black to play 21.

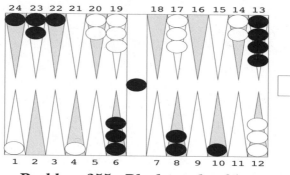

### Problem 355: Black to play 31.

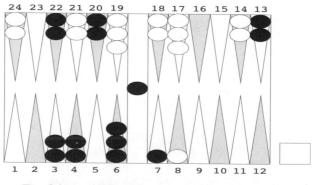

### Problem 356: Black to play 52.

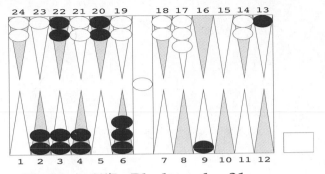

Problem 357: Black to play 21.

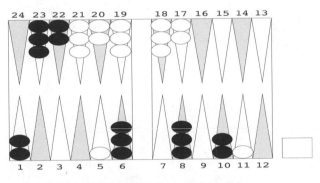

Problem 358: Black to play 33.

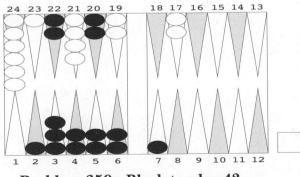

Problem 359: Black to play 42.

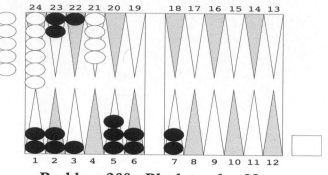

### Problem 360: Black to play 32.

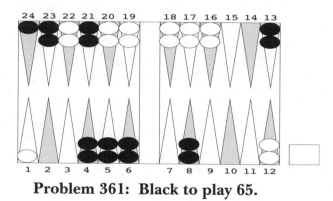

### Problem 361: Black to play 65.

### Problem 362: Should Black double?
### Should White take if doubled?

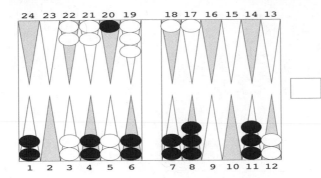

**Problem 363: Should Black double?
Should White take if doubled?**

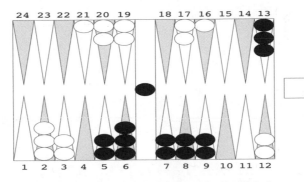

**Problem 364: Should Black double?
Should White take if doubled?**

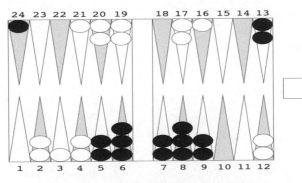

**Problem 365: Should Black double?
Should White take if doubled?**

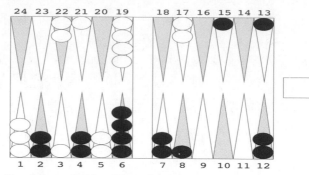

### Problem 366: Should Black double?
### Should White take if doubled?

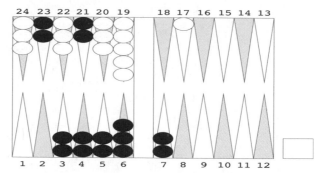

### Problem 367: Should Black double?
### Should White take if doubled?

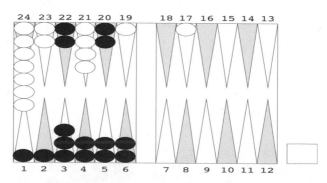

### Problem 368: Should Black double?
### Should White take if doubled?

## SOLUTIONS

### Problem 336: Black to play 41.

Don't be afraid to stick your opponent in a back game.

Black should just play 16/12* 16/15. If White can pull out a well-timed back game from this mess, so be it. Some players try to get fancy with plays like 7/3* 10/9, refusing to send back a fourth man, but that namby-pamby style just costs Black a lot of gammons down the road. Back games are treacherous, so make your opponent show that he can play them!

### Problem 337: Black to play 61.

Blocking points are the key to defeating a back game.

Black can hit on either the 20-point or the 15-point, but the right play is 13/7 8/7. Until Black makes a prime, the back game is a huge threat. Once the prime is in place, Black will be able to hit more checkers with relative impunity.

### Problem 338: Black to play 41.

Black has a choice between two plays in Position 338. He can make a strong blocking point with 13/9 10/9, at the cost of leaving a blot exposed to aces and some combination shots, or he can play safe with 10/6 2/1. Which is better?

Some good advice: Don't volunteer a direct shot if your opponent's position is about to crumble. Wait, and assess the new situation later. Perhaps a shot will never be necessary. Here White holds three good points, but will have to give up something next turn. Black should play safe, 10/6 2/1, and await developments.

### Problem 339: Black to play 62.

Don't let your opponent establish the second back game point if you don't have to.

Black could escape his last checker with 24/16, but if White then rolls a deuce, Black will have to contend with a 5-2 back game. True, that's not one of the best back games, but it's good enough to cause a lot of problems.

A better play is 24/22 8/2*!, nipping the back game in the bud. Now White's very unlikely to establish the second point in Black's board. Black could run into trouble if this blot gets hit, but that's a long shot, not really worth worrying about.

**Problem 340: Black to play 32.**

Black actually played 13/8 here, which looks pretty but misses the point. If your opponent is about to establish a third back game point, you must try to stop him. That third point gives him tremendous flexibility and is extremely dangerous for you.

Here Black needs to go after the 3-point with 6/3* 15/13. Even if he's hit back, it's no big deal, while the upside is enormous.

**Problem 341: Black to play 32.**

Here's an advanced technique for crippling your opponent's timing in a back game — the recirculation, or "dump" play.

Black should move 10/8 4/1!, hoping that White will roll an ace next turn and hit the blot. Black would then require several turns to bring that checker around the board, while White's forward position would probably collapse. There's a small risk that the checker might get trapped in White's home board with some awkward numbers, but it's a risk worth taking.

**Problem 342: Black to play 11.**

*A point cleared is a point not to be feared*. Thus spoke Kit Woolsey, and he's right. Each point cleared removes one possibility of leaving a shot. Black should take this opportunity to clear two points. The right play is 6/5(2) 4/3(2).

**Problem 343: Black to play 32.**

When bearing in against a backgame, it's usually right to clear your points from the back. This keeps your checkers connected and usually makes clearing future points easier. In problem 343, Black should follow this rule and clear the 8-point, playing 8/6 8/5.

**Problem 344: Black to play 32.**

Here's an exception to the previous rule. Black should clear the 7-point rather than the 8-point, playing 7/4 7/5. Why? Note that whichever point he clears this turn, the remaining point will be equally easy to clear next turn. (He'll have four landing points in his board in either case.) However, if Black clears the 8-point this turn and then leaves a blot on the 7-point next turn, that blot will be subject to a double shot (6s and 4s.) If Black clears the 7-point first, then leaves a blot on the 8-point, that blot will only be subject to a **single** shot (5s). For the best long-term safety, Black should clear the 7-point first.

**Problem 345: Black to play 51.**
Don't strip points if there's a possibility of attacking inside. Here Black could prepare to clear his 6-point with the routine 6/off, but a better play is 5/off 1/off, which leaves three builders to make the 3-point.

**Problem 346: Black to play 64.**
When bearing off against a back game, remember a few simple rules:
1) Clear your back point when you can.
2) Strip your back point (remove all spares) so you can clear it next turn.
3) Don't strip interior points. Keep spares there.
This position illustrates point (3). The right play is 6/off 5/1, keeping a spare on the 4-point. That's about 5% less likely to eventually get hit than the other play, 6/off 4/off.

**Problem 347: Black to play 41.**
When your opponent's back game has collapsed, try to squeeze the most out of the position.
Black could play safe with 14/10 5/4, but that misses the point. White has no game left, so Black wants to give himself the best possible gammon chances. Take a look — any six by White except 62 will force him to run off the 3-point, probably exposing two blots in the process. That's the swing variation, and Black wants to be in the best possible position if that happens. By playing 10/5, Black will have a good chance to make the 3-point, plus he'll have a shot in the outfield if White runs out with 61, 63, or 64. When the game's totally under control, play against the other guy's worst shots!

### Problem 348: Black to play 31.

Don't be in a hurry to clear points if a gammon is in the air.

Black could play for maximum safety with 6/3 6/5, but that might let the gammon slip away. Correct is 4/1*/off!, which slows White down, while many of White's entering numbers also break his board.

### Problem 349: Black to play 32.

In the actual game, Black played Bar/22 24/22, building the 22-point and trying to play a 4-3 back game. It's a poor play on several counts:

• Black doesn't have time to play a back game since his front checkers are too far forward. Black needs to force a decision in the middle game, where his strong board will be an asset.

• Putting both back checkers on the same point reduces the number of potential shots at an outfield blot.

• White's board is weak, so there's less need for another anchor.

• Black has a better play: Bar/22 3/1!, simply strengthening his board.

### Problem 350: Black to play 52.

When you've got a terrible game but only one rear point, it's worth almost anything to get the second back game point.

Here Black should play 24/22 8/3*. By moving up to the 22-point, Black can get a 2-3 back game if he throws an ace next turn. He might also get the point if White hits him on the 1-point or 3-point and he reenters with a 3. His back game won't have great timing, but it offers much better chances than a hopeless 2-point game.

### Problem 351: Black to play 31.

When playing a back game, every play is crucial. When you lose, you'll probably lose a gammon or a backgammon, so every throw has to be played precisely.

Take a look at position 351. A superficial player might quickly play 6/2. This is actually a serious error. The right play is 23/22 7/4. Why? The first rule in backgames is: Preserve your timing. This means that any spare back checkers must leap into the outfield at the first opportunity. If you can't leap a spare, make sure that your spares are in the best possible position to leap in the future.

Right now Black's spare on the 23-point can only get into the outfield with 6s. By playing 23/22, the checker can reach the outfield with 5s as well. That's a big difference. With the three, the next idea is to start the strongest remaining point in the home board. Here, that's the 4-point. Don't be concerned about building low points in your board. That's a very low priority, usually only important once an enemy checker has been hit.

**Problem 352: Black to play 62.**

In a back game, the top priority is to keep your checkers moving.

Black seems to be developing a reasonably timed back game, so he might be tempted to slot his bar-point with 13/7 13/11. If he gets hit, it's no big deal, right?

That's true, but recirculating the spare checkers that are already back is a higher priority. Getting a trapped checker into the outfield guarantees more timing, whether the checker gets hit or not. Black should just play 24/16.

**Problem 353: Black to play 63.**

The move 15/6 looks inviting, providing a third cover number for the 3-point, but...

The top priority in playing a back game is preserving your timing. You've got to get every spare mobile, so that a stray 44 or 55 doesn't destroy your position. The right move is 21/12.

**Problem 354: Black to play 21.**

If you're stuck in an untenable back game, look for a chance to bail out.

There's no way Black can hope to preserve his timing in this 1-3 back game. Rather than wait for his board to collapse, Black transposes into a straight 3-point game with 24/22 24/23! This move won't help him win the game — his chances of winning are tiny in any event — but it gives him a realistic shot at running off the gammon.

**Problem 355: Black to play 31.**

Once you've established two back game points, and your opponent doesn't have a prime yet, you should play as purely as possible. If your blots aren't hit, you'll build a front position more quickly. If they are hit, you'll reenter, perhaps build a third back game point, and recirculate your men.

Here the right play is Bar/22 and then 6/5! preparing to make the 5-point. Black won't lose by being hit, but he may gain a lot if he's not hit.

**Problem 356: Black to play 52.**

When playing a back game that can't be primed, try to win by going forwards first.

Black made what he thought was a clever play: Bar/20 7/5, refusing to hit. He thought this would keep White moving forward and help his back game timing.

But Black's timing is in excellent shape in any event, since his back game can't be primed. Instead, he should take the opportunity to see if he can first win with a front game, by playing the obvious Bar/23 13/8*. The front game may succeed all by itself. If it doesn't, White will only get out by hitting more blots, further helping Black's timing.

This is an example of what's called a two-way game: Black can win going either forwards or backwards. It's a very powerful strategy.

**Problem 357: Black to play 21.**

Playing a two-way game gives tremendous flexibility. Here Black should play 13/11 6/5! If White dances, Black is just a move away from a double. If White hits, Black's back game timing is improved. In a two-way game, you can directly slot your key points without fear of being hit.

**Problem 358: Black to play 33.**

If you're playing a back game with dubious timing, don't slow your opponent down! Let him play his full roll. If you get a little lucky, he might roll big numbers, restoring your timing.

Black can use his 33 to attack, with a play like 8/5*(2) 10/7(2). That creates a couple of good points for a moment, but so what?

White will still enter and escape soon, and Black's timing will be closer to disappearing.

The right play is to leave White alone and just play 10/4(2). Now White has to move, and if he rolls numbers like 55 or 66, his men rush home and Black's timing might just hold up. If Black hits and White rolls one of those numbers, he doesn't even move. That's a disaster for Black.

### Problem 359:  Black to play 42.

When it's time to run off one of your back game points, leave from the front point.

Black can only hold both back game points by playing 7/1, but in that case he'll have to leave next turn anyway, and meanwhile his messy board will cause big problems if he hits a shot. The right play is 20/14 immediately.

### Problem 360:  Black to play 32.

When playing a back game, remember that winning requires both hitting a shot and then containing the hit checker. Breaking the 23-point will have Black some shots when White rolls a deuce next turn. However, playing 5/3 7/4 gives Black a better chance of closing his board after he hits a shot. With the middle points in his board open, Black's top priority this turn is closing his board, so 5/3 7/4 is best.

### Problem 361:  Black to play 65.

Preserving timing is so important in a back game that he sometimes requires running off the back game points themselves. Here Black has some unappetizing choices. He could play 13/7 13/8, or even 13/2, but both plays use up some valuable timing while completely committing Black to winning from a back game.

The right idea is 21/10, which preserves lots of timing, gives Black some possibility of winning in a priming game, and more or less forces White to attack on the 21-point, a strategy which might quickly backfire since White's attacking points are all stripped. Keep an eye out for such unusual but powerful plays.

**Problem 362: Should Black double?**
**Should White take if doubled?**

Beware of doubling a back game too quickly. Black has an advantage in position 362, but it's much too soon to double. White could develop a strong back game, but he could also end up going forward if Black can't build any new blocking points. You have to have at least the semblance of a prime to double a back game.

**Problem 363: Should Black double?**
**Should White take if doubled?**

Remember two key rules for back games:

• If your opponent has a well-timed back game, threats to hit blots aren't threats at all.
• Don't double if you can't lose your market!

What's Black's best sequence here? Perhaps a 21, playing 20/18*/17*, followed by White's dancing? In that case, Black could double and White would still have an easy take!

Black should astutely refrain from doubling here.

**Problem 364: Should Black double?**
**Should White take if doubled?**

White's in a lot of trouble in position 364. Although he's got a 2-3 back game, he can't release a checker anytime soon, and Black won't have to break his prime for a long time — take a look at the checker on the bar and Black's three checkers on the midpoint. Those four men provide plenty of time for Black to hold his position while White moves forward. White's timing is very questionable, and that's a good reason to give up a back game. Double and pass.

**Problem 365: Should Black double?**
**Should White take if doubled?**

This position might look similar to the previous one. In both cases White has a back game, and the timing looks roughly similar. But in fact there are some big differences:

1) White has a 2-4 back game instead of a 2-3. The more advanced the back game points are, the less timing is required, because shots will appear sooner. White's timing was dubious before, but here it's quite a bit better.

2) White's advanced anchor is at the edge of Black's prime. This is good because spares can get to the lead anchor and then have a direct route to the outfield. This also helps White's timing.

3) Black's not on the bar in this position. That means if he rolls 66 or 55, he has to destroy his position rather than just pick up his dice.

All these factors swing the evaluation a lot. This position is no double and easy take.

**Problem 366: Should Black double?**
**Should White take if doubled?**

The 1-5 back game isn't worth much. It plays out like an ace-point game in which Black never has to clear his 5-point, because he never had it in the first place. White has some small chances to get more than your basic 1-5 game here (he could get luck and get a 1-3-5 game, which is pretty good), but he probably won't. Double and easy pass.

**Problem 367: Should Black double?**
**Should White take if doubled?**

Black has played his back game, and now a shot appears before White has even managed to get all his men home. Black has a 5-prime waiting. He counts his shots: all 6s, all 4s, 51 and 31 — a total of 24 shots. "I'm a clear favorite!," he says. "I double."

Big mistake. Black is a favorite — if he keeps the cube. If he gives the cube away, his situation isn't nearly so good. Let's see why.

First let's suppose Black doesn't double, but keeps the cube at 2. He hits in 24 games, and because he owns the cube, he wins almost all of those games. Let's give him 23 wins out of those 24 games. In the other 12 games, Black misses. Since he owns the cube, he still wins a few of the remaining games. Let's say he wins 4 of these last 12. His total is 27 wins and 9 losses out of 36 games. That's a profit of 18 games with the cube on 2, or 36 points.

What happens if he doubles to 4 instead? In the 12 games where he misses, White immediately redoubles to 8 and Black will pass, so he loses all 12 of those games. In the 24 games where he hits, the game gets played to a conclusion. White, owning the cube, gets lucky and pulls out a few of those games. Let's say Black wins 20 and loses only 4. That gives Black a total of 20 wins and 16 losses. That's a profit of 4 games with the cube on 4, or 16 points.

Would you rather win 36 points by keeping the cube, or 16 points by doubling? Clearly holding onto the cube is right. White has a take, of course.

### Problem 368:  Should Black double?
### Should White take if doubled?

White had just left a double shot with a poorly timed 65. Black doubled. White took. Was White crazy?

Not at all. White's take was perfectly correct, as was Black's double. Let's see why.

Black has a pure triple shot – all 1s, 3s, and 5s hit. Any combination of two even numbers misses. That's 27 hits and 9 misses. Many players make the mistake of equating hits with wins. Don't fall into this trap! Suppose Black hits one checker, say with a 54, which he would play 22/17*/13. Now suppose White comes back with a 42, played Bar/2* and 19/23. Is the game over? Black's a mile behind in the race, with a checker on the bar and four other checkers back. Will White ever be able to win from this position? Of course! He'll be a favorite after one more good sequence.

Black's correct double is actually based on his gammon chances when he's able to close his board and pick up both checkers. Right now he's actually about 20% to win a gammon.

# THE CONTAINMENT GAME

All right. You've played an ace-point game or a back game, you got a shot, and you hit the shot. Now what?

Now you're in a game we call the containment game. You've got three goals here.

(1)  Prevent the checker you've hit from running around the board and getting home. You'll have to control the outfield so you can hit the checker whenever he jumps out.

(2)  Build a full 6-point prime to contain the checker.

(3)  Roll the prime home until the checker is closed out. At this point, you're in a post-ace-point game, the subject of the next chapter.

The best way to contain a checker is to build a full prime, and the easiest way to do that is to slot the back of the prime, then cover.

Doubling situations in containment games are tricky. One way to avoid errors is to ask yourself this question: "If I roll my best number, will my opponent still take a double next turn?" If the answer is "Yes," hold onto the cube.

## PROBLEMS

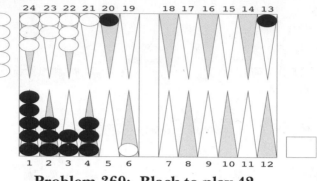

Problem 369: Black to play 42.

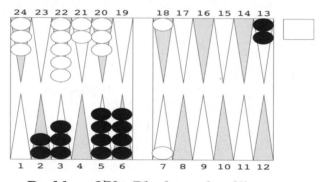

Problem 370: Black to play 65.

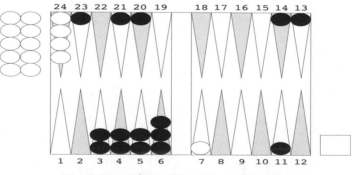

Problem 371: Black to play 42.

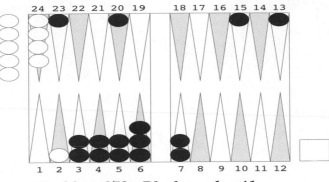

Problem 372: Black to play 41.

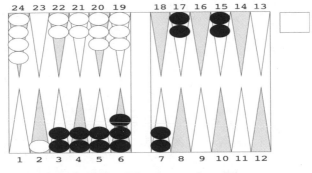

Problem 373: Black to play 43.

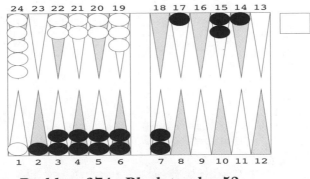

Problem 374: Black to play 52.

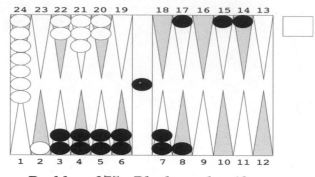

Problem 375: Black to play 42.

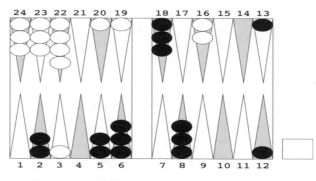

Problem 376: Black to play 51.

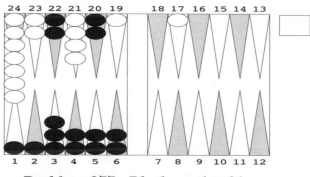

Problem 377: Black to play 31.

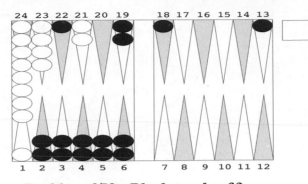

**Problem 378: Black to play 63.**

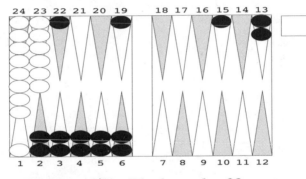

**Problem 379: Black to play 32.**

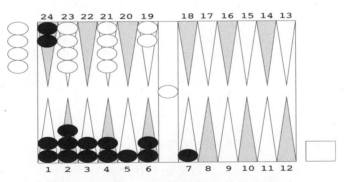

**Problem 380: Should Black double?
Should White take if doubled?**

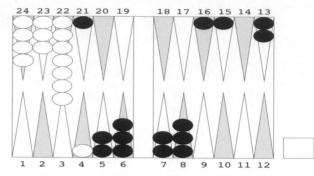

**Problem 381: Should Black double?**
**Should White take if doubled?**

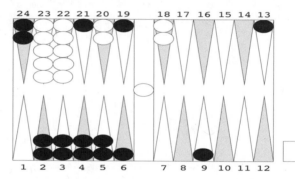

**Problem 382: Should Black double?**
**Should White take if doubled?**

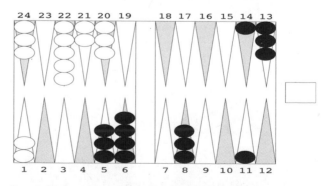

**Problem 383: Should Black double?**
**Should White take if doubled?**

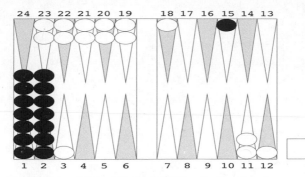

**Problem 384: Should Black double?**
**Should White take if doubled?**

## SOLUTIONS

**Problem 369: Black to play 42.**

Black has hit a checker but his chances still aren't very good. White has four men off, and Black's board is weak. With a 42 to play, Black has to keep two principles in mind for these positions: (1) Don't leave White a direct shot, and (2) Stay as far back as possible. The right play is 20/16 4/2!

**Problem 370: Black to play 65.**

White has almost escaped, but Black managed to hit with this 65. He has a choice between playing completely safe with 13/7*/2, or taking a small risk to have a better chance to make the 4-point by playing 13/7* 13/8. What's right?

In the case the safe play is correct. If Black knew he wasn't going to get hit after 13/7* 13/8, that would certainly be the right play. But White's returns of 43 and 61 are pretty clear winners (44 doesn't count since it would win for White in any case). That means the bold play loses an extra 10% of the time on the very first shake. It's hard for long-term flexibility to make up for such a big loss right off the top, so the safe play is best.

**Problem 371: Black to play 42.**

When you're struggling to contain a checker, the key idea is to build a prime, and to build it as soon as possible. The trick is to slot the back of the prime, rather than the front, then cover the blot quickly. After Black hits with 11/7*, the right deuce is 14/12, enabling Black to build a 5-point prime next turn with fives or sixes. It looks risky, since White could roll a 16 or 25 next turn. But in the long run, Black minimizes his overall risk by building a prime as quickly as possible.

**Problem 372: Black to play 41.**

Black's first job is to make sure White doesn't leap into the outfield next turn, so he hits, 6/2*. For the best ace, Black needs to give himself the best chance if White throws his best shot, 26. So he plays 15/14, giving himself 5s and 6s to hit if White gets free.

### Problem 373: Black to play 43.

The normal play in this sort of position is to prevent White from escaping by hitting him on the edge of the prime with 6/2*. But this is an unusual position because White's board is very strong now and Black won't have many direct cover numbers after hitting. The best play is just 17/14 15/11, covering the outfield and giving Black many shots if White rolls a 6 which doesn't hit.

### Problem 374: Black to play 52.

When containing a checker, try not to give it a direct path to the outfield. Black could play 7/2 7/5, building the 2-point and covering a blot, but the right move is 15/8, preparing to build the prime from the back. This way White needs to roll two specific numbers, a one and then a six, to get to the outfield. That's much harder than just rolling a direct six.

### Problem 375: Black to play 42.

Don't let a contained checker escape with tempo.

Black could play Bar/23 17/13, leaving the 8-point slotted, which guarantees a win if White doesn't roll an immediate six. But when White does roll a six, the cost is way too high: Black often gets quickly gammoned. Instead, just play Bar/23 8/4. You won't lose on an immediate six, and you'll mostly win when White stays put anyway.

### Problem 376: Black to play 51.

Attack weakness; prime strength.

If White had a good board, Black might have to proceed cautiously with this roll and just make the 7-point. But with White's board in tatters, Black can just play for the direct closeout with 8/3* 12/11. Some of White's return hits (36 is the worst) are disasters for him.

### Problem 377: Black to play 31.

This is a great shot with three plausible plays: (A) the double-hit with 20/19* 20/17*; (B) hit and no blots, 22/19* 2/1; (C) hit and make a 5-prime, 22/19* 3/2.

In a containment game, your primary goal is first hitting a checker, then containing it. Since all three plays hit at least one checker, you might be inclined to pick either play (B) or play (C), which are the best plays for containing a single checker.

But when two checkers are up for grabs, your emphasis shifts a bit. Containing and closing out one checker will almost always win the game, but with very few gammons in the mix. Containing and closing out two checkers, however, hits the jackpot. With two checkers closed out, your gammon chances will rise into the 35% range.

Here there is only one play that guarantees you will hit two checkers, and that's play (A). You're likely to hit two checkers after (B) or (C), but it's not a certainty. With White's weak board, you're likely to eventually close out the two checkers you hit, although it will take some time and patience. Go for the throat and hit both men.

### Problem 378: Black to play 63.
If only one roll beats you, and you have a solid grip on the position, block that roll.

Here the only great roll for White is 66. Black should block that with 19/13, then play 18/15 for good outfield coverage.

Note that Black leaves the checker on the 22-point where it is. If White's next roll is 52 or 53 or 42 or 43, Black will have a shot at a new blot.

### Problem 379: Black to play 32.
When containing a single checker, you'd ideally like your waiting checkers to be in the range of 11-14 pips away from the checker they're containing. In this way there's little chance of being hit, but maximum chance of hitting when your opponent makes a run for it.

Here Black can get a nearly ideal formation by playing 19/14, which leaves him with 66 blocked and double or triple shots anytime White runs into the outfield.

### Problem 380: Should Black double?
### Should White take if doubled?
Be careful with this position. Black looks like he's doing well, with deuces covering his 5-point to give him a closed board. But notice that not all deuces work. If Black rolls 25, 23, or 11, he can close the 5-point only to break the 6-point. In reality, only seven deuces work for him: 26, 24, 21, and 22. Since White has four men

off and will have some chances even if he's closed out, Black can't double yet. White should beaver if he is doubled.

### Problem 381:  Should Black double?
### Should White take if doubled?

Black was on his way to losing a sure gammon when he hit a last-ditch shot.  Now the game is turning around.  Should Black whip the cube over?

Not yet.  Black's become a favorite, but he's not quite at a doubling point.  White has an easy take, and in fact could still win a gammon with one lucky sequence.  Black has to wait and improve his position a bit more.

### Problem 382:  Should Black double?
### Should White take if doubled?

Black is about to close his 6-point, which would give him an overwhelming advantage.  If Black closes the point, most of White's entering numbers (15, 14, 13, and 12) will expose another blot to a double shot.  These variations are potentially quite gammonish, so Black definitely wants to double now.

Can White take?  Not really.  Black covers the blot on the 6-point with 19 numbers.  (All 3s, 21 and 11, 61 and 52, plus 55.)  If Black doesn't cover, he leaves the point slotted and brings more builders to cover.  For White to enter, he'll have to roll a six after Black misses, which happens only about one time in six.  That's not enough to take in a position with significant gammon chances.

### Problem 383:  Should Black double?
### Should White take if doubled?

White's been hit by an awkward series of big doubles, and he's completely lost control of the outfield. Black has good chances to build a prime before White can get his back men moving, so he has an easy double. For White's part, he needs to be careful and not fall into a subtle trap. He apparently has two big assets, his racing lead (now 38 pips) and his stronger board. But once Black builds a prime, White's racing lead will slowly vanish, and Black has such good distribution that he doesn't need to take big chances to improve his game. White should pass.

**Problem 384:  Should Black double?**
**Should White take if doubled?**

When the game gets down to the last roll, double if you're a favorite.

This isn't quite a last-roll position, but it's very close.  In most variations, Black moves around and gives White a direct shot, which White will be an underdog to hit.  If White hits, he wins;  if he misses, he loses.  There's a few other stray variations — Black hits a second checker and wins a gammon, or Black gives up a double shot, but mostly the game is wrapped up on the next shake.  Since Black is a clear favorite, he doubles, and White has enough hitting chances to take.

# POST-ACE-POINT GAMES

Okay: you've played your ace-point game, you got a shot, you hit the shot, you built your prime, and finally you closed your board. Now you're in the realm of the post-ace-point game.

These positions are tricky, but with the help of the examples in this chapter, you'll be able to play them almost perfectly. Keep a couple of rules in mind:

• You should start thinking about redoubling when you've borne off five fewer checkers than your opponent.

• If you're way behind in the race, you may have to expose blots as you try to bear off quickly.

**PROBLEMS**

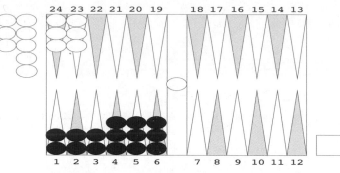

**Problem 385: Should Black double?**
**Should White take if doubled?**

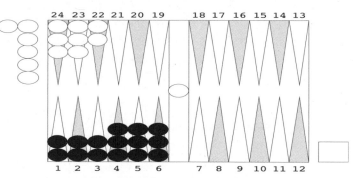

**Problem 386: Should Black double?**
**Should White take if doubled?**

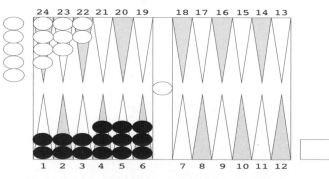

**Problem 387: Should Black double?**
**Should White take if doubled?**

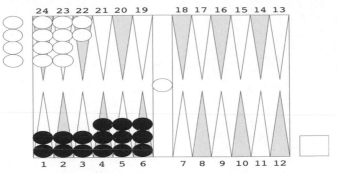

**Problem 388: Should Black double?**
**Should White take if doubled?**

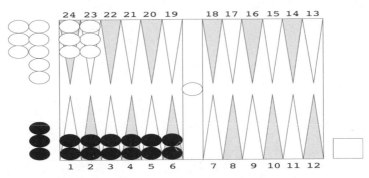

**Problem 389: Should Black double?**
**Should White take if doubled?**

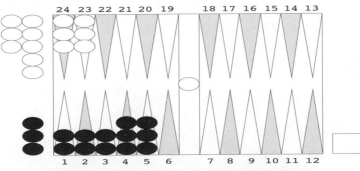

**Problem 390: Should Black double?**
**Should White take if doubled?**

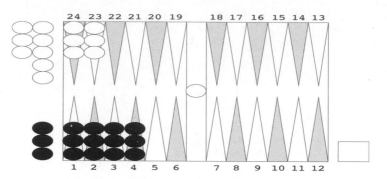

**Problem 391: Should Black double?**
**Should White take if doubled?**

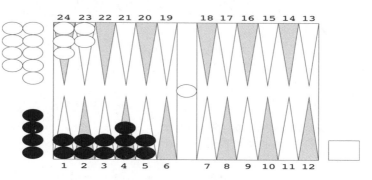

**Problem 392: Should Black double?**
**Should White take if doubled?**

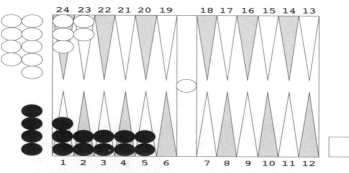

**Problem 393: Should Black double?**
**Should White take if doubled?**

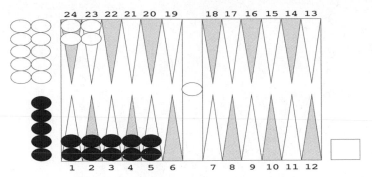

**Problem 394: Should Black double?**
**Should White take if doubled?**

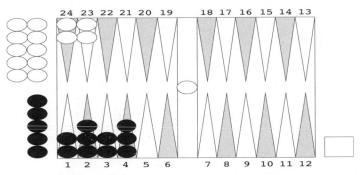

**Problem 395: Should Black double?**
**Should White take if doubled?**

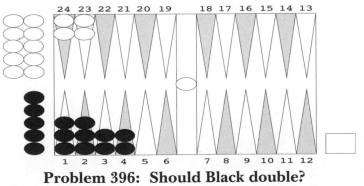

**Problem 396: Should Black double?**
**Should White take if doubled?**

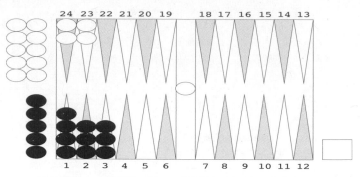

**Problem 397: Should Black double?**
**Should White take if doubled?**

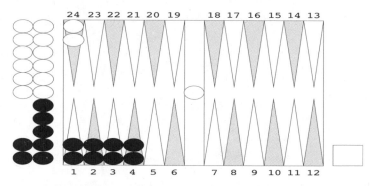

**Problem 398: Should Black double?**
**Should White take if doubled?**

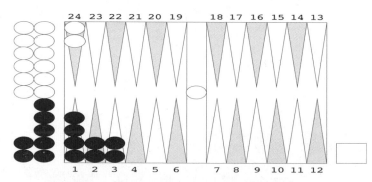

**Problem 399: Should Black double?**
**Should White take if doubled?**

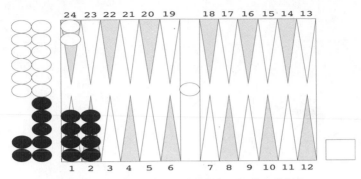

**Problem 400: Should Black double?**
**Should White take if doubled?**

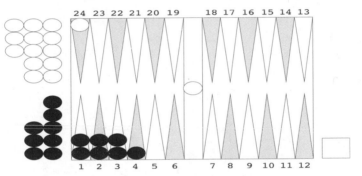

**Problem 401: Should Black double?**
**Should White take if doubled?**

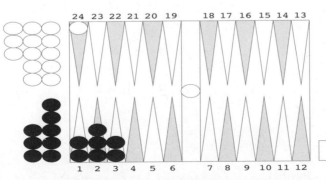

**Problem 402: Should Black double?**
**Should White take if doubled?**

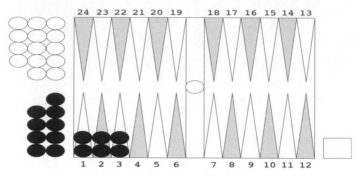

**Problem 403: Should Black double?**
**Should White take if doubled?**

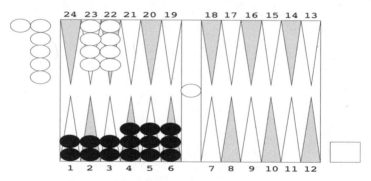

**Problem 404: Should Black double?**
**Should White take if doubled?**

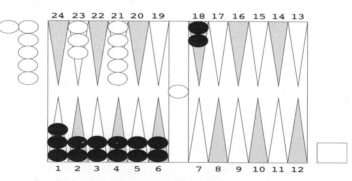

**Problem 405: Should Black double?**
**Should White take if doubled?**

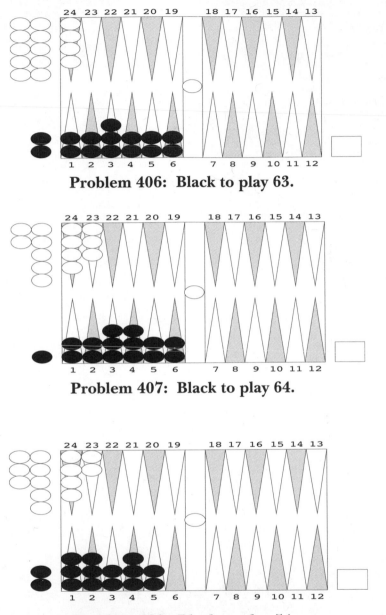

Problem 406: Black to play 63.

Problem 407: Black to play 64.

Problem 408: Black to play 54.

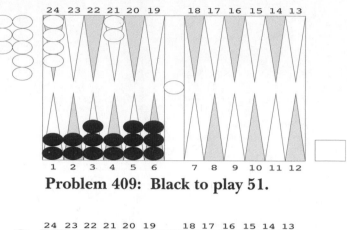

**Problem 409: Black to play 51.**

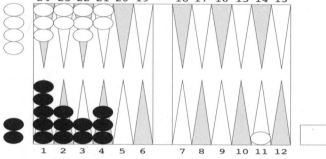

**Problem 410: Should Black double?
Should White take if doubled?**

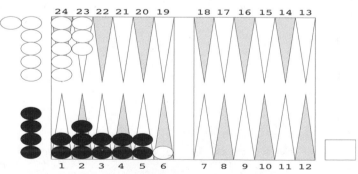

**Problem 411: Should Black double?
Should White take if doubled?**

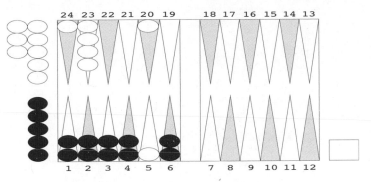

Problem 412: Black to play 21.

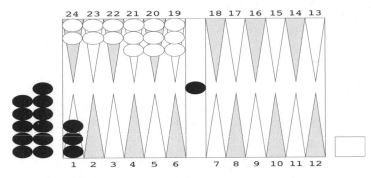

Problem 413: Should Black double?
Should White take if doubled?

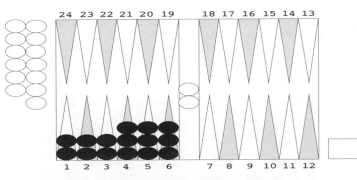

Problem 414: Should Black double?
Should White take if doubled?

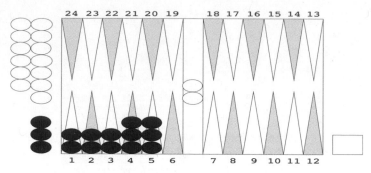

**Problem 415: Should Black double?**
**Should White take if doubled?**

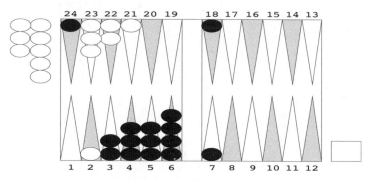

**Problem 416: Should Black double?**
**Should White take if doubled?**

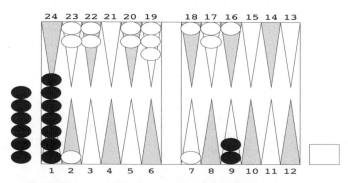

**Problem 417: Should Black double?**
**Should White take if doubled?**

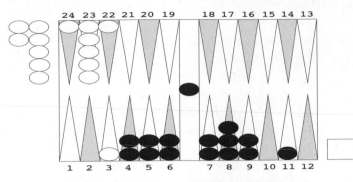

**Problem 418: Should Black double?**
**Should White take if doubled?**

## SOLUTIONS

**Problem 385: Should Black double?**
**Should White take if doubled?**

Black has played some sort of holding game — perhaps a back game, perhaps an ace-point game, perhaps he had one or two checkers on the bar. White bore off some checkers. Now Black hits a shot and closes his board. When should he double? That's one of the central questions in post-ace-point games.

Here White bore off eight checkers before being hit. Black has no one off yet, but an excellent bear-off formation. Should he double now? No way! If White owned the cube here, he'd be a solid favorite, and he could actually beaver!

**Problem 386: Should Black double?**
**Should White take if doubled?**

Here Black is closer. White only managed to bear off six checkers before getting hit. Black's now a favorite (his winning chances are in the range of 68%-69%, with White owning the cube), but he should try to get a little closer to 75% before doubling. No double and take.

**Problem 387: Should Black double?**
**Should White take if doubled?**

This is Black's optimal doubling point. He's trailing by five checkers with White closed out and on the bar. Black's bear off formation is perfect. He has an excellent double, and White just has a bare take. This is a crucial backgammon position which you must commit to memory. Over the years, knowing this position will earn (or save) you a lot of points.

**Problem 388: Should Black double?**
**Should White take if doubled?**

Here White only got four checkers off before being hit. Now it's a double and a big pass. Black is well over 80% to win here.

**Problem 389: Should Black double?**
**Should White take if doubled?**

Suppose White has more than five men off. In that case Black won't be able to double until he gets some of his own men off. How many men will he need off to double? That's a very tough question.

Here's a pretty good rule of thumb for handling these positions. If Black has a fast bearoff, he can double when he has five fewer men off than White. If he has a slow bearoff, he needs four fewer men off than White to double. White will almost always have a take when Black doubles in these situations.

In problem 389, Black has three off, White has eight off. Black's within five checkers, but he has a slow bearoff. Next turn he'll be breaking a point, and he may not even get a checker off. He shouldn't double yet.

**Problem 390: Should Black double?**
**Should White take if doubled?**

Black's doing better than in the previous problem (he rolled, broke a point, and White didn't enter) but his spares are all on his high points, slowing down his bearoff. He still doesn't have a double.

**Problem 391: Should Black double?**
**Should White take if doubled?**

Now Black's in a faster position. He has spares on all his points, and his pip count is less than before. He has a double, and White has a take.

**Problem 392: Should Black double?**
**Should White take if doubled?**

Black has four off, White has nine off. Black is within five again, but he has a very slow bearoff. He's not close to a double.

**Problem 393: Should Black double?**
**Should White take if doubled?**

Black has a faster bearoff than before, but he still has several checkers on his high points. No double.

**Problem 394: Should Black double?**
**Should White take if doubled?**

Black has five off, White has ten off. Black's within five, but again he has a slow bearoff. No double yet.

**Problem 395: Should Black double?**
**Should White take if doubled?**

To double when within five, conditions need to be just optimal. Black has a faster bearoff than in the previous position, but now he has a new problem: he has a good chance of leaving a shot next turn. Again, no double and take.

**Problem 396: Should Black double?**
**Should White take if doubled?**

Black is within five and now has a nice, fast bearoff with no shots next turn. Double and take.

**Problem 397: Should Black double?**
**Should White take if doubled?**

Black is within five but now has a super-fast bearoff. That's too much. Black doubles and White has to give up.

**Problem 398: Should Black double?**
**Should White take if doubled?**

As you get closer to the end of the game, 'within-five' becomes a stronger situation, because White has fewer turns left to throw a good number and turn the game around. Here Black has 7 off and White has 12 off. White will probably need a double to win, but he doesn't have as many turns to throw it as before. Although Black has a relatively slow bearoff position, this is double and take.

**Problem 399: Should Black double?**
**Should White take if doubled?**

With a slightly faster board for Black than in the last problem, the position becomes double and narrow pass.

**Problem 400: Should Black double?**
**Should White take if doubled?**

With a very fast board and no chances of missing, White's recovery chances almost vanish. It's now double and huge pass, with Black's chances nearly 90%.

**Problem 401: Should Black double?**
**Should White take if doubled?**

Now Black has 8 off and White has 13 off. As we get closer to the end, White's chances deteriorate. Black has a good double, and White can only take because he has good possibilities of getting a shot next turn.

**Problem 402: Should Black double?**
**Should White take if doubled?**

In a more normal position without immediate shot chances, 8 off vs 13 off is double and pass.

**Problem 403: Should Black double?**
**Should White take if doubled?**

With 9 off vs 14 off, even a relatively slow bearoff is double and pass.

**Problem 404: Should Black double?**
**Should White take if doubled?**

In the real world, White's bear off position won't always be as smooth as in the previous examples. Here White got hit from an ace-point game, and a gap remains on the 24-point. That will slow down White's bearoff when he finally reenters from the bar. Although Black trails here by six checkers (zero off vs six off), it's a good double and a take.

**Problem 405: Should Black double?**
**Should White take if doubled?**

Here both sides have problems compared to the more normal positions we've looked at. Black has a spare checker on his ace-point, which won't help his bearoff. He doesn't know yet where his two outside checkers will end up. But White's problems are worse. He got hit from an ace-three back game, so his bearoff will be slowed down by the gaps in his home board. Even though White got six checkers off before being hit, it's double and bare take.

### Problem 406: Black to play 63.

The obvious play here is 6/off 6/3, bearing off a checker and picking up a blot. That's usually the right play, but this is an unusual position. Black is so far behind in the race that he's very likely to lose if White throws a six next turn, whether Black's left a blot on the 6-point or not.

Here's a simple rule for these positions: Start by counting the number of crossovers for each side. Black has 13 checkers in his home board, so he needs 13 crossovers to bear off all his men. White needs 4 crossovers to get his checker on the bar into his home board, then 5 more to bear off his 5 checkers, a total of 9. If Black trails by four or more crossovers, take off two checkers. If Black trails by two crossovers or less, play safe. If Black trails by exactly three, it's a tossup.

Here Black trails by 4 (13-9), so he should bear off quickly, with 6/off 3/off.

### Problem 407: Black to play 64.

Black needs 14 crossovers and White needs 12. Black's close in the race, so he can play safe. The right move is 6/off 6/2.

### Problem 408: Black to play 54.

Black can play safely with 5/off 5/1, or boldly with 5/off 4/off. Again we count the crossovers. Black needs 13 to bear off all his checkers, White needs 4 to get his checker on the bar to his inner board, then 7 more to bear off, a total of 11. Black is within two, too close to volunteer a shot. The right play is 5/off 5/1.

### Problem 409: Black to play 51.

If Black's asleep he might play something like 6/off or 6/1 5/4. But he can do much better with the alert 5/off 1/off! If White stays out, Black's happy because he got an extra checker off. If White reenters with 11, 21, or 31, Black will get a shot at a second checker. If White rolls 41 or 51, Black will enter and perhaps hit loose on the 1-point, or stay back and see if White breaks the 21-point. Only 61 is a crushing shot, and that's a small price to pay.

**Problem 410: Should Black double?**
**Should White take if doubled?**

Suppose you never got to double while your opponent was on the bar, but things improved after he entered? In that case, look at crossovers.

Here both sides have fast home boards. Black needs 13 crossovers to bear off 13 men. White needs 2 crossovers to get his outside man home, then 11 more to bear off all his men, a total of 13. When crossovers are equal, the correct action is usually double and take. That's the case here.

**Problem 411: Should Black double?**
**Should White take if doubled?**

Here Black needs 11 crossovers, White needs 12 crossovers. Black's ahead in the crossover count, which is bad news for White. Double and pass.

**Problem 412: Black to play 21.**

Cube ownership is very important, and the location of the cube can sometimes determine the correct checker play. In general, when you own the cube you avoid high-volatility plays where a good roll by your opponent can nullify the value of the cube.

If White owned the cube, the best play would be 6/4 6/5*, which gives Black the best overall chance to win. But with the cube on White's side, he should play 2/off 1/off, a low-volatility play which gives him variations where he can use the cube later to win.

**Problem 413: Should Black double?**
**Should White take if doubled?**

Sometimes the guy on the bar can double! Here Black was playing for a gammon, bore off 11 men, and then got hit. Now the position is double for Black and take for White. Mostly Black will get in and run around the board to win by a roll or two. But sometimes he'll stay on the bar just long enough for White to pull the game out. White's chances will be a lot better if he's read this chapter, of course!

**Problem 414: Should Black double?**
**Should White take if doubled?**

White managed to bear off 13 checkers, but Black hit and closed out White's last two checkers in a maneuver known as the "coup classique." Now Black's men are all home and in an ideal bearoff position. Should he double?

The answer is no. Black's a favorite in the game (about a 2-1 favorite, actually) but he can get closer to his optimal doubling point before turning the cube. He should wait. If doubled, White has a very easy take.

**Problem 415: Should Black double?**
**Should White take if doubled?**

Diagram 415 shows a proper double in this situation. Black has borne off three men, and White is still on the bar. Now Black has a very strong double. White just barely has a take.

**Problem 416: Should Black double?**
**Should White take if doubled?**

Don't get overly excited just because you get a shot at a second checker. Make sure you're still winning the game if you never hit the second checker.

Here White has eight checkers off and Black has a ways to go to close out the first checker. Black shouldn't double yet and White has an easy take.

**Problem 417: Should Black double?**
**Should White take if doubled?**

Beware of taking cubes where you have to hit a shot to turn the game around, and your opponent will gammon you if you don't.

Here Black already has six men off. Black may leave a single or a double shot next, but if White misses he'll be gammoned. It's a powerhouse double and a pass.

**Problem 418:  Should Black double?**
**Should White take if doubled?**

Black has a double shot at two White blots. If he misses the shot, he's still a favorite in the game, (although he's now unhappy he doubled). If he hits either blot, he'll mostly have lost his market by a mile. He should double. White's doing well enough when Black misses that he can take the double.

# PLAYING FOR THE GAMMON

When your game is very strong, don't be afraid to play aggressively for the gammon. Scoring four points instead of two can demoralize your opponent and soften him up for the rest of the session!

When evaluating an aggressive checker play, keep the following relationship in mind. A play which turns a single win into a gammon win gains you (if the cube has already been turned) two points — the difference between +2 and +4 on the scoresheet. If the aggressive play backfires and turns a single win into a loss, it costs you four points — the difference between +2 and -2. When you make an aggressive, potentially risky play to win a gammon, you need to believe that you'll win more than twice as many extra gammons as you'll lose single games.

## PROBLEMS

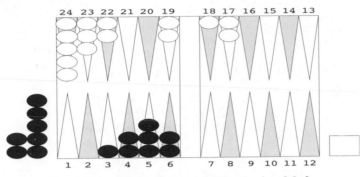

Problem 419: Should Black double?

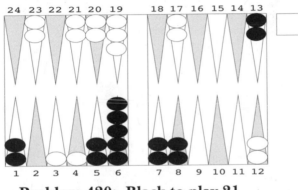

Problem 420: Black to play 21.

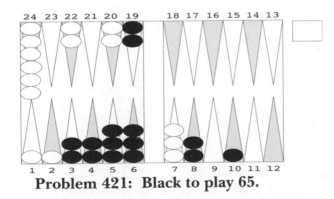

Problem 421: Black to play 65.

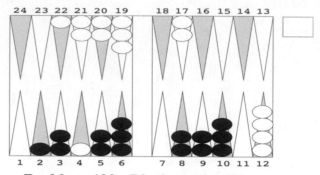

**Problem 422: Black to play 55.**

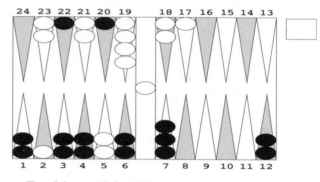

**Problem 423: Black to play 66.**

## SOLUTIONS

**Problem 419: Should Black double?**

When you've been playing for a gammon and it looks like you're not going to make it, don't concede too quickly. Here Black can still win a gammon, after the sequence Black: 66, White: any non-double, Black: 66 or 55. Not very likely, but it's worth throwing the dice one more time.

**Problem 420: Black to play 21.**

If a gammon chance presents itself, don't be afraid to go for it.

Black can play safe by clearing either the 7-point or the 8-point. But a much better play is 6/4*/3*, putting two of White's checkers on the bar, and leading to a very possible gammon. Even if Black gets hit, he hasn't lost the game yet. Remember: winning four points is a lot better than winning two points!

**Problem 421: Black to play 65.**

When in complete control, strike for the gammon in the most direct way possible. Black should play 8/2* 6/1*, putting two men on the bar and minimizing the chance that White can anchor again.

**Problem 422: Black to play 55.**

If the gammon's just sitting there, and the risk isn't too great, just go for it. Most players are much too conservative in playing for the gammon. Remember that if a play wins twice as many gammons as it costs you in extra losses, it's worth going for.

In the actual game, Black made the weeny play: 10/5(3) 6/1. It's completely safe, but it lets White keep moving, and Black's board is now so weak that he can't contemplate attacking later.

The right play is 9/4*(2) 10/5(2), putting White on the bar and aiming to close the board before White can move another man. If it works, Black should win an easy gammon. But even if White rolls a deuce and hits, Black doesn't just lose. He'll have chances to hit on the 22-point, and at worst he'll just be back to even money. It's a risk worth taking.

**Problem 423: Black to play 66.**

When your opponent is on the ropes, go for the gammon.

With his first three sixes, Black should put a second checker on the bar: 20/2*. He could escape with the last six (22/16) and a lot of players would try that. But a better play is 12/6! It not only brings a second cover number to bear on the 2-point, but by staying back and taking aim at White's blot on the 17-point, Black gives himself a chance to pick up yet a third checker. That third blot could mean the difference between winning and not winning a gammon.

# SAVING THE GAMMON

Sometimes, despite all your best efforts, the game slips away and your only job becomes saving the gammon. It's not a happy job, but you might as well learn how it's done.

The basic rules are these:
- Try to bear your checkers in exactly to the 6-point in your home board. That way you won't waste any pips.
- When moving through the outfield, try to get as many cross-overs (moves from one quadrant to another) as possible.
- On the last roll, count the number of doubles that will let you bear off a checker.
- Remember to watch out for backgammons!

**PROBLEMS**

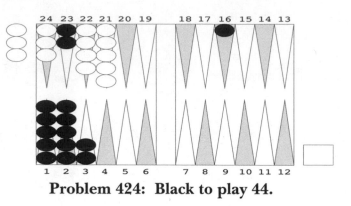

**Problem 424: Black to play 44.**

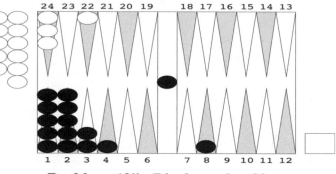

**Problem 425: Black to play 62.**

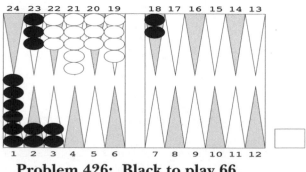

**Problem 426: Black to play 66.**

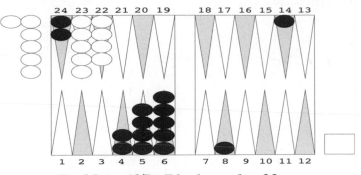

Problem 427: Black to play 33.

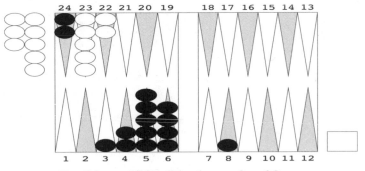

Problem 428: Black to play 32.

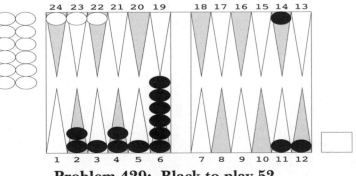

Problem 429: Black to play 52.

## SOLUTIONS

**Problem 424: Black to play 44.**

When racing to save the gammon, don't waste pips. If you can't bear in exactly to the 6-point, move in the outfield.

In the actual game, Black played 16/4 23/19, a subtle error. By playing a checker to the 4-point in his board, Black has wasted two pips which may come in handy later. A better play is 23/11 16/12. Now Black only needs to roll 28 pips on the dice to bring his remaining checkers to his inner board (the 6-point), rather than 30 with his actual play. These two pips might mean the difference between saving and losing a gammon.

**Problem 425: Black to play 62.**

The rule about bringing your men to the 6-point is a great rule, but there are a few exceptions. Here's one.

Saving the gammon may not be the biggest problem in the position. Bar/19 8/6 gets a checker to the 6-point, but Black has to play Bar/19/17, getting out of White's home board entirely so that he doesn't get backgammoned next turn if White throws a large double!

**Problem 426: Black to play 66.**

Here's another exception, which requires a little imagination to see.

Black can play two men directly to the 6-point: 18/6(2), building a better board in the process. The right play? Not here. Imagine what happens if Black's next roll is, say, 44. In that case he doesn't get to move any back men at all, while he has to destroy the board he just made. In fact, any roll not containing a five or a six fits this category.

A better play is 23/11 18/6. Now Black can play 4s and 3s effectively next turn, while he's actually wasted no pips at all.

**Problem 427: Black to play 33.**

When saving the gammon is a realistic possibility, it's usually best to go for it.

The best play to win later, after hitting a shot, is 6/3(2) 5/2(2). But that sacrifices a lot of pips in the gammon-saving effort. Since

Black rates to save the gammon in a straight race about 1/3 of the time, his best play is to run for it. He should move 24/12, keeping one checker back for a possible later shot but wasting no pips in his inner board.

**Problem 428: Black to play 32.**

Once your opponent is down to eight checkers or less, you have to start to leave the 24-point to save the backgammon. Here the right play is 24/21 8/6. If White rolls a double next, Black will still have time to run off the backgammon in most variations.

**Problem 429: Black to play 52.**

When you've just got one roll left to save a gammon, count the doubles that work for you.

Black played 11/6 14/12, the only way to get two crossovers. But with just one roll left, crossovers aren't necessarily going to point to the right play. You have to actually count the doubles that save the gammon.

After Black's actual play, only 66 saves a gammon next turn. But if he moves 11/6 12/10, then 44, 55, and 66 all work — triple the number of gammon-saving shots! Don't guess, count!

# BEARING OFF AGAINST CONTACT

When the game is mostly won, and you're bearing your last few checkers home, you'll need to balance two goals:

- Playing safe to avoid losing.
- Putting yourself in the best position to win a gammon.

Here's a few examples of typical problems in these endings.

## PROBLEMS

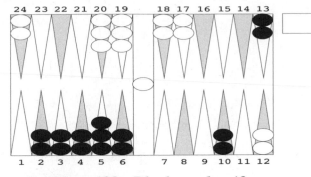

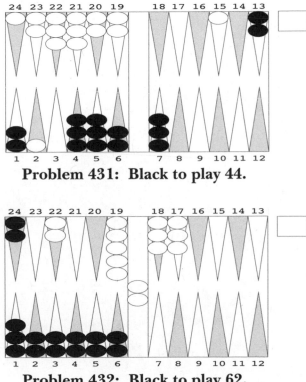

Problem 430: Black to play 43.

Problem 431: Black to play 44.

Problem 432: Black to play 62.

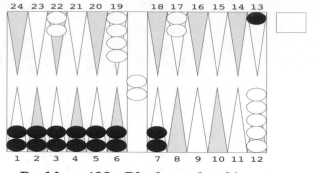

Problem 433: Black to play 61.

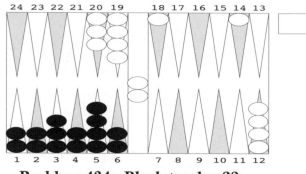

Problem 434: Black to play 22.

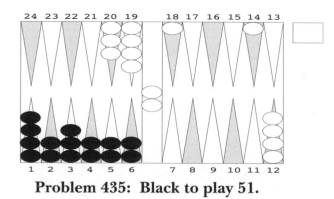

Problem 435: Black to play 51.

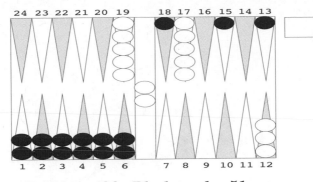

Problem 436: Black to play 51.

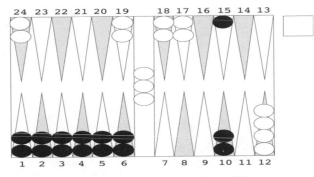

Problem 437: Black to play 54.

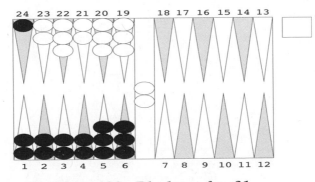

Problem 438: Black to play 61.

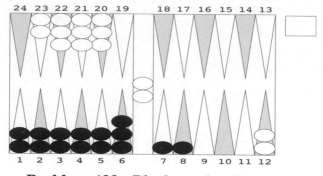

Problem 439: Black to play 51.

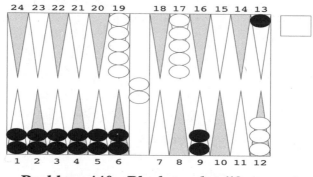

Problem 440: Black to play 53.

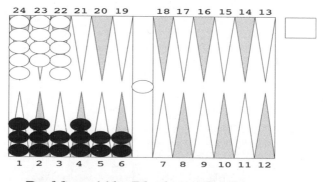

Problem 441: Black to play 31.

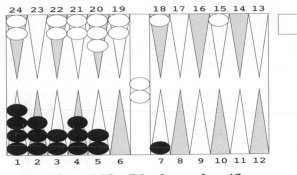

Problem 442: Black to play 42.

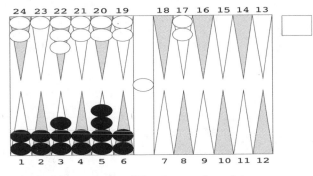

Problem 443: Black to play 44.

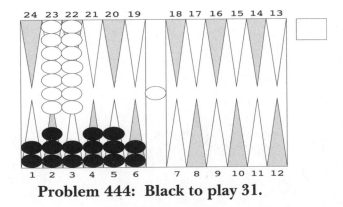

Problem 444: Black to play 31.

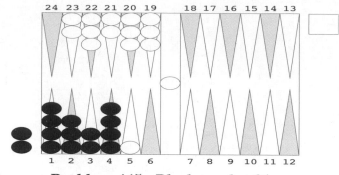

**Problem 445: Black to play 31.**

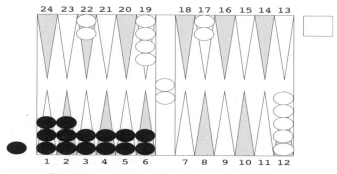

**Problem 446: Black to play 21.**

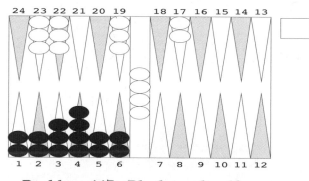

**Problem 447: Black to play 42.**

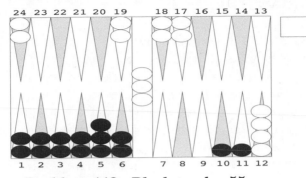

Problem 448: Black to play 55.

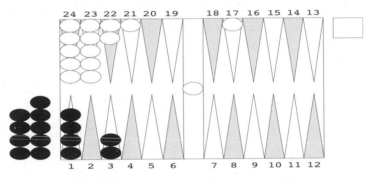

Problem 449: Black to play 61.

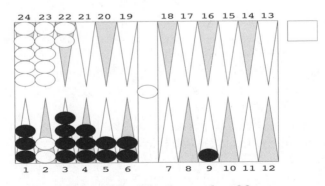

Problem 450: Black to play 33.

## SOLUTIONS

**Problem 430: Black to play 43.**

When the game seems to be won, stay alert! There will still be plenty of non-trivial decisions ahead of you.

Black has a couple of goals in this position. The first is to close his board as quickly as possible, both to increase his gammon chances by leaving as many White men as possible stuck in the outfield, and to eliminate White's counterplay. The second is to do so prudently, so as not to give Black too many immediate winning chances.

The safest play is 13/9 13/10, giving White no shots. But that play doesn't make progress toward making the 1-point. A better play is 10/6 10/7, which brings two more builders to bear on the 1-point, while giving White only two shots from the bar. It's a good trade-off.

**Problem 431: Black to play 44.**

When coming home against a single blot, don't overlook the power of switching points.

Black can play safe in a number of ways: 13/5(2) or 7/3(3) 5/1, for example. But the best move is the switch, which crushes all resistance in most variations: 6/2*(2) 7/3(2)! By building a 5-point board and moving the open point higher in the board, Black effectively compresses White's winning chances into hitting a difficult fly shot over the next couple of rolls. This offers more long-term safety than letting White hang around on the 2-point.

**Problem 432: Black to play 62.**

Black can't move the checkers on the 24-point, so he's got to play a two in his board, leaving a shot. His choices are 3/1, 4/2, 5/3, or 6/4. What's right?

When you have to break up your board, the right strategy is: Break from the back. Breaking your rear points first will give you fewer awkward rolls in the future, and lets you keep what remains of your board longer. The right play is 6/4.

**Problem 433: Black to play 61.**

When bearing in, avoid putting checkers on the low points in your board whenever possible. Keeping checkers away from the 1-point and 2-point will give you more flexibility later on.

Black should play 13/6, keeping alive the possibility of starting the bearoff with all spares on high points, rather than 7/1 7/6.

## Problem 434: Black to play 22.

In the actual game from which this position was taken, Black played 5/1(2). This might look safe but it's really not. Black could easily get into trouble if his next roll is 61 or 51, which would leave him odd-ended on his high points. Another error would be 4/off(2). This creates a gap on the 4-point, which will force a shot if his next roll is 62, and which will lead to trouble on later sequences as well.

The right play is 6/off 6/4, which does three good things: It bears off a checker, it clears the rear point (allowing White to enter behind Black), and it leaves Black with spares on his high points, allowing for future flexibility.

## Problem 435: Black to play 51.

Black has thrown one of his worst numbers, and now has to play it correctly so as to minimize the damage. He has two choices: 6/1 6/5, leaving himself odd-ended, and 5/off 5/4, leaving a gap.

The right play can usually be found by counting the number of rolls that leave a shot next turn after either play. If Black clears the 5-point, he leaves a shot next turn with three doubles (66, 55, and 44) and four non-doubles (61 and 51), for a total of seven shot-leaving numbers. If he clears the 6-point instead, he leaves a shot with the same three doubles plus six non-doubles (65, 64, and 54), a total of nine numbers. Clearing the 5-point is safer, so that's the right play.

## Problem 436: Black to play 51.

When you're bearing your checkers around to your closed board, and there's still contact, make sure that you place your checkers so that doubles don't break your board.

Black played 18/13 15/14, and then was shocked when his next roll popped out — 11! The right play was just 15/9, after which Black can handle any double.

## Problem 437: Black to play 54.

After you've closed your opponent out and your moving your checkers home, keep two rules in mind.

Rule 1: Arrange your checkers so that 66 on your part won't leave a blot. (If 66 won't leave a blot, then no other roll will.)

Rule 2: Keep your checkers spread out on different points, for maximum flexibility.

In problem 437, Black quickly played 15/6 and picked up his dice. He was wrong on two counts: his play was vulnerable to 66 next turn, leaving a blot on the 6-point, and his two outside checkers were on the same point.

A better play was 15/11 10/5, guarding against all those possibilities.

**Problem 438: Black to play 61.**

When bearing in against checkers on the bar, try to make sure that 66 plays safely next turn. If it does, your other rolls should be safe as well. If Black plays 24/18 6/5, then 66 will expose a blot next turn. The right play is 24/18 5/4, after which 66 (and all other rolls) play safely.

**Problem 439: Black to play 51.**

When bearing off with a closed board against one or two checkers on the bar, keep these rules in mind:

(1) Make sure that you won't leave a shot if you roll 66 next.

(2) Keep your spare checkers on separate points.

(3) Before bearing off, try to get a spare to the 5-point.

If you follow these rules, you should minimize accidents in the bearoff. Here one play obeys all three rules: 8/3 6/5. It's the best move.

**Problem 440: Black to play 53.**

Do you see the right play here? It's 13/10 9/4 — spares on different points, and safe against 66 next turn.

**Problem 441: Black to play 31.**

Don't get too cute; remember that backgammon is basically a race. I've seen players play 6/5 6/3 in this position, on the theory that it was good to let White in, to eliminate the possibility of a later hit. A clever idea, but White becomes an immediate favorite after a 66, while other sixes leave the race a little too close. Just take a checker off with 4/off, and wrap up the race before White can enter.

**Problem 442: Black to play 42.**

Don't make the mistake of playing too safely when bearing off. If a small extra risk can increase your gammon chances by a lot, it's a risk worth taking.

In Position 442, the safest play for Black is to pre-clear the 5-point with 5/3 5/1. This lets White enter from the bar quickly, minimizing the chances of Black's leaving a shot down the road. Unfortunately, it often lets White run off the gammon.

A better play is 7/3 4/2, which is still very safe (even-ended on the two highest points), and by keeping White on the bar longer, helps Black win more gammons. It's a better play.

Best of all, however, is 7/3 2/off. By bearing off a checker, Black saves a whole roll in the bearoff. (He only needs seven more rolls rather than 8.) This wins even more gammons, at a slightly higher risk (Black leaves a shot next turn on 44, 55, and 66). The high gammon rate makes this the best play.

**Problem 443: Black to play 44.**

The super-safe play is 6/2(2) 5/1(2), taking no checkers off but preparing to clear the 5-point next. If winning the game were Black's only concern, it would be the right play.

But Black also has some small chances of winning a gammon, and it's worth keeping those alive if he can do so at very little risk. The right play is 6/2(2) 4/off(2), which gives him a couple of extra checkers off at the cost of a very small extra chance of being hit. It's worth it.

**Problem 444: Black to play 31.**

With winning a gammon a close issue, and losing very unlikely, Black should play very aggressively for the gammon. The right play is not the ultra-safe 5/1, but the aggressive 4/off.

**Problem 445: Black to play 31.**

If the gammon is a close affair, go for it. The risk is probably less than you think.

The gammon is close in problem 445. White is a favorite to save it, but Black can improve his chances with aggressive play. The right move is the bold 4/off!, leaving himself odd-ended. This keeps a 4-point board while reducing Black to 12 checkers, meaning he should bear off in 6 turns.

Can this play backfire? Sure, but here's what has to happen: White has to stay on the bar (probability 4/9), Black has to leave a shot (probability 1/3) and White has to hit (probability about 1/3). The total probability of this sequence of events is 4/9 x 1/3 x 1/3, or 4/81, about 4%. Even then Black doesn't necessarily lose, since he will have five checkers off at that point. It's a small risk for a potentially big reward.

**Problem 446: Black to play 21.**

If the gammon is a lock, just make the safest play.

When the gammon is in doubt, you usually want to bear checkers off when you have a chance. But if the gammon is really assured, play safe. Here the safest play is 6/4 6/5, allowing White to enter quickly, while providing a smooth bearoff for several turns to come. Taking two checkers off (2/off 1/off) opens up the possibility of later bad distribution (after 61 or similar rolls).

**Problem 447: Black to play 42.**

With more than three enemy checkers on the bar, the backgammon becomes a major issue. Avoid ultra-conservative play and aim for winning a backgammon.

Many players in this position would play 6/2 6/4, opening the board quickly to let White enter. This is the safest play but not the best play. Black should play the relatively safe but more aggressive 4/off 4/2, keeping White on the bar as long as possible. The extra backgammons this play will win more than compensate for the extra losses.

**Problem 448: Black to play 55.**

If you've closed out several of your opponent's checkers, the only way you can lose the game is to be hit in the bearoff. The faster you clear your rear points, the sooner your opponent will enter, and the sooner he'll be out of your hair.

Some players carry this strategy to extreme and start clearing points before they've even finished bearing their checkers in. In position 448, for example, Black played 11/6, 6/1(3). This technique is known as "pre-clearing".

While it looks oh-so-clever, pre-clearing is usually a blunder! It backfires in two ways. White may immediately throw the double that enters all his men, after which you might leave a shot as you try to get your last checker home. Or White might just escape the gammon or the backgammon because he gets to enter from the bar more quickly.

Don't get too cute. The right play is just 11/1 10/off.

**Problem 449: Black to play 61.**

Black should play 3/off 1/off, aiming for the gammon. He could leave fewest shots with 3/off 3/2, leaving White only twos to hit (instead of threes plus 21 with the better move). But Black is unlikely to lose even if he gets hit, while remaining with four checkers instead of five leaves him with a much better chance to win a gammon.

**Problem 450: Black to play 33.**

The safest play — the play least likely to ever get hit — is 9/3 6/3(2). If safety were all that mattered, that would be the play. But Black has another goal: to win a gammon, not just a single game. White's board isn't a threat even if Black gets hit at some later point, so he should bear off aggressively: 9/off 3/off!

# VARIOUS ENDINGS

The very end of the game can lead to a lot of situations that are hard to characterize. Keep your wits about you and count shots. Here are a few examples.

## PROBLEMS

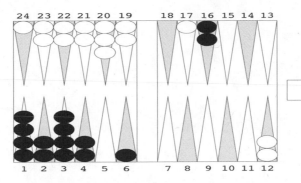

Problem 451: Black to play 62.

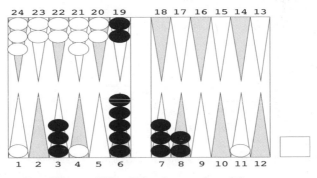

Problem 452: Black to play 31.

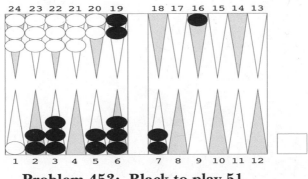

Problem 453: Black to play 51.

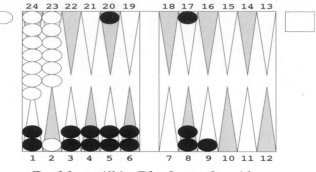

**Problem 454: Black to play 41.**

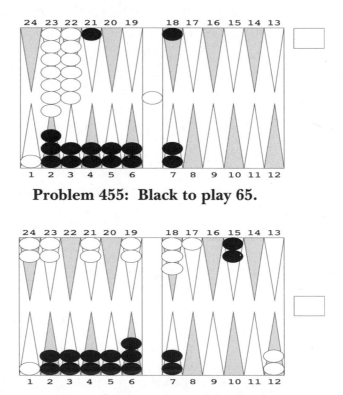

**Problem 455: Black to play 65.**

**Problem 456: Black to play 22.**

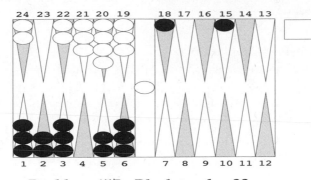

Problem 457: Black to play 22.

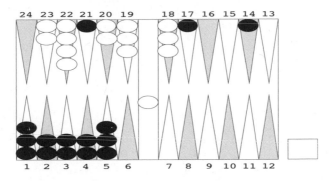

Problem 458: Should Black double?
Should White take if doubled?

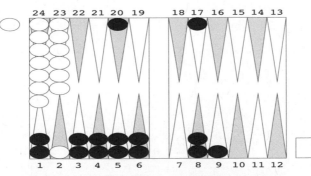

Problem 459: Should Black double?
Should White take if doubled?

## SOLUTIONS

**Problem 451:  Black to play 62.**

If you have to leave a shot at the end of the game, which will probably cost you the game if it's hit, try to leave the fewest shots.

If Black plays 16/10 16/14, he can be hit with any two, or 11, a total of 12 shots.  If he plays instead 16/8, he can be hit with any four, plus 31, 22, and 11, a total of 14 shots.  Playing 16/14 loses almost 6% less often!

**Problem 452:  Black to play 31.**

When your opponent's board is strong and yours is weak, survival is top priority.  Black can play 8/5 6/5, which is certainly the best play if Black knows he won't get hit.  But a hit is disastrous in light of White's 5-point board, so Black can't play this big.  The right play is 7/4*/3, gaining some time and waiting for a break next turn.

**Problem 453:  Black to play 51.**

White has one checker left, ready to run if he rolls a three. Black's job is to cover the outfield as best he can, hoping for maximum shots when White runs out.  The best play is 19/14 16/15, which guarantees Black a double shot if White runs out with 36 or 35, and a powerful single shot if White hops out with 34.

Note that hitting on the 1-point, 6/1* 19/18, is the wrong idea.  White is just as likely to get to the 4-point from the bar as he is from the 1-point, and by hitting, Black kills a builder for the crucial 4-point.

**Problem 454:  Black to play 41.**

Black wanted to hit on his 2-point, but he rolled a poor shot. Now he has to arrange his checkers to give himself the best possible chances next turn. His first job is to play 9/5 with the four. This does two good things: it avoids being hit with 5-2, but more important, it gives Black a whopping 29 hitting numbers in the likely case that White doesn't roll a five to escape.

After 9/5, he has a choice of 17/16 or 20/19 with his ace. The right play is 20/19, which forces White to hit if he rolls 5-5, giving Black a return shot from the bar!

**Problem 455: Black to play 65.**

Go for the gammon when the downside risk is small. Here Black should play 7/1* 18/13, trying to close out two checkers. Black's gammon chances against two checkers closed out is about 40%, while his chances if White anchors on the ace-point are only about 15%.

**Problem 456: Black to play 22.**

Always remember that winning instead of losing is twice as important as turning a simple win into a gammon win. The difference between a loss and a win is 4 points (-2 to +2), whereas the difference between a win and a gammon is just 2 points (+2 to +4).

In this position, some players might try switching with 3/1*(2) 15/13(2), which indeed wins the most gammons when White stays on the bar a while. But if White immediately enters with a three, the win itself is in jeopardy. Just play 15/7 instead, keeping the full prime with an almost certain win and some gammon chances to boot.

**Problem 457: Black to play 22.**

Black has the game well under control and only needs to worry about one thing — a 44 by White next turn.

Black looks to see what pips are covered by 44. White could reach the 8-point, the 12-point, or the 16-point. Black avoids those spots and correctly plays 18/14 15/11!

**Problem 458: Should Black double?**
**Should White take if doubled?**

Here's a common endgame situation. White is on the bar against a 5-point board, with a high point open. Black is coming around with his last few stragglers. A good rule of thumb is that Black can double as long as he's closer than 10 pips down in the race. White can take as long as Black is not solidly ahead in the race.

Here Black leads by two pips 88-90. He has a good double, and White can just squeeze out a take.

**Problem 459:  Should Black double?**
**Should White take if doubled?**

Let's start by considering White's chances of winning.  To win quickly, Black has to fail to hit on the 2-point, then White needs to leap with a five.  If we count the number of rolls that hit on the 2-point, we should get 22 rolls.  (All 6s, 52, 43, and 55 hit.  Black also switches points with 11, which is just as good as a hit.  So Black doesn't hit with 13 rolls (out of 36), or about 35%.  Of those rolls, White jumps out with a five about 30% of the time.  The total chance that Black misses and White then escapes is 35% x 30%, or just about 10%.  Even after White escapes, Black might still hit in the outfield.  White has some small chances to win in other variations, but he's not close to the 25% chances needed to take, so Black should double and White should pass.

# THE RACE

When both sides escape all their back men and all contact between the armies is broken, we're in a straight race.

Doubling strategy in races is very important, since races arise so frequently. Fortunately, there's a powerful rule for race doubling, which will give you a big edge over your less-knowledgeable opponents. Here it is:

• Count your pips, then your opponent's. If your lead is at least 8% of your pip count, you can double. If it's more than 9% of your pip count, you can redouble.

Suppose you get doubled? Here's the rule for that:

• If you trail by more than 12% of your opponent's pip count, pass the cube. If you're closer than that, take.

**PROBLEMS**

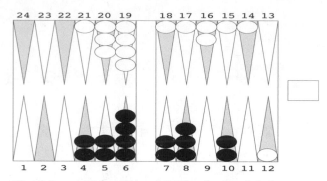

**Problem 460:  Should Black double?**
**Should White take if doubled?**

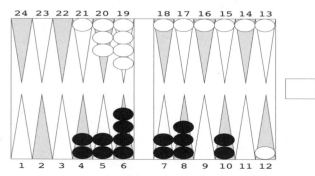

**Problem 461:  Should Black double?**
**Should White take if doubled?**

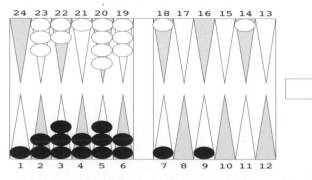

**Problem 462:  Should Black double?**
**Should White take if doubled?**

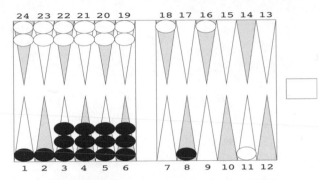

**Problem 463: Should Black double?**
**Should White take if doubled?**

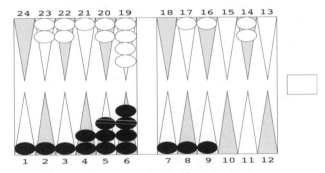

**Problem 464: Should Black double?**
**Should White take if doubled?**

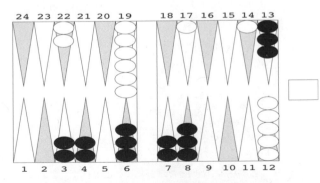

**Problem 465: Should Black double?**
**Should White take if doubled?**

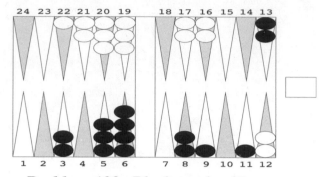

Problem 466: Black to play 33.

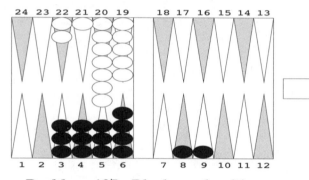

Problem 467: Black to play 31.

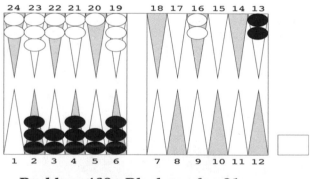

Problem 468: Black to play 21.

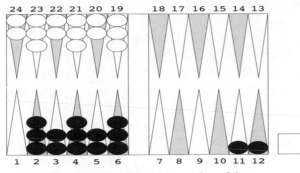

Problem 469: Black to play 61.

## SOLUTIONS

**Problem 460: Should Black double?**
**Should White take if doubled?**

Problem 460 shows a pure racing position. If we know the pip counts for both sides, we can decide on the correct cube action for both players. The rule for medium to long-sized racing positions is this: If the side on roll is ahead by at least 8%, he has an initial double and his opponent has a take; if he's ahead by 9%, he has a redouble and his opponent has a take; and if he's ahead by more than 12%, his opponent should pass.

Remember this rule: It's very powerful, and it will be a useful guide, since racing positions come up very frequently.

Black's pip count is 100, and White's is 111. Black leads by 11% (his lead is 11 pips, and his count is 100, so the ratio 11/100 = 11%). By our rule, Black can double, and White is close enough to take.

**Problem 461: Should Black double?**
**Should White take if doubled?**

A very similar position. The pip counts are now Black: 100, White: 114. Now Black leads by 14%. That's too much, so by our rule, Black should double and White should pass.

**Problem 462: Should Black double?**
**Should White take if doubled?**

The race here tells the whole story. Black's pip count is 65, White's is 72. Black leads by just over 10%, which is enough for a good double.

Since White trails by less than 12%, he has a good take.

**Problem 463: Should Black double?**
**Should White take if doubled?**

Here's another problem with the same pip count: Black 65, White 72. Is this also a take? Not quite. There's a crucial difference. Black only requires one crossover before all his checkers are in his inner board, ready to start bearing off. White needs four crossovers before he can start his bearoff. Black rates to have three or four checkers off before White starts bearing off. That makes Black 7-pip lead more like an 11 to 12 pip lead.

That's enough to push White well into pass territory after Black doubles.

### Problem 464: Should Black double?
### Should White take if doubled?

In this race, Black's pip count is 77, White's is 87. Black leads by 10 on a count of 77. Our rule says White can take if he trails by no more than 12%. What's 12% of 77?

A tip for quick calculation: Calculate something close that's easier to do, then make a common-sense adjustment. 77 is close to 80, so 12% of 77 is a little less than 12% of 80, which is 9.6. Making an educated guess, 12% of 77 should be about 9.3. Since 10 is more than 9.3, White is a little too far behind to take. Two additional considerations: Black's distribution is a little smoother than White's, and White needs one more crossover to get his checkers home. Both factors argue for an even more convincing pass.

### Problem 465: Should Black double?
### Should White take if doubled?

To size up this race, all we have to do is count the pips. Black's pip count is 109; White's is 126. Black leads by 17. Since 12% of 109 is about 13 pips (it helps if you practice to do these calculations in your head), White trails by about 4 pips too many. Black doubles and White passes.

Don't make questionable racing takes just because you've rolled some big numbers that day. Play the percentages, and you'll be a winner in the long run. Flaunt the percentages, and they'll crush you like a bug.

### Problem 466: Black to play 33.

In long races, try to arrange your men evenly across the 4, 5, and 6-points.

Here the right play is 13/4 13/10. Black gets three crossovers and starts putting men on the open 4-point. He could get four crossovers by playing 8/5(2) 13/10(2), but who knows if the 4-point would ever get filled in that case?

**Problem 467: Black to play 31.**

The ideal structure for starting the bearoff is a triangle of checkers in the inner board, with 5 checkers on the 6-point, trailing down to 1 checker on the 2-point. (This was shown in an article in *Inside Backgammon*, the world's leading magazine of backgammon theory and practice. For back issues of *Inside Backgammon*, contact the Gammon Press at P.O. Box 294, Arlington, MA 02476.) The closer you can come to starting the bearoff with this formation, the more efficient your bearoff will be. The best play to reach this structure is 9/6 3/2.

**Problem 468: Black to play 21.**

In races, use spare aces to unstack and fill gaps in your home board; don't waste them limping pathetically through the out-field.

Black should play 13/11 and 2/1!, unstacking and filling a gap. It's slightly better than getting two crossovers with 13/11 13/12.

**Problem 469: Black to play 61.**

Black should play 12/6 2/1. 12/6 is crucial since it's the only way that checker can reach the inner board in half a roll. After playing 12/6, 2/1 is better than 6/5 since it fills a gap. (Black's sure to roll an ace at some point in the bearoff.) Avoid playing the ace 11/10 unless your inner board is already perfectly smooth for the bearoff.

# THE BEAROFF

When all the checkers are in the inner boards, you're in the final stage of backgammon — the bearoff. Watch out: the action is fast, and a single good roll can suddenly give you a powerhouse double. The bearoff is the most volatile section of the game, and you'll need to keep your wits about you.

Here's some quick advice for doubling in the bearoff:

• In a long bearoff (40 or more pips on both sides), the 8-9-12 doubling rule we learned in the chapter on racing is still a pretty good guide.

• In short bearoffs (under 30 pips on both sides), being on roll with the same pip count as your opponent probably means you have a double. Most of these are also takes, unless the bearoff is really short.

• With just a couple of checkers left, count the number of rolls that actually bear off your checkers before doubling.

**PROBLEMS**

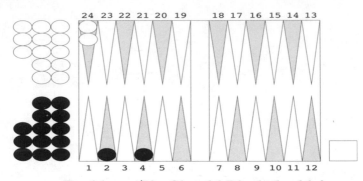

### Problem 470: Should Black double?
### Should White take if doubled?

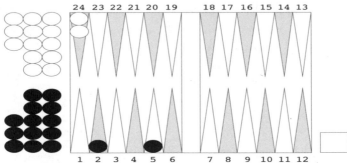

### Problem 471: Should Black double?
### Should White take if doubled?

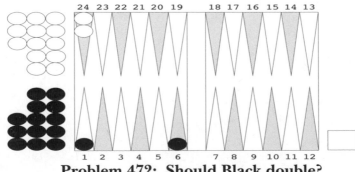

### Problem 472: Should Black double?
### Should White take if doubled?

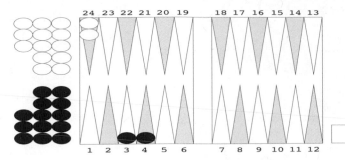

## Problem 473: Should Black double?
## Should White take if doubled?

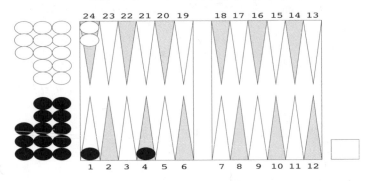

## Problem 474: Should Black double?
### Should White take if doubled?

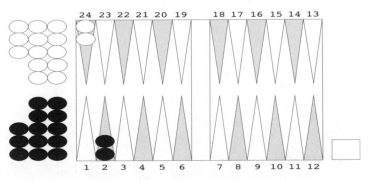

## Problem 475: Should Black double?
## Should White take if doubled?

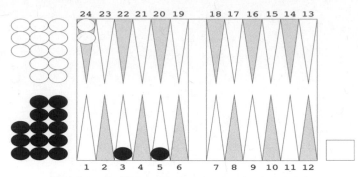

**Problem 476: Should Black double?**
**Should White take if doubled?**

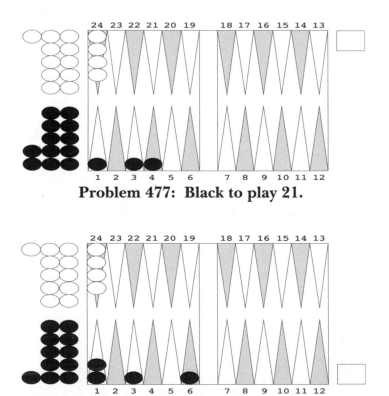

**Problem 477: Black to play 21.**

**Problem 478: Black to play 11.**

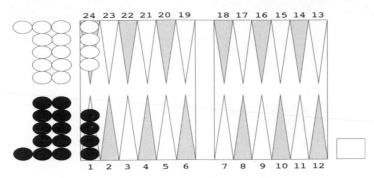

**Problem 479: Should Black double?**
**Should White take if doubled?**

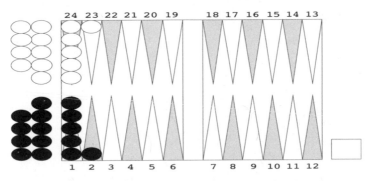

**Problem 480: Should Black double?**
**Should White take if doubled?**

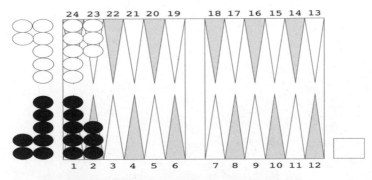

**Problem 481: Should Black double?**
**Should White take if doubled?**

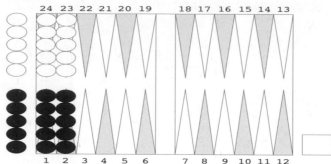

**Problem 482: Should Black double?**
**Should White take if doubled?**

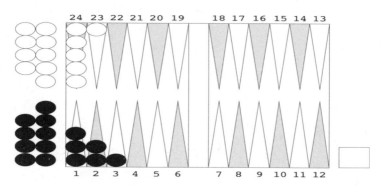

**Problem 483: Should Black double?**
**Should White take if doubled?**

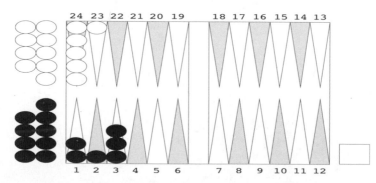

**Problem 484: Should Black double?**
**Should White take if doubled?**

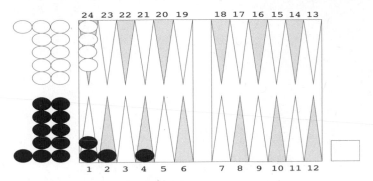

## Problem 485: Should Black double?
## Should White take if doubled?

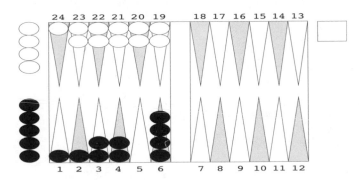

## Problem 486: Black to play 61.

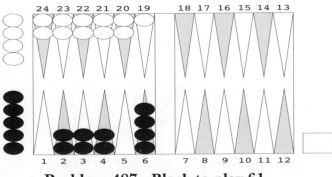

## Problem 487: Black to play 61.

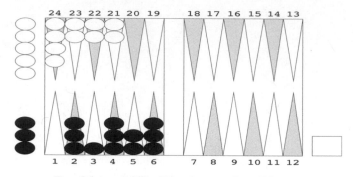

**Problem 488:  Black to play 51.**

**Problem 489:  Black to play 51.**

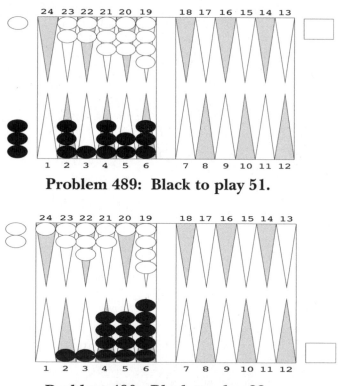

**Problem 490:  Black to play 32.**

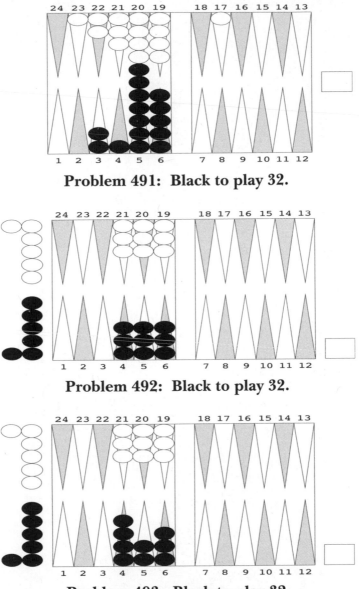

Problem 491: Black to play 32.

Problem 492: Black to play 32.

Problem 493: Black to play 32.

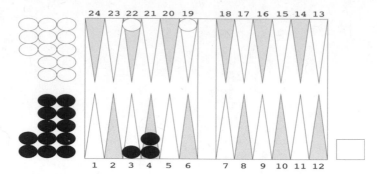

**Problem 494:  Should Black double?**
**Should White take if doubled?**

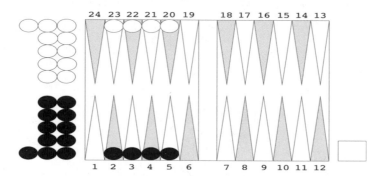

**Problem 495:  Should Black double?**
**Should White take if doubled?**

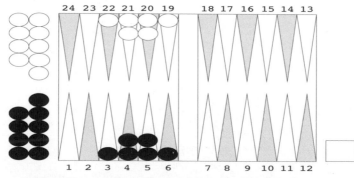

**Problem 496:  Should Black double?**
**Should White take if doubled?**

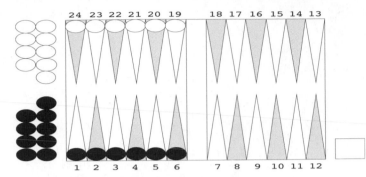

**Problem 497: Should Black double?**
**Should White take if doubled?**

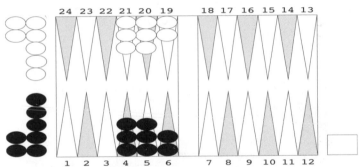

**Problem 498: Should Black double?**
**Should White take if doubled?**

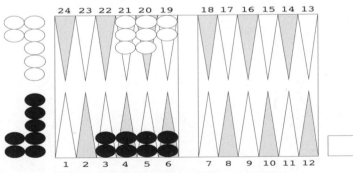

**Problem 499: Should Black double?**
**Should White take if doubled?**

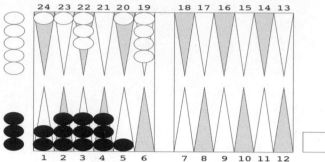

**Problem 500: Should Black double?**
**Should White take if doubled?**

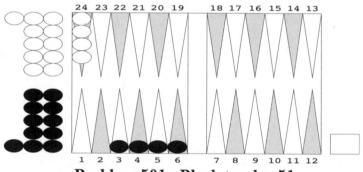

**Problem 501: Black to play 51.**

## SOLUTIONS

### Problem 470:  Should Black double?
### Should White take if doubled?

When only one roll remains in the game, deciding whether or not to double is a simple matter.  If more than half your rolls bear off your checkers, you're a favorite and you should double.  Sometimes the easiest way to count the rolls that bear off is to first count the rolls that don't bear off, then subtract the answer from 36.  Here Black fails to bear off with any roll containing a one (there are 11 such rolls), plus the 32 roll, for a total of 13 misses.  That means he has 23 bear off numbers, so right now he's a 23 to 13 favorite to win.  In that situation, he should be happy to double the stakes.

Should White take?  That depends if he can win more than 25% of the time.  Since 25% of 36 is 9, White should take if Black has 9 or more misses.  Since Black has 13 misses, it's an easy take.

### Problem 471:  Should Black double?
### Should White take if doubled?

Black's chances aren't as good as in the last problem, but he's still winning.  He has 19 rolls that bear off both checkers, and 17 rolls that miss. (Try counting this one yourself.)  As a slight favorite, he's still happy to double the stakes with just one roll left.  White has far more than the minimum nine wins needed, so he takes.

### Problem 472:  Should Black double?
### Should White take if doubled?

If a checker on the 5-point and a checker on the 2-point is a double, how about this position?  Black's pip count is just the same as before (7 pips) so this must be a double too, right?

Wrong!  This position shows how important it is to actually count the rolls that win and the rolls that lose.  Black wins with 65, 64, 63, 62, 61, 66, 55, 44, 33, and 22 — a total of just 15 rolls.  He loses on the other 21.  So no double for Black, and White can beaver if Black is foolish enough to double him.

### Problem 473: Should Black double?
### Should White take if doubled?

If 5 and 2 was a double, and 6 and 1 was not, what's this position? Let's see.

The winning rolls are 65, 64, 63, 54, 53, 43, plus the bigger doubles: 66, 55, 44, 33, and 22. The total is 17 winning rolls, which means there must be 19 losers. No double for Black, beaver if White gets doubled.

### Problem 474: Should Black double?
### Should White take if doubled?

Here the easiest thing is to count Black's misses. The only rolls that miss are 31, 21, 32, and 11. All other rolls bear off both checkers. That's 29 winning rolls and just 7 misses. Since Black is a 3-1 favorite when he has 27 winning rolls and 9 misses, he's much better than that here — actually over 80%. Black doubles and White should pass.

### Problem 475: Should Black double?
### Should White take if doubled?

Here Black has 26 winning numbers on his next roll. (Any ace misses, except 11, which gets both checkers off.) It's an easy double. White wins after the 10 miss numbers, which is just slightly more than the 9 he needs to take.

### Problem 476: Should Black double?
### Should White take if doubled?

Let's count how many winning rolls Black has. Among the doubles, he bears off both checkers with 66, 55, 44, and 33. That's four rolls. If one die is a six, he bears off both men with 65, 64, and 63. That's six more rolls, for a total so far of 10 winners. If his highest number is a five, he can bear off both men with 54 and 53, four more rolls, for a grand total of 14 winners out of 36 rolls. He's a slight underdog, so he shouldn't double.

If White got doubled in this position, he shouldn't just take, he should beaver!

**Problem 477: Black to play 21.**

Black should play 1/off with his ace, then consider his best deuce: 3/1 or 4/2. If he plays 4/2, he fails to bear both checkers off next turn with any roll containing an ace. There are 11 such rolls. If he plays 3/1, he misses with the rolls 21, 31, 32, and 11, a total of 7 rolls. The right play is 1/off, 3/1.

**Problem 478: Black to play 11.**

First rule of bearoffs: Always bearoff checkers with a single number if you can. In other words, if you roll an ace and you have a checker on the ace-point, bear it off. If you roll a three, take a checker off the 3-point. (There are exceptions to this rule, but they're so rare and unusual you could play for a lifetime and never see one.)

In problem 478, Black uses this rule to quickly bear off his two checkers on the 1-point. Then he has two aces left, and has to decide on the best arrangement of his last two checkers. Should he play 3/1, or 6/5 3/2, or 6/4?

The answer is easy if Black remembers positions 471, 472, and 473. The only arrangement of two checkers totalling seven pips that leaves Black a favorite on his last shake is position 471 — a checker on the 5-point and a checker on the 2-point. Black should move into this position by playing 3/2 and 6/5 with his last two aces.

**Problem 479: Should Black double?**
**Should White take if doubled?**

Problem 479 is what is known in the trade as a "two-roll position." If neither side rolls a double, each side will be off in exactly two rolls. A two-roll position is a double for Black and a pass for White. White's winning chances can be calculated directly: For White to win, Black must first throw a non-double (probability 5/6) and White must then throw a double (probability 1/6). So White's probability of winning is exactly 5/6 x 1/6, or 5/36. That's far below the 9/36 needed to take, so White drops.

**Problem 480: Should Black double?**
**Should White take if doubled?**

Problem 480 is a "three-roll position." Both sides will bear off in three rolls, barring doubles. Calculating winning chances isn't as easy as in the previous problem, but Black is about 79% to win. He should double, and White should pass. This position and the next one are important to memorize for over-the-board play.

**Problem 481: Should Black double?**
**Should White take if doubled?**

Now we're looking at a four-roll position. In this position Black is only about 74% to win. He has a good double, but White has a perfectly correct take. Make sure you know these three positions cold, as they frequently appear at the end of many bearoffs.

**Problem 482: Should Black double?**
**Should White take if doubled?**

A five-roll position isn't even a redouble; it's an initial double only. The basic reason is that Black has trouble losing his market. If both sides take two checkers off (the most likely sequence), it's still double-take.

**Problem 483: Should Black double?**
**Should White take if doubled?**

In real life we don't usually see these perfect positions with everyone stacked neatly on the one-points. Here's a more typical example. White is certainly off in three rolls. So is Black, but he's lost some winning chances compared to a true three-roll position. Notice that if his first roll is 11, he doesn't automatically win the game. Instead he bears off three checkers, but then still needs two more rolls to bear off his last three men. The 11 roll wasn't really a double — it didn't do anything for him that a non-double like 65 wouldn't have done. Notice that 22 works the same way.

Still, these flaws aren't enough to change the verdict. Black is better than 79% to win in a true three-roll position, and each ineffective double clips only a little more than a percent off Black's winning chances. It's still double and pass.

## Problem 484: Should Black double?
## Should White take if doubled?

Again it's six checkers against six checkers, but now we're a long way from a true "three roll vs three roll" position. Black has lots of new ways to lose here. For example:

- 11 doesn't work as a double.
- 22 only takes one checker off, and loses immediately. (White will then be in a true three-roll position, and will double!)
- If Black throws two consecutive deuces (for example, 62 followed by 52), he'll lose.
- If he throws three consecutive aces, he'll miss and lose with the last ace.

All these missing sequences clip a quick 12% off Black's raw winning chances. Now it's barely a double, and an easy take.

## Problem 485: Should Black double?
## Should White take if doubled?

This might look like a two-roll position, but look again. Black loses right away if he rolls 31 or 32. That happens one time in nine, or about 11%. That's enough to give White a take. (Black still has a double, of course.)

## Problem 486: Black to play 61.

If you can bear off checkers with both parts of your roll, do it. Black should play 6/off 1/off. Playing 6/off 6/5, filling a gap, looks clever but mostly just loses half a roll or transposes.

## Problem 487: Black to play 61.

If you can't bear off checkers with both parts of your roll, the next priority is filling a gap. In this case the best play is 6/off 6/5, rather than 6/off 2/1. If Black doesn't fill the gap on the 5-point next turn, he may never get another chances, while the 1-point may be filled naturally later on.

## Problem 488: Black to play 51.

Black will play 5/off with his 5, then look around for his best ace. Since he trails by a wide margin, he needs to cater to sequences which are possible winners. 2/1 protects against missing with an ace, but sequences with aces are likely losers in any event. The right ace is 6/5, catering to sequences with 55 as the first or second roll, which are possible winners.

**Problem 489: Black to play 51.**

Compared to the previous sequence, Black is now a heavy favorite, so his priorities shift. Sequences with large numbers are likely to win for him no matter how he plays his ace. Now he needs to guard against missing with small numbers, which could conceivably cost him the game. The right ace is now 2/1.

**Problem 490: Black to play 32.**

If you can take a checker off with each half of your roll, do it. Here Black should play 3/off 2/off, rather than any move which smooths his distribution.

**Problem 491: Black to play 32.**

When bearing off, it's easy to forget that your roll comes in two separate parts. A roll of 32 is a 3 and a 2, not a 5.

Black played the quick 5/off. He should have played 3/off, then looked around for the best deuce. The gap on the 4-point is the critical weakness in his position, since once that point is vacant, Black will waste fours for the rest of the game. The right deuce is 6/4.

**Problem 492: Black to play 32.**

Suppose you roll a number where you can only take a checker off by using both halves of the number — like position 492, for instance. Here it turns out that you should use the whole roll to bear off in most cases, but not in all. If using the whole roll leaves you with an awkward distribution, you might want to consider smoothing your position instead.

Here the right play is the obvious 5/off, since Black's position afterwards is still nice and smooth.

**Problem 493: Black to play 32.**

But here it's a different story. Now playing 5/off leaves Black with a weakness on the 5-point and a stack on the 4-point, which might lead to wastage later on. That's enough of a problem so that the right play is 6/3 4/2!

**Problem 494: Should Black double?**
**Should White take if doubled?**

It's easy to get confused in positions like problem 494, but a little common sense can get us to a pretty good estimation of Black's winning chances.

First, note that if Black doesn't bearoff all his men this turn (and he has only 3 rolls that bear off), White will be on roll with 10 rolls that bear off both his men. That means that White will win about 25% of the games next shake, so we know that White can take this double.

Now notice that in addition to those games, Black will lose if he throws two consecutive rolls containing an ace. (61 followed by 61, for instance, doesn't bear off for him). The chance of that happening is about another 10%. So White's winning chances are at least 35%.

Notice that White has other winning sequences: if Black starts with 21, for instance, he's already an underdog in the game! These other winning chances bring White's total chances up to about 40%. So Black is only about a 60-40 favorite from this position. He should hold the cube, and perhaps offer a good double next shake.

**Problem 495: Should Black double?**
**Should White take if doubled?**

In a bearoff where both sides have the same position, the side on roll has a double if the race is close to a finish, with only about 25-30 pips left on both sides. If the race is longer than that, the advantage of just the roll is usually not enough to double.

Here the positions are even, and both sides have just 14 pips. Black has a good redouble. White has a clear take, based on the fact that Black might miss and take three rolls to get off, while White could be off in two with good rolling.

**Problem 496: Should Black double?**
**Should White take if doubled?**

Another symmetrical position, but now the pip counts are 30 for both sides. Black shouldn't redouble, although it would be an initial double if the cube were in the center. (Black wouldn't be giving up cube ownership in that case.)

**Problem 497: Should Black double?**
**Should White take if doubled?**

Here's a symmetrical position with just six checkers each. The pip count is 21 to 21. That's low enough so that Black has a good double, and White has a take.

**Problem 498: Should Black double?**
**Should White take if doubled?**

In this symmetrical position, the pip count is 39 to 39. With no lead, it's an easy take for White, and Black shouldn't double.

**Problem 499: Should Black double?**
**Should White take if doubled?**

Now Black has a three-pip lead, 36 to 39. That's almost 10% of his pip count, enough for a good double. White has a clear take.

**Problem 500: Should Black double?**
**Should White take if doubled?**

Black's pip count is 34, White's is 41. Using our 8-9-12 rule, a 4-pip lead for Black in a bearoff where his count is 34 should be enough to make the game a marginal pass. Here his lead is 7 pips. That looks like a pass, but this is an unusual position, and we need to apply some corrections to the basic pip count before we're done.

Black has 12 checkers, White only 10. Every extra checker hurts the pip count by about 2 pips. So Black loses 4 pips, reducing his lead to just 3 pips.

Black has two checkers on his ace-point, White only one. Checkers on the ace-point exaggerate the pip count, since they will usually be borne off with larger numbers. You should subtract a pip for each extra checker on the ace-point. Here we subtract one pip for Black, reducing his lead to just 2 pips. Looks now like a take, but there's one more correction...

White has a gap on the 4-point which will probably never be filled, and 5 checkers above that gap. The significance of a gap that won't be filled (in pips) is about half the number of checkers above the gap. Here we add 2 1/2 pips to White's total, increasing Black's lead back to 4 1/2 pips.

Evaluation: strong double and pass.

**Problem 501: Black to play 51.**

Black should play 5/off with the five, then look for the best ace. He'll have at most one more roll in the game, so he'll have to roll a double to bear off his three remaining checkers. If he plays 6/5, then 66, 55, and 44 will bear off his checkers. If he plays 3/2, the same three large doubles will work. But if he plays the accurate 4/3, then 33 will bear off his checkers in addition to 44, 55, and 66. The right play of the ace increases Black's winning chances by 33%!

# NEXT STEPS

Congratulations! You've worked your way through this book, and it was a big job. Now what?

The two keys to success at backgammon are Study and Practice. You've done the studying, now it's time for some practice. You need to go out and find some people to play with, so you'll have a chance to exercise some of the ideas you've just learned.

If you have some friends in your area to play with, do so. If not, you might want to track down some clubs or tournaments. There are backgammon clubs and tournaments going on all over the country. For a complete list, send $1.00 to the Gammon Press, P.O. Box 294, Arlington, MA 02476. Most major cities have one or more active clubs.

You can also play backgammon online. The best site is Games-Grid, where you can get a rating, play matches against players of your own strength, or watch some of the world's best play against each other. To join, get on the Web at www.gamesgrid.com and follow the directions for downloading their software.

After a month or two has passed, try reading this book again. You won't absorb everything in the first pass. Work hard, and you'll find yourself improving (and winning) steadily. Good luck!